ENC
== OF ==

HITS

The 1950s

ENCYCLOPEDIA
OF
HITS
The 1950s

Dave McAleer

BLANDFORD

Dedication

Not only to the successful songwriters, producers, arrangers, musical directors, record companies and recording artists from the 1950s, but also to the thousands more who also dedicated themselves to their music in that era but never made the big time.

A Blandford Book

First published in the UK 1997 by Blandford

A Cassell Imprint

Cassell Plc, Wellington House,
125 Strand, London WC2R 0BB

Distributed in the United States by Sterling Publishing Co., Inc.,
387 Park Avenue South, New York, NY 10016–8810

British Library Cataloguing-in-Publication Data
A catalogue entry for this title is available from the British Library

ISBN 0-7137-2659-8

Compiled and entries fully created by Dave McAleer on disk using Word for Windows 6
Design, typesetting and page make up from the above by Ben Cracknell Studios on an Apple Macintosh

Printed and bound in Great Britain by Hartnolls Limited, Bodmin, Cornwall.

Contents

Acknowledgements

Thanks for their help on this project to Stuart Booth, Billie, Jon Philibert and Colin Morgan of *In Tune* magazine, 12 Caer Gofaint, Groes, Nr Denbigh, Clwyd LL16 5YT, Wales.

Thanks for their input in the 1950s to Tony Ballard, Anne Brasnell, Derek Brecknock, David Brown, Carol Burdette, Paul Burton, Ricky Carrick, Christine Dawes, Ray English, Dave Horsely, Norah, Sandy and Ken McAleer, Keith Millis, Anthony Philibert, Tony Walters and Graham Winter.

Also a tip of the hat to the *NME* and *Billboard* journalists of the era and writers Lee Cotten, Jim Dawson, Pete Frame, Galen Gart, Dr Anthony J. Gribin, Brian Henson, Terry Hounsome, Dick Jacobs, Wayne Jancik, John Javna, Leslie Lowe, Joseph Murrells, MRIB mob, *Now Dig This* team, Al Pavlow, Paul Pelletier, Steve Propes, Dr Matthew M. Schiff, Bob Shannon, *Stak-O-Wax* stalwarts, Steve Sullivan, Steven Suskin, Jay Warner, Joel Whitburn and the many artists, producers, writers and record business associates who have passed on stories to me over the years.

Introduction

The 1950s was the decade that changed the face of popular music forever, and the aim of this volume of *Enclyclopedia of Hits* is to cover the whole era from crooners and big bands to rock'n'roll singers and teen idols, with equal prominence being given to all styles.

For the first time, every one of the 1,200-plus US and UK Top 10 hits from this important period are included in one book. The chronological trip covers the myriad musical trends of the 1950s and features information on all the top stars, including early 1950s chart regulars Frankie Laine, Doris Day and Johnnie Ray, ground-breaking rockers Bill Haley & The Comets, Chuck Berry and Elvis Presley, and later teen idols such as Ricky Nelson, Cliff Richard and Connie Francis.

At the start of the decade it was quite normal for a handful of artists to record the same song – in fact, it was rare that only one version of a popular tune charted. In addition, in the early 1950s it was not unusual for artists to release two or three singles a month, and they were not unduly worried if some fell by the wayside. It is also worth noting that record buyers (especially in the UK) were often enticed into purchasing a certain version of a popular composition by its B side. In other words, if the artist sang two well-known numbers on a single there was a better chance of increasing sales; sometimes, therefore, the song was more important than the singer.

When rock'n'roll arrived the number of covers dropped dramatically, but it was still common practice in the UK for local acts to record US hit songs through to the late 1960s. In fact, the majority of British artists who had UK hits in the 1950s did so with such recordings. On that subject, in the early and mid-1950s many American pop acts successfully covered R&B and country records, which reversed the earlier trend, when it was normal for R&B and country acts to cut pop hits for their own markets.

It is also interesting to note that non-American acts seldom scored transatlantic hits in the 1950s, and that many tracks which were recorded as 'throwaway' B sides went on to become Top 10 hits.

In the second half of the decade, independent labels flourished as the average age of record buyers decreased and the importance of disc jockeys increased. Top DJs like Alan Freed and Dick Clark could break a hit record almost single-handedly, and this power inevitably led to charges of payola. With a high percentage of late 1950's hits being tarnished by 'pay-for-play' accusations, it is mind-boggling to think how different the charts may have looked if money had not changed hands.

Also during the 1950s, the first official gold records were presented in the US, and for the first time some singles sold over a million copies in the UK alone. It was a time when the Grammy Awards were introduced, stereo challenged the supremacy of mono, singles still reigned supreme and the R&B and country markets grew dramatically.

The whole spectrum of 1950s music can be viewed by delving into this book. Song by song, record by record, it comprehensively charts the many musical changes that took place over the fascinating ten-year period when some of the century's most outstanding pop songs were written, and when rock'n'roll's arrival altered the path of popular music.

How to Use This Book

This volume in the *Encyclopedia of Hits* contains information about every single that reached the US or UK Top 10 during the 1950s. The records are listed chronologically and when two or more entered the chart simultaneously the highest entry is listed first and the lowest last. If a record appeared in both the US and UK Top 10, the information appears under the entry in the artist's home country.

Included are details about original versions, cover recordings, follow-ups, record-breaking feats, composers, answer records and success on the other side of the Atlantic. When a chart placing is mentioned within the text, it refers to the country where the entry appears unless stated otherwise. When the R&B or country chart is mentioned, this refers to the US charts.

The heading for each entry shows the artist's name, record title, label, peak position and the act's total number of Top 10 entries up to that point (these running totals being calculated from the first published charts in the 1950s), plus the record's placing in the Top 250 singles of the decade, if applicable. The book also includes separate listings of these Top 250 singles and of the Top 100 acts on both sides of the Atlantic, and full artist and title indexes.

Please note that where a word is spelt differently in the US and the UK, the British spelling is used, eg favourite (not favorite) or colour (not color).

Also note that the word 'doo-wop' has been used even though it was not a recognized term in the 1950s.

Top 100 Artists

The positions in these lists (see pages 217–18) are calculated by a complex points system which takes into consideration each record's weekly chart position, peak position, weeks in the Top 10 and time spent at No 1. All points earned by records that debuted in the Top 10 during the decade are included.

Top 250 Singles

It is impossible to obtain completely accurate sales figures for the era and these lists (see pages 219–26) are therefore based on each record's chart performance. It is thus 'longevity biased', so that a record which spent a long time in the Top 10 will score more points than a bigger-selling single that made a quick exit.

The positions are calculated by a complex points system which takes into consideration a record's weekly chart position, peak position, weeks in the Top 10 and time spent at No 1. All points earned by records that debuted in the Top 10 during the decade are included.

NB Points and record heading information for top UK artists and singles are calculated from November 14, 1952 when the first record sales chart was published.

Terms and Abbreviations

'Demo' means a demonstration recording, usually made by a composer or his publisher in order to interest an artist in recording the song.

'Cover' means a recording of a song that has already been released by another artist.

'Cut' is another word for a recording.

NME New Musical Express

Record Heading Information

The heading for each record contains the following information:

Example

> **TERESA BREWER**
> MUSIC! MUSIC! MUSIC! ♪
> *London*
> ▲ 1
> ⑩ 1
> 58/250

TERESA BREWER	Act name	▲ 1 Peak position in country concerned
MUSIC! MUSIC! MUSIC!	Song title	⑩ 1 Number of Top 10 entries act has had in country concerned to this point, in this case 1 – when followed by ● indicates it was also the last Top 10 hit
♪ Song entered UK Top 10 Sheet music chart (applicable only to US hits up to and including October 1952)		58/250 Position in country's Top 250 for the decade, in this case 58, where applicable
London Record label in country concerned		

Extra Chart Information

For most of the 1950s there were separate US charts for bestsellers, jukebox plays and airplay. In this book, only the bestsellers' chart positions have been used.

Before the UK record sales chart was introduced in November 1952, the popularity of singles could only be gauged from the bestselling sheet music chart. In order to give you a good idea of the songs that were popular in the UK between January 1950 and October 1952, we have therefore indicated on the US Top 10 entries if a song also reached the Top 10 on the UK sheet music chart; however, this does not mean that that the US hit version was also the bestselling version in the UK. Added to that, we have included a bestselling 'single of the month' (outside the US hits already marked) selected by Colin Morgan (editor of the bible of the pre-rock years, *In Tune*).

Please note that in the early days of the UK record sales chart, it was not unusual for two or more records to share the same position, and so occasionally there were more than ten records in a particular week's Top 10.

US chart information © BPI Communications Inc used courtesy of *Billboard* magazine. *Billboard* ® is a registered trademark of BPI Communications. All rights reserved and are used under licence from VNU Business Press Syndication International BV.

UK chart information courtesy of *NME*.

UNITED STATES
January 1950

DINAH SHORE
DEAR HEARTS AND GENTLE PEOPLE ♪
Columbia

▲ 7
⑩ 1
—/250

As the revolutionary 1950s dawned and President Truman gave the go-ahead for the H-bomb, it seemed that everyone on both sides of the Atlantic was singing about those gentle people whose weekends were spent reading the 'good book' in their picket-fence-fronted houses. One of the most popular versions was by Tennessee-born Shore, who had previously hit the top with 'I'll Walk Alone' and 'Buttons And Bows'.

TONY MARTIN
THERE'S NO TOMORROW
RCA

▲ 2
⑩ 1
157/250

The veteran romantic balladeer and actor from California (born Alvin Morris Jr) scored one of his biggest hits with an English lyric version of 'O Sole Mio', which was featured in Martin's movie *Two Tickets To Broadway*. Ten years later, his RCA label-mate Elvis Presley successfully updated the renowned Italian aria under the title 'It's Now Or Never'.

RICHARD HAYES
THE OLD MASTER PAINTER
Mercury

▲ 7
⑩ 1
—/250

Just days after leaving his teens, this New Jersey-born vocalist's interpretation of the much recorded song outsold treatments by such stalwarts as Frank Sinatra and Peggy Lee, and gave Hayes his Top 10 debut. Like many stars of the era, he found fame via Arthur Godfrey's *Talent Scouts* show and, like countless others, Hayes' hits were produced by Mitch Miller.

DICK HAYMES
THE OLD MASTER PAINTER
Decca

▲ 5
⑩11•
—/250

This Argentine-born baritone reached his artistic peak in the 1940s, when he recorded such enduring singles as 'Till The End Of Time', 'Little White Lies' and the a cappella 'You'll Never Know'. The movie and radio star, who had replaced Frank Sinatra in both the Harry James and Tommy Dorsey Bands, last entered the Top 10 with a song that Sinatra took only into the lower reaches of the chart.

AMES BROTHERS
RAG MOP
Coral

▲ 1
⑩ 1
119/250

One of the most recorded songs of the year was also a bestseller in the R&B and C&W areas. It was penned by country bandleader Johnnie Lee Wills, although the publishers of Henry 'Red' Allen's 1946 composition 'Get The Mop' thought differently. 'Rag Mop' was the first major hit for this family foursome from Massachusetts, who became one of the early 1950s bestselling recording acts and charted in every year of the decade.

RED FOLEY
CHATTANOOGIE SHOE SHINE BOY ♪
Decca

▲ 1
⑩ 1•
65/250

As a rule, country records sold poorly in the pop marketplace, but an early exception came from a Kentucky-born performer who first made his mark in the 1930s. Penned by two top executives at the very influential country radio station WSM, this catchy foot-tapper topped the country chart for three months. Foley, one of the era's leading C&W singers, went on to host the long-running TV show *Ozark Jubilee* and he was elected to the Country Hall of Fame shortly before his death in 1968.

UNITED KINGDOM
January 1950

DINAH SHORE & BUDDY CLARK
BABY, IT'S COLD OUTSIDE
Columbia

Among the great all-time duets songs was the Academy Award-winning Frank Loesser composi-

tion from the Esther Williams movie *Neptune's Daughter*. In the US, both this version and one by Margaret Whiting and Johnny Mercer reached the Top 5 in 1949. Clark (of whom Al Jolson said 'Frank Sinatra was not fit to shine his shoes') died in a plane crash soon after this record was released.

UNITED STATES
February 1950

JACK TETER TRIO
JOHNSON RAG
London

▲ 6
🔟 1*
—/250

A revival of interest in Dixieland jazz in 1950 helped propel Teter's trio into the Top 10 with a re-make of a ragtime tune that Larry Clinton had first made famous in 1940. The record, which was picked up by London from the Sharp label in 1949, was covered at the time by such notables as Russ Morgan and R&B star Amos Milburn. Subsequent singles, including the follow-up 'Kansas City Kitty', sold in far smaller quantities.

TERESA BREWER
MUSIC! MUSIC! MUSIC! ♪
London

▲ 1
🔟 1
58/250

One of the year's best-loved songs introduced petite Ohio teenager Brewer (born Breuer) to the

big time and earned many a nickel on jukeboxes around the world. The photogenic performer, whose career dated back to the late 1930s, was joined on the sing-along number by The Dixieland All Stars. The record was a transatlantic topper and Brewer was voted Top New Artist of the Year.

TONY MARTIN & FRAN WARREN
I SAID MY PAJAMAS (AND PUT ON MY PRAY'RS)
RCA

▲ 5
🔟 2
—/250

Several top singers (including Doris Day, Margaret Whiting and Ethel Merman) released renditions of this novelty number. However, none proved to be more popular than the interpretation by Hollywood heart-throb Martin and New York song stylist Warren.

FRANKIE LAINE
THE CRY OF THE WILD GOOSE
Mercury

Few artists in the early 1950s outsold this power-house performer (born Frank LoVecchio) from Chicago. The internationally renowned vocalist followed two successive No 1 hits with a memorable Mitch Miller production that cleverly combined actual goose cries with French horns. Like Laine's previous hit, 'Mule Train', the Terry Gilkyson composition had earlier been recorded by Tennessee Ernie Ford.

SAMMY KAYE & HIS ORCHESTRA
IT ISN'T FAIR
RCA

▲ 3
🔟 1
134/250

Since 1937, when 'Swing And Sway' gave him his first taste of fame, this bandleader from Ohio had kept America 'swinging and swaying' with his unique brand of sweet music. Stylish vocalist Don Cornell, a cornerstone of Kaye's band since 1942, sang on the big ballad, which had first been recorded by its composer Richard Himber and his Orchestra in the 1930s. Cornell went solo soon after and re-recorded the song in 1959, when it fared less well.

LIONEL HAMPTON & HIS ORCHESTRA
RAG MOP
Decca

Without doubt, jazz vibraphonist Hampton and his boogie woogie band helped lay the foundation stone of rock'n'roll, with such tracks as 'Flying Home' (1943) and 'Hey! Ba-Ba-Re-Bop' (1946). The band's version of 'Rag Mop', which featured guitarist Wes Montgomery, was one of three to reach the R&B Top 10 (the others being by Joe Liggins and Doc Sausage & His Mad Lads). The durable performer from Kentucky, whose recording career started in 1924, was rightly elected into the Grammy Hall of Fame in 1996.

BING CROSBY
CHATTANOOGIE SHOE SHINE BOY ♪
Decca

Only Elvis Presley and The Beatles can match the record sales of the King of the Crooners. During Crosby's long and very successful career, the supreme song stylist from Washington released over 2,500 tracks, put 300 of them into the US Top 20 and sold over 300 million records. The 'old groaner', who was no stranger to country music, had his first US chart entry of the decade with this distinctive treatment of Red Foley's current country smash.

UNITED KINGDOM
February 1950

AL MORGAN
JEALOUS HEART
London

British Decca launched their London label with a country-slanted lost-love lament performed by the singer/pianist from Chicago. The single, which was first issued by Universal Records, had been a major US success some months before. Morgan's subsequent solo singles (which included many songs with 'heart' in the title), on such major labels as Decca, RCA and Columbia, went nowhere.

UNITED STATES
March 1950

JOHNNIE LEE WILLS & HIS BOYS
RAG MOP
Bullet

▲ 10
🔟 1•
—/250

Ten years after he left his brother Bob Wills' trail-blazing western swing outfit, The Texas Playboys, Johnnie Lee penned one of the most recorded songs of the era. His band's version not only reached the upper rungs of the country chart, but was also joined by six others on the pop lists. This very popular dance tune, with its simplistic spell-out-the-title lyric, was the only crossover success for the fiddle-and-banjo-playing Texas troubadour's band.

BING CROSBY (THE ANDREWS SISTERS)
QUICKSILVER
Decca

▲ 8
🔟 2
—/250

Teaming the world's top-selling male soloist with the No 1 female group proved to be an inspired idea. The quartet had a string of hits in the 1940s, including the chart-topping 'Pistol Packin' Mama' (1943) and 'Don't Fence Me In' (1944). Their biggest seller together in the 1950s was a catchy

Irving Taylor-penned foot-tapper that also sold well by Doris Day.

EILEEN BARTON
IF I KNEW YOU WERE COMIN' I'D'VE BAKED A CAKE
National/Mercury

▲ 1
🔟 1•
91/250

Eileen was a one-time child protégé whose father, ex-vaudeville artist Ben Barton, was Frank Sinatra's agent. She found fleeting international fame with an irresistibly commercial pop sing-along penned by two masters of that genre, Bob Merrill and Al Hoffman. The dixieland-influenced record was released on both Mercury and R&B label National. Barton never found the ingredients for another huge hit, and even a 1959 re-recording of her No 1 gave the singer little cause for celebration.

RALPH FLANAGAN & HIS ORCHESTRA
RAG MOP
RCA

▲ 10
🔟 1•
—/250

Another recording artist who cleaned up with 'Rag Mop' was Sammy Kaye's one-time arranger, Ralph

Flanagan, and his popular orchestra. In the early 1950s the Glenn Miller-influenced outfit also had successful versions of such hit songs as 'Nevertheless', 'Harbour Lights' and 'Slow Poke'.

GUY LOMBARDO & HIS ROYAL CANADIANS
ENJOY YOURSELF ♪
Decca

▲ 10
🔟 1
—/250

'Enjoy yourself – it's later than you think' was the timely advice offered in the popular Carl Sigman and Herb Magidson-penned song – after all, it looked as if a war in Korea was imminent and the Russians now had the A-bomb! This undeniably catchy toe-tapper (which featured vocalist Kenny Gardner) added to the Lombardo band's long line of hits, which stretched back to 1927 when 'Charmaine' gave them the first of their many chart toppers.

UNITED KINGDOM
March 1950

BILLY COTTON & HIS BAND
I'VE GOT A LOVELY BUNCH OF COCONUTS
Decca

One of Britain's longest-running and best-loved bands had the biggest-selling version of a popular cockney novelty number, which was also recorded by such headliners as Danny Kaye and Dick James. Unlike the fairground showman in the song (who says 'every ball you throw will make me rich'), composer Fred Heatherton made little from the transatlantic hit, having, allegedly, sold his rights for just £25 ($100)!

UNITED STATES
April 1950

ANTON KARAS
THE THIRD MAN THEME ♪
London

▲ 1
🔟 1•
3/250

Austrian zither player Karas wrote and recorded this haunting melody as the title song for an Orson Welles movie. Incidentally, the combined sales of the tune (which is roughly based on a practice piece in a zither tutor book) are said to be over 40 million. In the UK, where it was known as 'The Harry Lime Theme', it sold a record-breaking 900,000 copies in 1949. Later in life, this one-hit wonder opened a wine bar in Austria called, not surprisingly, 'The Third Man'.

MARY MARTIN & ARTHUR GODFREY
GO TO SLEEP, GO TO SLEEP, GO TO SLEEP
Decca

▲ 8
🔟 1•
—/250

While packing in the crowds at New York's Majestic Theater, where she was starring in *South Pacific*,

Miss Martin had a rare hit single. One of America's best-known TV celebrities, Arthur Godfrey (whose talent shows launched the careers of numerous chart makers) joined her on this Sammy Cahn song. Mary, who was born in Texas, subsequently played the lead in the stage musical *The Sound Of Music* and was the mother of Larry Hagman (J.R. of *Dallas* fame).

GUY LOMBARDO & HIS ROYAL CANADIANS
THE THIRD MAN THEME♪
Decca

For seven weeks the only single that stopped this from heading the chart was the original Anton Karas version of the celebrated film theme. The Lombardo band's recording showcased the work of guitarist Don Rodney.

MERVIN SHINER
PETER COTTONTAIL
Decca

Steve Nelson, the composer of 1948's biggest country song 'Bouquet Of Roses', targeted this novelty item at a younger audience. His aim was true, and both Shiner's and Gene Autry's recordings of it sold over a million copies. The Bethlehem (Pennsylvania)-born singer failed to follow up this success even with such pre-teen titles as 'Francis The Talking Mule' and 'Sonny The Bunny', and had to wait 17 years before hopping back into the country chart.

GENE AUTRY
PETER COTTONTAIL
Columbia

Four versions of this children's novelty number reached the pop and country charts. On both listings the biggest seller was by the original 'Singing Cowboy', who coupled it with another rabbit-related recording, 'Funny Little Bunny'. The single also returned to the Top 20 a year later by the movie star/singer and astute businessman. Interestingly, several old Autry hits re-charted in the 1950s: 'Blueberry Hill', 'Sail Along Silvery Moon' and 'There's A Gold Mine In The Sky'.

GORDON JENKINS & HIS ORCHESTRA
MY FOOLISH HEART♪
Decca

At times, this bandleader from Missouri had three singles situated together in the US Top 10. One of them was Jenkins' rendition of the Ned Washington and Victor Young-composed title song from a film starring Susan Hayward and Dana Andrews. His recording, which featured singer Sandy Evans and a vocal chorus, just pipped Billy Eckstine's interpretation. In the UK, local balladeer Steve Conway's interpretation narrowly beat the US opposition.

AMES BROTHERS
SENTIMENTAL ME♪
Coral

Ed, Gene, Joe and Vic Ames (born Urick) earned their second gold disc of the year with a track that had amazingly first appeared on the B side of the group's previous million seller, 'Rag Mop'.

BILL SNYDER
BEWITCHED♪
Tower

Rodgers & Hart's melodic and haunting song from the 1942 musical *Pal Joey* transported the Chicago pianist and bandleader into the charts for the only time. The success of this nightclub entertainer's arrangement inspired other revivals, seven of which joined him in the US Top 30. In early 1952 *Pal Joey* triumphantly returned to Broadway, thanks in part to the renewed interest in 'Bewitched'.

MILLS BROTHERS
DADDY'S LITTLE GIRL♪
Decca

Black vocal groups had changed a lot since the Mills Brothers first appeared on the scene in the late 1920s. However, this legendary family quartet were still winning DJ polls and clocking up hits on both sides of the Atlantic in the early 1950s. In the US, they narrowly out-pointed a version of the song by Canadian Dick Todd, while in the UK, Steve Conway's sensitive cover easily overcame all opposition, which included future headliner Frankie Vaughan.

UNITED KINGDOM
April 1950

EVE YOUNG & THE HOMESTEADERS
IF I KNEW YOU WERE COMIN' I'D'VE BAKED A CAKE
London

In the US, Eileen Barton's 'Cake' won all the prizes. However, in the UK her version of the unbelievably contagious composition didn't rise as high as the one by this Idaho-born songstress (real name Eve Nadauld). Young, who sang with the Benny Goodman Band in the late 1940s, was married to noted arranger/conductor Jack Pleis.

UNITED STATES
May 1950

BILLY ECKSTINE
MY FOOLISH HEART ♪
MGM

| ▲ 6 |
| ⑩ 1 |
| —/250 |

This song stylist from Pittsburgh possessed a distinctive deep baritone voice with an unmistakable vibrato. After leaving his own pioneering be-bop band (which included legendary musicians Charlie Parker, Dizzy Gillespie, Miles Davis and Art Blakey) in 1947, he became one of the most in-demand singing stars of the time. Eckstine's unique treatment of the much recorded film theme earned him a sixth gold single and sold well on both sides of the Atlantic.

PERRY COMO (& THE FONTANE SISTERS)
HOOP-DE-HOO
RCA

| ▲ 4 |
| ⑩ 1 |
| 243/250 |

Top tunesmith Frank Loesser composed Como's first hit of the decade. The singer, whose earlier No 1s included 'Till The End Of Time' (1945), 'Prisoner Of Love' (1946) and 'Some Enchanted Evening' (1949), was one of few to chart in every year of the 1950s. The ultra-relaxed Pennsylvania-born performer was joined on the track by The Fontane Sisters, who were currently regulars on his *Chesterfield Supper Club* show.

RUSS MORGAN & HIS ORCHESTRA
SENTIMENTAL ME ♪
Decca

| ▲ 10 |
| ⑩ 1• |
| —/250 |

From the mid-1930s, the US public could not get enough 'music in the Morgan manner' and kept the bandleader/vocalist at the top. Among the sweet music maestro's best-known hits were 'I've Got A Pocketful of Dreams' (1938), his own composition 'So Tired' (1948) and 'Cruising Down The River' (1949). Morgan, who hailed from Pennsylvania, last charted with a song that the Ames Brothers fared even better with. Curiously, in 1958 the orchestra appeared in the rock'n'roll film *The Big Beat*.

GORDON JENKINS & HIS ORCHESTRA
BEWITCHED ♪
Decca

▲ 6
⑩ 2
—/250

Decca's noted musical director and his orchestra joined Bill Snyder and Doris Day in the Top 10 with this lush version of the show-stopping song from *Pal Joey*. Vocals on the track were handled by Bonnie Lou Williams.

UNITED KINGDOM
May 1950

STEVE CONWAY
MY FOOLISH HEART
Columbia

This distinctive balladeer from London (born Walter Groom), who had been popular in Britain since 1945, had the UK's top version of the much recorded film theme. The coupling, a stand-out Norman Newell number, 'My Thanks To You', also attracted its fair share of sales.

UNITED STATES
June 1950

ANDREWS SISTERS
I WANNA BE LOVED
Decca

▲ 3
⑩ 2•
176/250

Maxene, Laverne and Patty Andrews had no rivals among girl groups in the pre-rock years. The trio's recordings, such as 'Boogie Woogie Bugle Boy', 'Rum and Coca-Cola' and their cover of Ella Mae Morse's 'Shoo-Shoo Baby', were an integral part of the soundtrack of World War II. Before they broke up, these world-renowned Minneapolis ladies are said to have sold a total of over 75 million records. The sisters' revival of a Billy Rose song from the mid-1930s was the trio's last notable success.

DORIS DAY
BEWITCHED ♪
Columbia

▲ 10
⑩ 1
—/250

Apart from being bewitched, bothered and bewildered, the photogenic singer from Cincinnati (born Doris Von Kappelhoff) was also very busy, splitting her time between the recording and film studios. Before going to Hollywood in 1948, she sang on the Les Brown's Orchestra chart-topping 'Sentimental Journey' and 'My Dreams Are Getting Better All The Time'. In 1950, she released four films and half a dozen bestselling singles.

NAT 'KING' COLE
MONA LISA ♪
Capitol

▲ 1
⑩ 1
20/250

After a two-year absence, this Academy Award-winning ballad reinstated the velvet-voiced vocalist from Alabama in the Top 10. The song that brought a smile back to his face came from the film *Captain Carey, USA* (known as *After Midnight* in the UK). As the single topped the US chart, Cole was playing to record-breaking crowds at the prestigious London Palladium. The timeless tune returned to the transatlantic charts in 1959 recorded by Conway Twitty.

UNITED KINGDOM
June 1950

SPORTSMEN
ME AND MY SHADOW
Capitol

Thanks, initially, to repeated plays by Britain's No 1 DJ Jack Jackson, this US vocal group scored a UK-only hit with an update of a well-known standard. The song, which lists Al Jolson among its composers, had originally been made famous by 'Whispering' Jack Smith in 1927. The Sportsmen, who supported Mel Blanc on his 1948 million seller 'Woody Woodpecker', were backed on their single by Billy May's Orchestra.

UNITED STATES
July 1950

BILLY ECKSTINE
I WANNA BE LOVED
MGM

▲ 9
⑩ 2
—/250

Mr B, as the influential vocal stylist was widely known, joined the Andrews Sisters in the Top 10 with his version of an engaging song from the 1934 musical revue *Casino De Paris*.

GORDON JENKINS
(& HIS ORCHESTRA)
& THE WEAVERS
TZENA, TZENA, TZENA ♪
Decca

▲ 2
⑩ 3
173/250

Amazingly, both sides of the first hit by influential folk group The Weavers reached the Top 3 simultaneously. Orchestra leader and noteworthy composer Jenkins arranged his version of the well-known Jewish folk song.

GORDON JENKINS
(& HIS ORCHESTRA)
& THE WEAVERS
GOODNIGHT IRENE ♪
Decca

▲ 1
⑩ 4
2/250

Even though few people at Decca believed in the potential of The Weavers, Jenkins signed them to the label before Columbia's Mitch Miller beat him to it. The combination of the distinctive folk quartet and Jenkins' big band produced a two-million-selling single and kick-started a folk music trend. Suddenly, it seemed that every singer wanted to say goodnight to Irene, and Leadbelly's World War I blues composition became one of the most recorded songs of the 1950s. Sadly, the composer died penniless months before this record was released.

GARY CROSBY & FRIEND (BING CROSBY)
PLAY A SIMPLE MELODY
Decca

▲ 3
⑩ 3
165/250

A bouncy Irving Berlin song from the World War I days catapulted chart newcomer Gary and his world-famous father up the transatlantic charts and earned Bing's twenty-first gold record.

KAY STARR
BONAPARTE'S RETREAT
Capitol

▲ 5
⑩ 1
210/250

As a teenager, this distinctive song stylist (born Katherine Starks) from Oklahoma sung with such celebrated bands as those of Joe Venuti, Glenn Miller, Charlie Barnet and Bob Crosby. She went solo in 1945, and notched up her first Top 10 entry with a cover of the lively, knee-slapping Pee Wee King composition, which the country bandleader had taken up the country chart earlier in the year. 'Bonaparte's Retreat' was the first of four best-sellers for songsmith King in the early 1950s.

GARY CROSBY & FRIEND (BING CROSBY)
SAM'S SONG ♪
Decca

▲ 3
⑩ 4
160/250

At times, both sides of this family duet stood together in the Top 5. The jaunty, jazzy song, on which father and son were joined by Matty Matlock's dixieland band, was an ideal vehicle for the casual Crosbys.

UNITED KINGDOM
July 1950

DINNING SISTERS
ONCE IN A WHILE
Capitol

One of the late 1940's leading girl groups notched up a UK-only hit with their revival of a sad lost-love lament that Tommy Dorsey's Orchestra had taken to the top of the US bestsellers in 1937. It was the last charter for Chicago-based Ginger, Lou and Jean; however, the trio's younger brother Mark achieved a US No 1 in 1959. Coincidentally, Mark's ex-babysitter, Patti Page, took the song up the US chart in 1952. 'Once In a While' re-appeared in the Top 20 in 1961 by doo-wop outfit The Chimes.

UNITED STATES
August 1950

HUGO WINTERHALTER & HIS ORCHESTRA & CHORUS
COUNT EVERY STAR
RCA

▲ 10
⑩ 1
—/250

Few recording artists can claim to have appeared on as many hits in the 1950s as Hugo Winterhalter & His Orchestra, who can be heard playing on scores of the decade's top sellers. Their treatment of this melodic Sammy Gallop composition narrowly outpaced others by Ray Anthony and Artie Shaw (with Dick Haymes). The romantic ballad subsequently charted for doo-wop groups The Rivieras (1958) and Donnie & The Dreamers (1961).

JOE 'FINGERS' CARR
SAM'S SONG ♪
Capitol

▲ 8
⑩ 1•
—/250

'Sam's Song' also charted by Capitol Records in-house producer Lou Busch, whose honky tonk treatment was released under the pseudonym Joe 'Fingers' Carr. In the 1930s, the keyboard wizard from Louisville played on numerous hits by both the Hal Kemp and George Olsen Bands. He joined the fledgling Capitol label in the 1940s, and his orchestra can be heard on singles by such singers as Kay Starr and Margaret Whiting (who later became Mrs Busch).

LES PAUL
NOLA
Capitol

▲ 9
⑩ 1
—/250

This ground-breaking guitarist and master of multi-tracking scored with a revival of the Vincent Lopez Orchestra's theme song, which was composed during World War I by Felix Arndt. The track was recorded by Paul (real name Lester Polfus) at his purpose-built home studio and included such innovative recording ideas as sped-up guitar tracks and numerous guitar overdubs.

MITCH MILLER & HIS ORCHESTRA & CHORUS
TZENA, TZENA, TZENA ♪
Columbia

▲ 10
⑩ 1
—/250

No producer in the 1950s racked up more transatlantic hits than the one-time classical oboe player, who had headed A&R at Mercury before joining Columbia in 1950. After Decca beat Miller to the signature of The Weavers, his orchestra successfully covered the group's version of the old Jewish folk tune. Interestingly, Vic Damone (a vocalist Miller signed to Mercury) also charted with the song. This was one of several 33⅓ rpm singles that Columbia released at the time.

VIC DAMONE
TZENA, TZENA, TZENA ♪
Mercury

▲ 8
⑩ 1
—/250

One of the three versions of this fast-paced folk song that simultaneously squeezed into the Top 10 was by a New York balladeer, born Vito Farinola. Damone, who had hit No 1 exactly a year earlier with 'You're Breaking My Heart', was voted Most Promising Male Singer of the Year by US radio DJs.

TONY MARTIN
LA VIE EN ROSE ♪
RCA

▲ 9
⑩ 3
—/250

France's foremost female performer Edith Piaf penned and originally recorded this song in 1946. Two years later, it was a British success ('Take Me In Your Heart Again' – UK lyric title), and in 1950, it quickly returned ace showman Tony Martin to the heights ('You're Too Dangerous, Cherie' – US lyric title).

AMES BROTHERS
CAN ANYONE EXPLAIN
Coral

▲ 7
🔟 3
—/250

America's most popular vocal group of the early years of the decade had the highest-hitting version of a song that also transported another half a dozen recording artists into the chart. It was composed by the prolific pair Bennie Benjamin and George Weiss.

UNITED KINGDOM
August 1950

BING CROSBY & THE ANDREWS SISTERS
HAVE I TOLD YOU LATELY
THAT I LOVE YOU
Brunswick

In 1946, four performers took Scott Wiseman's famous composition into the country Top 5: Gene Autry, Tex Ritter, Red Foley and Foy Willing. The update by this fabulous foursome was a top seller in the UK , although in the US it was its equally popular B side, 'Quicksilver', that hit the heights. Ricky Nelson returned the song once more to the US Top 40 in 1957.

UNITED STATES
September 1950

JO STAFFORD
NO OTHER LOVE
Capitol

▲ 8
🔟 1
—/250

Few female vocalists sold more records in the 1940s than the Californian songstress, who had gone solo in 1944 after making a name for herself in Tommy Dorsey's vocal quartet The Pied Pipers. It was in Dorsey's band that she met her husband, Paul Weston, whose orchestra supplied the backing on most of Stafford's singles. He also supplied the lyrics for this haunting ballad, which was based on Chopin's 'Etude No 3 In E'.

KAY STARR & TENNESSEE ERNIE FORD
I'LL NEVER BE FREE
Capitol

▲ 3
🔟 2
201/250

Countless pop, R&B and country artists recorded the notable Benjamin and Weiss ballad which took Starr into the country chart for the only time. The distinctive duo's B side, 'Ain't Nobody's Business But My Own', also made a dent on both charts. A re-recording by Starr in 1961 reached the lower rungs of the US chart.

VICTOR YOUNG (& HIS ORCHESTRA & CHORUS) & DON CHERRY
MONA LISA ♪
Decca

▲ 10
⑩ 1
—/250

One of the big screen's most in-demand composers briefly joined Nat 'King' Cole in the Top 10 with a string-soaked interpretation of this outstanding Livingston & Evans film theme. Young also wrote such standards as 'Stella By Starlight', 'Love Letters', 'Ghost Of A Chance With You' and, in the 1950s, 'My Foolish Heart', 'Blue Star' and 'When I Fall In Love'.

RICHARD HAYES & KITTY KALLEN
OUR LADY OF FATIMA
Mercury

▲ 10
⑩ 2•
—/250

Ex-big-band vocalist Kallen joined Hayes on a semi-religious song that country singer Red Foley also escorted up the chart. Hayes, voted second Most Promising New Male of 1950 by US DJs, later took up record spinning himself, and even replaced the legendary Alan Freed as host of *Big Beat* on WABC in 1959. In the early 1970s, he reappeared as the presenter of TV's *Name That Tune*.

PATTI PAGE
ALL MY LOVE ♪
Mercury

▲ 2
⑩ 1
180/250

After Page's first four releases sank without trace, this Oakie from Muskogee found a winning formula when she multi-tracked her voice on the 1948 release 'Confess'. The single started a run of hits that continued throughout the 1950s. This unique interpretation of 'All My Love', an English lyric version of the French song 'Bolero' (originally recorded by Jacqueline Francois), outsold several other renditions, and helped Page pick up the award for Most Promising Female Singer of 1950.

SAMMY KAYE & HIS ORCHESTRA
HARBOUR LIGHTS
Columbia

▲ 1
⑩ 2•
55/250

At times, Kaye's and Guy Lombardo's revivals of this pre-war British song were docked at Nos 1 and 2 on the US chart. Vocals on the track were supplied by Tony Alamo and The Kaydets. In the mid-1950s, when Kaye had side-stepped success-fully into music publishing, he was a surprise defender of rock'n'roll music.

UNITED KINGDOM
September 1950

EVE YOUNG & THE HOMESTEADERS
SILVER DOLLAR
London

Astoundingly, the B side of Young's earlier smash, 'If I Knew You Were Comin' I'd've Baked A Cake', became a top hit in its own right in the UK some months later. The song topped the sheet music chart and this version outsold those by lauded local groups The Stargazers, Keynotes and Five Smith Brothers. The American performer's only noteworthy US bestseller came after she changed her name to Karen Chandler.

UNITED STATES
October 1950

DON CHERRY
THINKING OF YOU
Decca

▲ 4
🔟 2
220/250

After losing a chart battle with Nat 'King' Cole over 'Mona Lisa', the Texas entertainer outsold acclaimed newcomer Eddie Fisher with his rendition of an old Kalmer & Ruby classic, which was featured in the current film *Three Little Words*. The song was also known as the theme for Kay Kyser's Orchestra.

UNITED KINGDOM
October 1950

**MARGARET WHITING &
BOB HOPE**
BLIND DATE/HOME
COOKIN'
Capitol

This double-sided novelty teamed Britain's best-known export to Hollywood, Bob Hope, with a Hollywood-based chart regular. The former side took a humorous look at what people say and what they actually think on meeting their blind date. The coupling was a Jerry Livingston and Ray Evans gem taken from Hope's hit movie *Fancy Pants*. The pair were joined on the transatlantic Top 20 entry by The Starlighters (vocals) and Billy May's Orchestra.

UNITED STATES
November 1950

**GUY LOMBARDO & HIS
ROYAL CANADIANS**
HARBOUR LIGHTS
Decca

▲ 2
🔟 3
178/250

As soap rationing ended in the UK, this British song cleaned up on the US charts, with versions at times holding the top two spots. It was one of over 200 tracks that Canadian-born Lombardo and his band scored with Stateside.

PERRY COMO
PATRICIA
RCA

▲ 7
⑩ 2
—/250

Among the dozens of hits Mr C (as he was known) clocked up was his interpretation of this catchy number penned by Benny Davis. The venerable songwriter also had success in the 1950s with his compositions 'Baby Face', 'Carolina Moon' and 'With These Hands'.

PAUL WESTON & HIS ORCHESTRA
NEVERTHELESS ♪
Columbia

▲ 9
⑩ 1•
—/250

In the late 1940s, this celebrated arranger/ conductor and composer's orchestra was seldom off the chart. As an in-house band at Capitol, they backed many of the label's acts and scored several hits of their own. After the Massachusetts-born musician moved to Columbia, his orchestra had its biggest seller with a song from Fred Astaire's film *Three Little Words* – a biopic of composers Bert Kalmar and Harry Ruby. Among the singers Weston (born Wetstein) backed and wrote for was his very successful wife, Jo Stafford.

EDDIE FISHER
THINKING OF YOU
RCA

▲ 8
⑩ 1
—/250

None of the RCA roster (including Elvis Presley and Perry Como) had more Top 10 entries in the 1950s than Fisher. The 22-year-old from Philadelphia, who first came to the public's attention on Eddie Cantor's radio show in 1949, was voted Most Promising Male singer by American DJs in 1950. His debut hit followed Don Cherry's version up the chart and, like Paul Weston's song above, was featured in the film *Three Little Words*.

PHIL HARRIS
THE THING ♪
RCA

▲ 1
⑩ 1•
66/250

At the time no one knew what the 'thing' was that the Indiana entertainer could not get rid of on this novelty number that rocketed to the top of the transatlantic charts. His follow-up, 'Oh What A Face' revealed that it was a locket containing a picture of an ugly girl. Interestingly, Harris' re-recording in 1958 – complete with Chipmunk-like vocals – didn't mean a thing. The veteran entertainer was better known to later generations as the voice of Baloo the bear in Disney's *Jungle Book*.

PATTI PAGE
THE TENNESSEE WALTZ ♪
Mercury

▲ 1
⑩ 2
11/250

A track that started life as the B side to Page's cover of Mabel Scott's 'Boogie Woogie Santa Claus' went on to sell a reputed 10 million copies. It topped the chart for nine weeks and became the biggest seller of 1951. Country performer Pee Wee King wrote and originally recorded his worldwide hit in 1948.

PERRY COMO (& BETTY HUTTON)
A BUSHEL AND A PECK
RCA

▲ 6
⑩ 3
—/250

In the Broadway smash *Guys And Dolls* this jaunty singalong song was performed by Vivian Blaine, but it was Como and film star Betty Hutton who had the biggest US hit. When the show was launched in the UK in 1953, only Blaine's recording reached the bestsellers.

UNITED KINGDOM
November 1950

TEDDY JOHNSON
BELOVED, BE FAITHFUL
Columbia

In the US, Russ Morgan had a minor hit with the Ervin Drake and Jimmy Shirl song that gave this

Surrey-born singer his biggest seller. Incidentally, when the influential Radio Luxembourg launched the UK's first Top 20 radio show in May 1949, Johnson, who was the station's sole English announcer, hosted the popular show.

UNITED STATES
December 1950

GUY MITCHELL
MY HEART CRIES FOR YOU♪
Columbia

▲ 2
⑩ 1
124/250

Legend has it that Mitchell was only drafted in at the last moment to record the song when Frank Sinatra refused to cut 'this crap'. Another nice story is that the traditional French air on which it is based, 'Chanson De Marie Antoinette', was actually composed by that eighteenth-century Queen of France. Either way, his version of the heart-wrenching ballad beat some heavy competition and earned the Detroit-born son of Yugoslav immigrants (real name Albert Cernick) the first of many transatlantic charters during the 1950s.

BING CROSBY
HARBOUR LIGHTS
Decca

▲ 10
⑩ 5
—/250

Lyn Murray's Hawaiian orchestra joined the influential crooner on his distinctive revival of the pre-war song. In 1960, The Platters reinstated 'Harbour Lights' in the Top 10.

MILLS BROTHERS
NEVERTHELESS♪
Decca

▲ 9
⑩ 2
—/250

These veteran vocalists from Ohio returned to the top rungs with their rendition of a song that had originally been made famous by Canadian band-leader Jack Denny in 1931 – the year the quartet's first hit, 'Tiger Rag', reached the top.

MARIO LANZA
BE MY LOVE♪
RCA

▲ 1
⑩ 1
40/250

Not since Enrico Caruso, in the first decades of the century, had an opera star reached the heights of popularity that this much acclaimed tenor from Philadelphia (real name Alfredo Cocozza) did in the early 1950s. The two-million-selling transatlantic hit was written for his second film, *Toast Of New Orleans*, by Sammy Cahn and Nicholas Brodszky. He was supported on the outstanding light operatic ode by the Jeff Alexander Choir and Ray Sinatra's Orchestra.

UNITED KINGDOM
December 1950

GENE AUTRY
RUDOLPH THE RED-
NOSED REINDEER
Columbia

Apart from Bing's 'White Christmas', no single had outsold this children's classic, which originally topped the US chart in 1949. It repeated that feat in the UK when finally released there a year later, and also pranced back into the US Top 20 in 1950, 1951 and 1952. The transatlantic hit sold over eight million copies and earned the legendary artist several very shiny discs.

UNITED STATES
January 1951

GENE AUTRY
FROSTY THE SNOWMAN
Columbia

▲ 7
⑩ 3•
—/250

Steve Nelson, composer of Autry's earlier hit 'Peter Cottontail', also penned this very popular children's Christmas song for the legendary Texan multi-millionaire. Autry, who first recorded in 1929 and last charted in 1993 (on the soundtrack of *Sleepless In Seattle*), was elected into the Country Hall of Fame in 1969.

DENNIS DAY
CHRISTMAS IN KILLARNEY ♪
RCA

▲ 10
⑩ 1•
—/250

For over 20 years this amiable Irish American tenor (born Eugene McNulty in New York) acted and sang on Jack Benny's top-rated comedy radio and TV shows. Day's handful of bestsellers included his treatment of this American-penned Irish yuletide ditty, on which he was backed by Henri Rene's Orchestra and supported vocally by The Mellowmen.

GORDON JENKINS & HIS ORCHESTRA (& THE WEAVERS)
SO LONG
Decca

▲ 6
⑩ 5
—/250

Both The Weavers and the song's composer Woody Guthrie helped change the face of late-twentieth-century music. They inspired such stars as the Kingston Trio, Peter, Paul & Mary and Bob Dylan, as well as many British skiffle acts including Lonnie Donegan, who subsequently recorded both sides of The Weavers' last major hit, 'So Long' and 'Lonesome Traveller'.

GUY LOMBARDO & HIS ROYAL CANADIANS
TENNESSEE WALTZ ♪
Decca

▲ 6
⑩ 4•
—/250

The orchestra that had supplied the 'sweetest music this side of heaven' since 1925, scored their last major hit with a polished performance of the popular country composition. The band were one of only a handful of recording artists who have sold over 100 million records and, strangely, Lombardo died within weeks of Elvis and Bing, who also belonged to that select club.

PERRY COMO
IF ♪
RCA

▲ 1
⑩ 5
35/250

Seven other versions of this big UK hit from the 1930s trailed behind the distinctive baritone's chart-topping interpretation. The B side, 'Zing Zing-Zoom Zoom', also graced the Top 20.

PERRY COMO (& THE FONTANE SISTERS)
YOU'RE JUST IN LOVE
RCA

▲ 5
⑩ 4
—/250

Both sides of this single came from Irving Berlin's final Broadway success, *Call Me Madam* (which starred the irrepressible Ethel Merman) – the B side being 'It's A Lovely Day Today'. It was the 62-year-old composer's third Top 20 entry within six months.

GUY MITCHELL
THE ROVING KIND ♪
Columbia

▲ 4
⑩ 2
—/250

Not only did the newcomer's recording outsell the original version by The Weavers, but at times it joined its other side, 'My Heart Cries For You', in the Top 5. The singalong song was based on an old English sea shanty, 'The Pirate Ship'.

UNITED KINGDOM
January 1951

BILLY COTTON & HIS BAND
THE FLYING SAUCER/
THE THING
Decca

Millions of Britons tuned in to *The Billy Cotton Band Show* every Sunday lunchtime. In the radio show,

his band would present a mix of novelty numbers and their versions of current hits. This single showcased both these musical areas. The A side was a novelty about visitors from outer space and was penned by Eric 'Coronation Street' Spear. The coupling was Cotton's anglicized adaptation of 'The Thing', featuring vocalist Alan Breeze, a permanent fixture of the band since 1931.

UNITED STATES
February 1951

MEL BLANC
I TAUT I TAW A
PUDDY TAT ♪
Capitol

▲ 9
⑩ 1•
—/250

Mel Blanc was the voice of many of Hollywood's top cartoon characters, including Bugs Bunny and Daffy Duck. A couple of years after clicking with 'Woody Woodpecker', the voice of Toon Town had another cartoon-based international hit: this time he utilized the voices of Tweety Pie (the bird) and Sylvester (the cat), and the resulting record flew up the transatlantic charts.

PATTI PAGE
WOULD I LOVE YOU
(LOVE YOU, LOVE YOU) ♪
Mercury

▲ 7
⑩ 3
—/250

In the mid-1940s Clara Ann Fowler had become the second 'Patti Page' hosting the Page Milk-

sponsored Oklahoma radio show *Meet Patti Page*. She retained the stage name, and by the time this track was recorded her voice was heard on radio stations worldwide.

LES PAUL & MARY FORD
TENNESSEE WALTZ ♪
Capitol

▲ 8
⑩ 2
—/250

Combining Paul's unique guitar sound with wife Mary's (born Colleen Summer) Patti Page-styled multi-tracked vocals proved to be an inspired idea, and the couple became America's top-selling artists of 1951. Their first major hit together was a cover of Page's revival of this country gem from the late 1940s.

UNITED KINGDOM
February 1951

TONY MARTIN & FRAN WARREN
TAKE A LETTER
MISS SMITH
HMV

Mixed duets were extremely popular on both sides of the Atlantic in the early 1950s, and the teaming of Martin and Warren had already proved successful ('I Said My Pajamas'). Despite the single's relatively poor showing Stateside, the George Tibbles and Ramey Idriss-composed 'secretary and boss' song was a big seller in the UK.

UNITED STATES
March 1951

CARLETON CARPENTER & DEBBIE REYNOLDS
ABA DABA HONEYMOON
MGM

▲ 3
⑩ 1•
229/250

These youthful movie stars featured the cute novelty number in the film *Two Weeks With Love*. The song had originally been successful 40 years earlier (by Arthur Collins and Byron Harlan), which was the period the film was set in. Eighteen-year-old Reynolds, a former Miss Burbank, became a popular actress in the 1950s and wed top singing star Eddie Fisher in 1955. Carleton appeared in several other films without making the big time.

LES PAUL & MARY FORD
MOCKIN' BIRD HILL ♪
Capitol

▲ 3
⑩ 3
146/250

On both sides of the Atlantic the song's cheerful 'Tra la la, twiddly de dum' chorus was heard everywhere, thanks to this version and Patti Page's cover (they previously covered her 'Tennessee Waltz'). Interestingly, it was first recorded by its composers, The Pinetoppers.

GUY MITCHELL
SPARROW IN THE TREE TOP ♪
Columbia

▲ 9
⑩ 3
—/250

Composer Bob Merrill's 'Sparrow' flew into the Top 10 between two Mockingbirds. It was the first of many of his songs that Mitchell took up the transatlantic charts in the early 1950s.

PATTI PAGE
MOCKIN' BIRD HILL ♪
Mercury

▲ 3
⑩ 4
171/250

Multi-track pioneer Page's cover of this utterly infectious ode earned the unstoppable artist her fourth gold disc. The B side was another successful country song, 'I Love You Because', which scored again in the 1960s when recorded by Al Martino and Jim Reeves .

UNITED KINGDOM
March 1951

TEDDY JOHNSON
TENNESSEE WALTZ
Columbia

The biggest-selling UK version of this country waltz was by the noted British balladeer, who soon afterwards recorded a duet, 'The Moment I Saw You', with leading American songstress Jo Stafford. In 1955 he married Pearl Carr, whom *Melody Maker* readers voted Top Female Singer of 1951. They became known as 'Britain's Mr and Mrs Music' and worked successfully together on the club and cabaret circuit for many years.

UNITED STATES
April 1951

LES PAUL & MARY FORD
HOW HIGH THE MOON
Capitol

▲ 1
⑩ 4
12/250

Six years after he had recorded a little noticed solo version of this 1940 song, Paul and his wife's innovative interpretation topped the lists for nine weeks. The single's guitar break was a blueprint for many later rock'n'roll hits, including 'Rock Around The Clock'.

WEAVERS
ON TOP OF OLD SMOKY ♪
Decca

▲ 2
⑩ 4•
117/250

Pete Seeger and Lee Hayes (who had earlier been in the Almanac Singers with Woody Guthrie) formed the nucleus of this most important and influential folk quartet. The group were joined on Seeger's adaptation of the traditional song by singer/composer Terry Gilkyson. Political black-listing in 1952 helped put The Weavers' career on ice for three years.

BILLY ECKSTINE
I APOLOGIZE ♪
MGM

▲ 8
⑩ 3•
—/250

The fashionable singer's unique reworking of Bing Crosby's 1931 hit was a top transatlantic seller. His 1959 re-recording went unnoticed, but in 1965, P.J. Proby's very similar interpretation reached the UK Top 20.

NAT 'KING' COLE
TOO YOUNG ♪
Capitol

▲ 1
⑩ 2
18/250

Thirty-four-year-old Cole (born Nathaniel Coles), who had been recording for almost half his life, last topped the chart with a standout love song that sold equally well in the UK by newcomer Jimmy Young. In 1972, 14-year-old Donny Osmond returned it to the heights.

UNITED KINGDOM
April 1951

FRED ASTAIRE & JANE POWELL
HOW COULD YOU
BELIEVE ME WHEN
I SAID I LOVE YOU
WHEN YOU KNOW
I'VE BEEN A LIAR
ALL MY LIFE
MGM

Without doubt the prize for longest title in the book goes to this Alan Jay Lerner and Burton Lane composition. The record teamed the twentieth century's best-known dance man, 51-year-old Astaire, with a 21-year-old ex-child actress (born Suzanne Burce). The song was featured in the pair's successful movie *Royal Wedding* which was retitled *Wedding Bells* in the UK.

UNITED STATES
May 1951

VAUGHN MONROE & HIS ORCHESTRA
SOUND OFF
RCA

▲ 4
⑩ 1
237/250

This big-voiced baritone from Ohio was a major recording star in the 1940s, clocking up such hits as 'There! I've Said It Again' (1945), 'Ballerina' (1947) and 'Riders In The Sky' (1949). He also started off the 1950s well by being voted Top Male Band Vocalist by American DJs. With the Korean war in progress, his rendition of the well-known army chant sold in large quantities.

BING CROSBY & GARY CROSBY
WHEN YOU AND I WERE
YOUNG MAGGIE BLUES
Decca

▲ 10
⑩ 6
—/250

Eighty-five years after the song was first performed on stage, the famous father-and-son team gave it a new lease of life. They coupled it with the relatively recent 1912 composition 'Moonlight Bay'.

MARIO LANZA
THE LOVELIEST NIGHT
OF THE YEAR ♪
RCA

▲ 3
⑩ 2
81/250

Who but Lanza (his stage name coming from his mother's maiden name Maria Lanza) could play the lead in *The Great Caruso*? From that film came this internationally successful poperatic aria which, like his previous million seller 'Be My Love', spent a staggering 32 weeks in the US Top 20. The song was adapted from 'Sabre Las Olas' by Juvenito Rosas.

FRANKIE LAINE
JEZEBEL ♪
Columbia

▲ 2
⑩ 2
125/250

Mr Rhythm, as he was known, had a big transatlantic hit with his impassioned performance of this dramatic ballad. The B side, 'Rose, Rose, I Love You', also reached the Top 10.

VAUGHN MONROE & HIS ORCHESTRA
OLD SOLDIERS NEVER DIE
RCA

▲ 9
⑩ 2
—/250

Composer Tom Glazer was inspired to write this song by one of General MacArthur's speeches. Orchestra leader/vocalist Monroe's recording of it soon marched up the chart and joined his other military-inspired success, 'Sound Off'.

FRANKIE LAINE
ROSE, ROSE, I LOVE YOU ♪
Columbia

▲ 6
⑩ 3
—/250

You can count the number of Chinese hits in the US on one set of chopsticks. This oriental ode (an English language version of 'May Kway O May Kway' by Miss Hue Lee) helped pay back the $25,000 that Columbia had given Mercury for Laine's contract.

UNITED KINGDOM
May 1951

STEVE CONWAY
GOOD LUCK, GOOD HEALTH, GOD BLESS YOU
Columbia

Conway was a unique and underrated vocalist, who specialized in solemn songs like 'Bless This House', 'At The End Of The Day' and this touching ballad (on which he was joined by the Hastings Girls' Choir). With cruel irony, Conway collapsed on stage in December 1951 with heart problems and died a few months later aged just 31.

UNITED STATES
June 1951

VAUGHN MONROE & HIS ORCHESTRA
ON TOP OF OLD SMOKY ♪
RCA

▲ 10
⑩ 3•
—/250

Monroe was joined by The Moon Maids and Moon Men on this recording of a folk tune that fared even better by The Weavers. The popular sing-along song was the last Top 10 hit for one of the 1940s most successful singers. When rock arrived, Monroe tried to board the bandwagon, but his face and powerful voice simply did not fit.

GUY MITCHELL
MY TRULY, TRULY FAIR ♪
Columbia

▲ 5
⑩ 4
—/250

This hand-clapping Bob Merrill singalong quickly lifted the one-time winner of Arthur Godfrey's *Talent Scouts* back into the transatlantic Top 10. Soon afterwards US DJs, not surprisingly, voted Mitchell the Most Promising Male Singer of 1951.

PATTI PAGE
MISTER AND MISSISSIPPI
Mercury

▲ 9
⑩ 5
—/250

Popular Miss Page continued her run of hits with an Irving Gordon-penned novelty which, like his 1960 success 'Delaware', was a play on the names of US States. Dennis Day and Tennessee Ernie Ford also charted with the song.

UNITED KINGDOM
June 1951

TENNESSEE ERNIE
THE SHOT GUN BOOGIE
Capitol

In the US, Frankie Laine's covers of Ford's country bestsellers, 'Mule Train and 'The Cry Of The Wild Goose', had taken the lion's share of pop sales.

However, in the UK, where Laine's versions were not available, Tennessee Ernie's singles sold in vast quantities. He added to his impressive UK hit list with a self-penned single which introduced British record buyers to country boogie – one of the main components of rockabilly and rock'n'roll.

UNITED STATES
July 1951

ROSEMARY CLOONEY
COME ON-A MY HOUSE
Columbia

▲ 1
⑩ 1
44/250

Mitch Miller spotted Clooney's potential when she sang with sister Betty in Tony Pastor's band. The single that made the distinctive singer from Kentucky a household name was a left-field novelty which also showcased harpsichordist Stan Freeman. Composer Ross Bagdasarian (who subsequently had hits as David Seville and as The Chipmunks) based it on an old Armenian air, and it was recorded previously by his wife Kay Armen. Clooney was to be seen singing it in the film *The Stars Are Singing*.

DINAH SHORE
SWEET VIOLETS ♪
RCA

▲ 3
⑩ 2•
203/250

Smoky-voiced Shore visited the transatlantic charts for the last time with her interpretation of an old folk song. The singer, who was seldom without a bestseller in the 1940s, hosted one of America's most popular variety TV shows in the 1950s, following it with an equally successful chat show in the 1970s.

TONY MARTIN
I GET IDEAS
RCA

▲ 3
⑩ 4
98/250

Martin added to his hit tally with a version of the Argentine tango, 'Adios Muchachos', although at the time many considered Dorcas Cochran's English lyric about dancing 'dangerously near' to someone to be perhaps a little risqué. Incidentally, both Peggy Lee and Louis Armstrong also clicked with the song.

TONY BENNETT
BECAUSE OF YOU ♪
Columbia

▲ 1
⑩ 1
6/250

Oscar Hammerstein's uncle, Arthur Hammerstein, composed the song that introduced this stylish New York-born performer (real name Anthony Benedetto) to the world. The Lanza-styled ballad was heard in the 1951 film *I Was An American Spy* (which starred veteran actress Ann Dvorak). Bennett's debut hit headed the pop chart for eight weeks (until his follow-up, remarkably, replaced it). A sax-led instrumental interpretation by Tab Smith topped the R&B chart.

UNITED KINGDOM
July 1951

HOAGY CARMICHAEL
MY RESISTANCE IS LOW
Brunswick

One of the twentieth century's most successful songsmiths was born in Indiana in the late nineteenth century. He also appeared in a handful of films and had several hit singles to his credit.

Among Carmichael's timeless tunes are 'Stardust', 'Georgia On My Mind', 'Heart And Soul' and 'Lazy River', all of which charted again in the early rock years. He sang the laid-back self-composed classic in the Jane Russell film *The Las Vegas Story*. In 1976, a carefully cloned revival by Robin Sarstedt was a huge UK-only hit.

UNITED STATES
August 1951

HENRI RENE
(& HIS ORCHESTRA)
FEATURING APRIL
STEVENS
I'M IN LOVE AGAIN
RCA

▲ 10
⑩ 1
—/250

Fifteen-year-old Stevens (born Carol Lo Tempio) from Niagara Falls made a big splash with her first

RCA release, on which she sang with Henri Rene's Orchestra. In the US, Cole Porter's composition first appeared in the 1924 version of *The Greenwich Village Follies* (performed by the Dolly Sisters) whereas in the UK it had been featured in the 1927 musical *Up With The Lark*. Later, in the 1960s, whispering-voiced Stevens, who was named Most Promising Female Vocalist of 1951, teamed with brother Nino, and their revival of 'Deep Purple' topped the chart.

DORIS DAY
SHANGHAI ♪
Columbia

▲ 9
⑩ 2
—/250

This freckle-faced film star had the biggest-selling recording of a bouncy Bob Hilliard ode that told of the problems a little white lie can cause. Among the versions left trailing in Day's dust was one by her ex-boss Bob Crosby.

LES PAUL
WHISPERING
Capitol

▲ 7
⑩ 5
—/250

The well-loved standard was returned to the chart by the 'Wizard of Wankesha' (his home town in Wisconsin), as the father of the solid-body guitar was known. Interestingly, the song revisited the US Top 20 in 1963 recorded by fellow 1951 hit maker April Stevens.

TONY BENNETT
COLD, COLD HEART
Columbia

▲ 1
⑩ 2
22/250

For a record-breaking ten weeks this single and Bennett's first hit, 'Because of You' held the top two rungs, his version of the Hank Williams country song following the singer's previous platter in the No 1 position. The single's success started a rush of pop covers of Williams' works.

UNITED KINGDOM
August 1951

JO STAFFORD &
FRANKIE LAINE
PRETTY-EYED BABY
Columbia

This dynamic duo's reworking of a song first recorded by ex-Ink Spot Deek Watson & The Brown Dots (who evolved into the Four Tunes), proved very popular in the UK. Their follow-up, 'In The Cool, Cool, Cool of the Evening', also made an impression on both sides of the Atlantic.

UNITED STATES
September 1951

LES PAUL &
MARY FORD
THE WORLD IS WAITING
FOR THE SUNRISE
Capitol

▲ 3
⑩ 6
199/250

As the war in Korea continued, the couple's unique update of an optimistic ode from the World War I era struck a chord with American record buyers. It also gave Mr and Mrs Paul a double-sided Top 10 single (with 'Whispering').

LES BAXTER & HIS ORCHESTRA
BECAUSE OF YOU ♪
Capitol

▲ 9
⑩ 1
—/250

Not only was this 1940 composition the vehicle that gave Tony Bennett his first hit, it was also the song that introduced this Texas-born, Hollywood-based orchestra leader/arranger to the bestsellers chart. Baxter, a member of Mel Torme's group The Mel-Tones in the 1940s, had earlier arranged Nat 'King' Cole's acclaimed recordings 'Mona Lisa' and 'Too Young'.

PATTI PAGE
AND SO TO SLEEP AGAIN
Mercury

▲ 10
⑩ 6
—/250

The distinctive Oklahoma vocalist scored her fifth Top 10 entry of the year with a compelling Joe Marsala and Sunny Skylar song. Among the other singers who cut the composition were Dick Haymes, Paul Weston and teenager April Stevens.

UNITED KINGDOM
September 1951

JIMMY YOUNG
TOO YOUNG
Polygon

Even though he recorded on the relatively small Polygon label, the Gloucester-born balladeer's version of the timeless song was as popular as Nat 'King' Cole's classic cut in the UK. Like many of his British peers in the early 1950s, the majority of Young's singles were covers of American hits.

UNITED STATES
October 1951

FOUR ACES
SIN
Victoria/Flash

▲ 4
⑩ 1
193/250

Pennsylvania's Four Aces set the standard for vocal groups in the early 1950s. The quartet, who started out as an instrumental outfit, put up their own money to record the song, which was written for them by two local composers. 'Sin' was leased to Dave Miller's new Victoria label (which quickly changed its name to Flash), who outbid Mercury for the master. A pack of other artists covered the Aces, but the youthful newcomers' version still sold over a million copies.

DEL WOOD
DOWN YONDER ♪
Tennessee

▲ 6
⑩ 1•
—/250

Nashville-born ragtime pianist Wood (real name Adelaide Hendricks) had a crossover pop and country hit with her honky-tonk treatment of an old vaudeville standard. It was the only record by a female American instrumentalist to sell over a million. Originally performed by its composer L. Wolfe Gilbert in the early 1920s, it returned to the transatlantic charts in 1960 by Johnny & The Hurricanes.

EDDY HOWARD
SIN
Mercury

One of the most popular crooners of the 1930s (when he was with Dick Jurgens Band) and 1940s had the highest-charting version of this much recorded song. Like the Californian vocalist's 1946 No 1 ,'To Each His Own', this single sold over a million copies. Howard's fan base had all but eroded by 1955, when the teen-targeted 'Teenager's Waltz' gave him his last Top 100 entry. He died aged 48 in 1963.

EDDIE FISHER
TURN BACK THE HANDS OF TIME
RCA

Before he was drafted into the special services, the photogenic young vocalist was already hugely popular with the bobby-sox brigade. In the US, no one successfully covered this singalong song; however, in the UK Fisher met stiff opposition from a celebrated local newcomer, Jimmy Young.

AMES BROTHERS
UNDECIDED
Coral

▲ 6
⑩ 4
—/250

The quartet, voted Top Vocal Group of 1951 by US DJs, were joined by Les Brown & His Band Of Renown on their winning revival of a well-loved Ella Fitzgerald jump tune from 1939.

UNITED KINGDOM
October 1951

JIMMY YOUNG
BECAUSE OF YOU
Polygon

Tony Bennett's rendition of the much recorded film song may have monopolized the top spot on the US charts, but in the UK the version by this popular newcomer outsold all others. Incidentally, the vocalist, who first came into the spotlight in 1949 when singing with the Ray Martin Orchestra, also covered the debut hit (both sides) of Johnnie Ray, another US newcomer.

UNITED STATES
November 1951

SAVANNAH CHURCHILL
(IT'S NO) SIN
RCA

This critically acclaimed jazz/R&B song stylist from Louisiana (born Savannah Valentine) had one of the three versions of 'Sin' in the Top 10. It was

Churchill's biggest-selling single since her composition 'I Want To Be Loved' (on which she teamed with The Sentimentals – subsequently known as The Four Tunes) headed the R&B charts in 1947. An injury caused by a drunk in the audience at a performance in 1956 all but ended the vocalist's career.

TONY MARTIN
DOMINO ♪
RCA

▲ 10
⑩ 5
—/250

Despite strong competition from Doris Day and Bing Crosby, it was screen star Martin's treatment

of the French song that took the honours on both sides of the Atlantic. The English lyric came from the pen of the underrated Don Raye.

FRANKIE LAINE
JEALOUSY (JALOUSIE)
Columbia

▲ 3
⑩ 4
228/250

A dynamic Danish composition from the mid-1920s added more gold to Laine's enviable collection. Interestingly, the B side, 'Flamenco', was co-written by top Atlantic Records' executive Jerry Wexler. In 1963, Billy Fury's update of 'Jealousy' reached the UK Top 3.

UNITED KINGDOM
November 1951

FRED WARING & HIS PENNSYLVANIANS
TULIPS AND HEATHER/
THE LOVELIEST NIGHT OF
THE YEAR
Brunswick

One of the most in-demand dance bands of the 1920s and 1930s scored a bestseller in the UK

with a single that coupled two current hits. Waring's famous Glee Club were featured on his version of Perry Como's 'Tulips And Heather', while Gordon Goodman was heard on the band's treatment of the song that Mario Lanza had originally made famous.

UNITED STATES
December 1951

JOHNNIE RAY
THE LITTLE WHITE CLOUD
THAT CRIED ♪
Okeh

▲ 2
⑩ 1
139/250

It may seem strange, but when this double-sided smash was released many people thought the vocalist was a female R&B artist, and the fact that

it was released on Columbia's R&B subsidiary, Okeh, did nothing to dispel the rumour. The single was such a success that at times the Ray-written song and the other side, 'Cry', held the top two rungs on the US chart. Backing vocals on both sides were handled by the Canadian newcomers The Four Lads.

JO STAFFORD
SHRIMP BOATS ♪
Columbia

| ▲ 2 |
| ⑩ 2 |
| 198/250 |

On both sides of the Atlantic, record buyers were hurry hurry hurrying to the shops to purchase this folk-flavoured ode about the returning fishing fleet. Jo's husband Paul Weston had a hand in writing the unusual but undeniably hooky song.

PEE WEE KING & HIS GOLDEN WEST COWBOYS
SLOW POKE ♪
RCA

| ▲ 3 |
| ⑩ 1• |
| 190/250 |

Q: What connects the big 1950s hits 'Tennessee Waltz', 'You Belong To Me', 'Bonaparte's Retreat' and 'Slow Poke'? A: They were all written by King (born Julius Kucyznski in Wisconsin), a fiddle and accordion player who fronted the award-winning band The Golden West Cowboys. For the the UK market, the band's singer and co-writer Redd Stewart re-vocalled the chorus, changing the title to 'Slow Coach', to avoid any confusion about its meaning. King was elected into the Country Hall of Fame in 1974.

JOHNNIE RAY
CRY ♪
Okeh

| ▲ 1 |
| ⑩ 2 |
| 4/250 |

Millions of transatlantic record buyers bought this revolutionary release, which introduced them to the most controversial singer of the early 1950s. The song, written by a night watchman, had earlier been cut by Ruth Casey. Ray's almost a cappella treatment was one of many versions around at the time. Earlier tearful tracks by such R&B vocalists as Jimmy Scott and Tommy Brown may have influenced Ray's performance, but that did not stop it becoming the first R&B No 1 by a white male vocalist.

EDDIE FISHER
ANY TIME
RCA

| ▲ 3 |
| ⑩ 3 |
| 126/250 |

America's bestselling country artist of the 1940s, Eddy Arnold, took this singalong Herb 'Happy' Lawson composition to the top of the C&W chart in 1948. Three years later, it earned Fisher his first gold disc. In the UK, the song is best known as comedian/singer Des O'Connor's theme.

UNITED KINGDOM
December 1951

LITA ROZA
ALLENTOWN JAIL
Decca

Roza, one of the UK's most popular female vocalists of the decade, had sung with the bands of Harry Roy and Edmundo Ros in the 1940s. She joined Ted Heath's band in 1950 and they provided the backing on her version of the western-styled Irving Gordon opus, which Jo Stafford had previously recorded. The Liverpool lass cut many of the era's best-known songs and took 'Hey There' (1955) and 'Jimmy Unknown' (1956) into the Top 20.

UNITED STATES
January 1952

FOUR ACES
TELL ME WHY ♪
Decca

▲ 2
⑩ 2
129/250

Lead singer Al Alberts penned this melodramatic ballad with the Aces' arranger Marty Gold. It was the foursome's first release on Decca and, like its predecessor 'Sin' (on Victoria/Flash), was widely covered. Interestingly, it featured 'doo-wah' backing vocals which, alongside 'doo-wop', became synonymous with the 1950s vocal group sound.

MANTOVANI & HIS ORCHESTRA
CHARMAINE
London

▲ 10
⑩ 1•
—/250

No UK-based artist sold more records in the US in the 1950s than this orchestra leader, born Annunzio Paulo in Venice (Mantovani being his mother's maiden name). Mantovani's treatment of the film theme from 1926 introduced the world to his 'cascading strings' sound, which made the orchestra internationally popular. Both 'Charmaine' and the B side, 'Diane', were written by Lew Pollock and Erno Rapee, and both were subsequently revived successfully by The Bachelors.

EDDIE FISHER
TELL ME WHY ♪
RCA

▲ 7
⑩ 4
—/250

America's most successful recording artist of 1952 joined The Four Aces in the Top 10 with his interpretation of a powerful ballad. A revival in 1964 by Bobby Vinton also sold extremely well.

LES PAUL & MARY FORD
TIGER RAG
Capitol

▲ 6
⑩ 7
—/250

World War I was raging when The Original Dixieland Jazz Band wrote and recorded this popular fast-paced foot-tapper. Interestingly, the rag that kept America's top duo hot had earned the Mills Brothers their first million seller some 20 years earlier.

BELL SISTERS
BERMUDA
RCA

▲ 8
⑩ 1•
—/250

Eleven-year-old Kay Strother and her 16-year-old sister Cynthia (their mother's maiden name was Bell) had their day in the sun, when a song written by Cynthia and the girl's father, Eugene, briefly made them a hot property. Later recordings by the Kentucky duo, including covers of 'Wheel Of Fortune' and 'Hambone', rang up relatively few sales for the 'Bermuda Kids' as they were affectionately known.

UNITED KINGDOM
January 1952

SIR HUBERT PIMM
I WANNA SAY HELLO
London

Although only a jukebox hit in the US, this American ragtime recording was very successful in the UK. On Pimm's No 1 single, the nattily named

pianist (reputed to be the composer Jimmy MacDonald) was joined by vocalist Ellen Sutton, but it was a case of 'hello/goodbye' for the performer, whose later tracks, which included 'Honky Tonk Train Blues' and 'Bye Bye Blues' failed to click.

UNITED STATES
February 1952

**LEROY ANDERSON &
HIS 'POPS' CONCERT
ORCHESTRA**
BLUE TANGO ♪
Decca

| ▲ 1 |
| 🔟 1• |
| 10/250 |

No record in the 1950s spent longer in the US Top 20 than the 36 weeks scored by this infectious Latin instrumental. Arranger/conductor Leroy Anderson, who had worked with the famous Boston Pops Orchestra in the 1930s and 1940s, also composed the internationally popular dance song. Bill Black's Combo returned 'Blue Tango' to the US Top 20 in 1960. Massachusetts-born Anderson (who hated lyrics of any kind being added to his music) is remembered equally well for the standout compositions 'Sleigh Ride', 'The Syncopated Clock', 'The Typewriter' and 'Forgotten Dreams'.

JOHNNIE RAY
PLEASE, MR SUN
Columbia

| ▲ 6 |
| 🔟 3 |
| —/250 |

How better to follow a double-sided debut smash than with another one – especially when all four

tracks are in the Top 10 together? Both Perry Como and Tommy Edwards had to be content to trail behind the 'Cry Guy' with their treatments of the 'hot' hit, although a re-recording by Edwards in 1959 reached the Top 20.

KAY STARR
WHEEL OF FORTUNE ♪
Capitol

| ▲ 1 |
| 🔟 3 |
| 13/250 |

Scores of pop and R&B artists gambled that this ultra-commercial Benjamin & Weiss composition would be lucky for them. The song, which Johnny Hartman had recorded first, was selling well by Eddie Wilcox and Sunny Gale when Starr's stunning cover version overtook them on both sides of the Atlantic.

UNITED KINGDOM
February 1952

FRANKIE FROBA & HIS BOYS
MISTAKES
Brunswick

In the month that King George VI died, this veteran pianist and bandleader had the UK's best-selling single with a revival of a British composition from 1928. Interestingly, Frankie Froba's (sometimes spelt Froeba) instrumental interpretation of the song sold far better than his recording featuring hit vocalist Al Morgan ('Jealous Heart'). The swing bandleader, who had previously worked with Benny Goodman, was co-writer of Cab Calloway's influential 1939 single 'The Jumpin' Jive'.

UNITED STATES
March 1952

JOHNNIE RAY
HERE AM I – BROKEN HEARTED
Columbia

| ▲ 9 |
| ⑩ 4 |
| —/250 |

This J.R. from Dallas (Oregon) cried all the way to the bank again, thanks to his emotion-packed revival of a Paul Whiteman pearl from 1927.

ELLA MAE MORSE
BLACKSMITH BLUES ♪
Capitol

| ▲ 3 |
| ⑩ 1• |
| 181/250 |

As Bill Haley released 'Rock The Joint' and Alan Freed launched his Coronation Ball, one of rock's earlier influences, Ella Mae Morse, had her last hit. The boogie woogie vocalist was not only the first white artist to head the R&B chart, but also sang on Capitol Records' first Top 10 entry 'Mr Five By Five' in 1942. Incidentally, a lawsuit showed that 'Blacksmith Blues' had actually started life in 1949 as 'Happy Payday'.

FOUR ACES
PERFIDIA
Decca

| ▲ 7 |
| ⑩ 3 |
| —/250 |

With Latin American music enjoying renewed poularity, the US' best-selling vocal group of 1952 played their cards right by reviving this Xavier Cugat classic from 1941. An instrumental interpretation by The Ventures reached the transatlantic Top 20 in 1960.

DORIS DAY
A GUY IS A GUY
Columbia

| ▲ 4 |
| ⑩ 3 |
| 206/250 |

A rewrite of a bawdy World War II song would hardly seem the ideal vehicle for America's best-loved girl-next-door. However, producer Mitch Miller managed to turn 'A Gob Is A Slob' into a transatlantic hit for her.

EDDIE FISHER
FORGIVE ME
RCA

▲ 7
🔟 5
—/250

Among the many songs that this teen idol

successfully revived was a noted 1927 composition which earlier superstar Gene Austin had originally made famous. It was one of five Top 10s for the popular performer in 1952.

UNITED KINGDOM
March 1952

GUY MITCHELL
THERE'S ALWAYS ROOM
AT OUR HOUSE
Columbia

In many British homes people found room for yet another happy-go-lucky Bob Merrill composition. Mitchell's version led the field, but Billy Cotton's treatment also sold well, thanks in part to its coupling, the equally popular 'I Wanna Say Hello'.

UNITED STATES
April 1952

GUY MITCHELL
PITTSBURGH,
PENNSYLVANIA ♪
Columbia

▲ 6
🔟 5
—/250

Yet another hit from the three M's: performer Mitchell, composer Bob Merrill and producer Mitch Miller. This toe-tapping transatlantic winner told of a young man who needed frequent visits to a pawnshop (on the corner in Pittsburgh, Pennsylvania) to be able to afford to take his angel out.

GEORGIA GIBBS
KISS OF FIRE ♪
Mercury

▲ 2
🔟 1
130/250

Rock writers tend to deride the ex-big-band vocalist for covering so many records during the decade, but if that is a crime, then Gibbs shouldn't be alone in the dock. The singer from Massachusetts (born Freda Gibbons) outsold six

other recording artists to top the chart with her version of the fiery Latin American song, on which she was backed by the Glenn Osser Orchestra. A re-recording in 1966 by Gibbs on Bell did not bring her career back to the boil.

DON CORNELL
I'LL WALK ALONE
Coral

▲ 7
🔟 1
—/250

Eight recordings of the haunting tune from the tear-jerking Jane Froman biopic, *With A Song In My Heart*, marched into the US chart. Striding ahead was the version by a New York balladeer and ex-boxer (born Luigi Varlaro, not Domenico Cornello as often quoted), who initially found fame as a vocalist with Sammy Kaye's band. When the song was first released during the war, Dinah Shore, Mary Martin and Martha Tilton had all taken it into the Top 10.

UNITED KINGDOM
April 1952

NAT 'KING' COLE
UNFORGETTABLE
Capitol

Nat 'King' Cole's theme song had a higher chart profile in the UK than in the acclaimed performer's homeland. Astoundingly, a quarter of a century after his death, a recording which mixed Nat's original version with daughter Natalie's treatment reached the US Top 20 in 1991, and earned a couple of Grammy Awards.

UNITED STATES
May 1952

HUGO WINTERHALTER & HIS ORCHESTRA & CHORUS
BLUE TANGO ♪
RCA

▲ 9
⑩ 2
—/250

Before heading RCA's A&R team, this orchestra leader from Pennsylvania wrote arrangements for such top stars as Vaughn Monroe, Billy Eckstine and Tommy & Jimmy Dorsey. He had one of his biggest hits with a string-laden interpretation of the Leroy Anderson chart topper.

DON CORNELL
I'M YOURS ♪
Coral

▲ 5
⑩ 2
—/250

The big-voiced baritone gave another heart-throb, Eddie Fisher, a good run for his money with this million-selling version of a top-drawer love ballad.

PERCY FAITH & HIS ORCHESTRA
DELICADO
Columbia

▲ 1
⑩ 1
73/250

Canadian composer/orchestra leader Faith had the first of three US chart toppers with his interpretation of an instrumental written and originally recorded by Brazilian composer/ orchestra leader Waldyr Azevedo. It featured noted harpsichordist Stan Freeman (of 'Come On-A My House' fame). As a musical director for Columbia, Faith & His Orchestra previously played on hits by such artists as Tony Bennett, Rosemary Clooney and Guy Mitchell.

EDDIE FISHER
I'M YOURS ♪
RCA

▲ 5
⑩ 6
—/250

This singing soldier's rendition of Robert Mellin's standout ballad joined Don Cornell's cut in the chart. Its B side, 'Just A Little Lovin'', had been a country No 1 for label-mate Eddy Arnold in 1948 – as had Fisher's earlier million seller, 'Any Time'.

AL MARTINO
HERE IN MY HEART
BBS

▲ 1
⑩ 1
63/250

Not long after The Four Aces charted with the first release on his Victoria label, Philadelphia entrepreneur Dave Miller had a transatlantic No 1 with the debut disc on his BBS label. Martino's (born Alfred Cini in Philadelphia) debut hit sold a staggering 100,000 copies in seven days and Miller quickly signed him to Capitol. It was the first

official No 1 in the UK. A re-recording in 1958 meant little, and another in 1961 entered the US Top 100.

UNITED KINGDOM
May 1952

JOHNSTON BROTHERS
BE MY LIFE'S COMPANION
Decca

The UK's most popular male vocal quartet of the early 1950s was formed by multi-talented music

publisher/composer/singer Johnny Johnston to sing on the soundtrack of the film *Portrait Of Jennie* in 1950. They had the top-selling British version of a Bob Hilliard and Milton De Lugg opus that the Mills Brothers and Rosemary Clooney had minor hits with in the US.

UNITED STATES
June 1952

TONY MARTIN
KISS OF FIRE ♪
RCA

▲	6
⑩	6
—	/250

For the second time in a year the romantic balladeer scored with a dramatic Argentine tango – this time it was based on the Latin American standard 'El Choclo'. Of the many versions on the market, only Georgia Gibbs' recording fared better.

JOHNNIE RAY
WALKIN' MY BABY BACK HOME ♪
Columbia

▲	6
⑩	5
—	/250

Female fan hysteria followed Ray wherever he performed – there had been nothing like it since the early days of Sinatra. He visited the Top 10 for the fifth time in as many months with a revival of a song Ted Weems had helped to popularize some 20 years earlier.

PERRY COMO & EDDIE FISHER
MAYBE
RCA

▲	8
⑩	6
—	/250

Two of RCA's biggest-selling stars teamed together on a revival of a memorable Ink Spots hit from 1940. It had been intended as the B side but soon surpassed 'Watermelon Weather' in popularity.

VERA LYNN
AUF WIEDERSEH'N SWEETHEART
London

▲	1
⑩	1
21	/250

See UK entry (July).

UNITED KINGDOM
June 1952

TED HEATH & HIS MUSIC
THE BLACKSMITH BLUES
Decca

During the 1950s, no British band was more popular on either side of the Atlantic than the one

led by an ex-street busker and one-time trombonist with the Jack Hylton, Ambrose and Geraldos' Bands. Over the years, the Londoner's band included many musicians and vocalists who went on to become solo stars. Among these was Lita Roza, who sang on their UK-aimed cover of Ella Mae Morse's US hit.

UNITED STATES
July 1952

ROSEMARY CLOONEY
HALF AS MUCH
Columbia

▲ 2
⑩ 2
114/250

As further proof that there was gold in them thar hillbillies, Mitch Miller recorded another Hank Williams country hit with one of his top pop acts. For the record, Hank had covered composer Curley Williams' original recording.

PEGGY LEE
LOVER
Decca

▲ 10
⑩ 1
—/250

Gordon Jenkins' 37 piece orchestra provided the spectacular mambo backing to Lee's (born Norma Jean Egstrom in North Dakota) revival of a Rodgers

& Hart waltz from the 1932 Maurice Chevalier and Jeanette MacDonald movie *Love Me Tonight*. It was the second gold disc for the ex-Benny Goodman Band vocalist, who had topped the chart in 1948 with her million-selling composition 'Mañana'.

ROSEMARY CLOONEY
BOTCH-A-ME
Columbia

▲ 2
⑩ 3
189/250

This captivating novelty song first surfaced in Italy during the war as 'Ba-Ba-Baciami Piccini'. The fresh-sounding vocalist's multi-language version added to her transatlantic charters, and at times stood in the US Top 3 with Clooney's previous single 'Half As Much'.

UNITED KINGDOM
July 1952

VERA LYNN
AUF WIEDERSEH'N
SWEETHEART
Decca

Seventy soldiers and airmen supposedly accompanied Britain's 'Forces Sweetheart' on a singalong song that sounded as if it had been written during the war, when actually it was penned in Germany in 1949. Not only did the record top the UK chart, but it also headed the US lists for nine weeks (despite being up against versions by some very big guns). It was the first UK single to top the US sales chart and the only one to achieve that feat in the 1950s.

UNITED STATES
August 1952

EDDIE FISHER
WISH YOU WERE HERE
RCA

▲ 3
⑩ 8
144/250

Harold Rome penned this hauntingly beautiful ballad for his 1952 musical of the same name. The track was recorded while the idol of the swoon set was on furlough from the special sevices. Over a year later, when the show was released, it was also a big UK hit.

NAT 'KING' COLE
SOMEWHERE ALONG THE WAY ♪
Capitol

▲ 8
⑩ 3
—/250

The leader of the 1940's 'coolest' combo (The King Cole Trio) added to his seemingly endless string of transatlantic hits with a classy Sammy Gallup composition.

FRANKIE LAINE
HIGH NOON
Columbia

▲ 5
⑩ 6
—/250

'Do not forsake me oh my darling' was the most memorable line from the dramatic Academy Award winning western film theme. This acclaimed Ned Washington and Dimitri Tiomkin song also bulleted up the chart by singing cowboy star Tex Ritter.

DORIS DAY & FRANKIE LAINE
SUGARBUSH
Columbia

▲ 10
⑩ 4
—/250

Joseph Marais based his composition on a folk song he learned as a child in South Africa. Its happy-go-lucky feel and catchy chorus, coupled with the popular performer's lively reading, made it instantly successful in both the US and UK.

JO STAFFORD
YOU BELONG TO ME
Columbia

▲ 1
⑩ 3
32/250

1951's Top Female Singer scored her highest-placed hit with this memorable musical travelogue. It was another stunner from the pens of country tunesmiths Pee Wee King and Redd Stewart. Stafford's transatlantic No 1 sold over two million copies and a 1962 revival by The Duprees also turned gold.

UNITED KINGDOM
August 1952

VERA LYNN
HOMING WALTZ
Decca

After 'Auf Wiedersehen' had spent ten weeks at the top of the UK sheet music chart, it was replaced by

Londoner Lynn's (born Vera Welsh) follow-up, 'Homing Waltz', which hogged the No 1 spot for a further nine weeks.

UNITED STATES
September 1952

PATTI PAGE
I WENT TO YOUR
WEDDING ♪
Mercury

▲ 1
⑩ 7
41/250

This moving Jessie Mae Robinson composition was one of the first R&B songs to make a real dent on the pop chart. Prior to Page's winning waxing, it had been recorded by Steve Gibson & The Original Red Caps (featuring Damita Jo). A cover by Hank Snow was also a major country hit.

LES PAUL
MEET MISTER
CALLAGHAN ♪
Capitol

▲ 5
⑩ 8
—/250

One of the world's most popular guitarists of the twentieth century had the biggest-selling version of the British movie theme. UK readers may be interested to note that composer Eric Spear also penned the theme to the long-running soap opera *Coronation Street*.

JO STAFFORD
JAMBALAYA
Columbia

▲ 3
⑩ 4
167/250

During her career this pure-toned vocalist often cut country compositions, and it was Stafford's version of the cajun classic that introduced the Hank Williams song to transatlantic pop record buyers. Interestingly, she had earlier released versions of Williams' 'Setting The Woods On Fire' and 'Hey, Good Lookin''.

SLIM WHITMAN
INDIAN LOVE CALL
Imperial

▲ 10
⑩ 1•
—/250

Recording a song from the popular operetta *Rose Marie* may have seemed a strange choice for a country yodeller, but it was this left-field idea that gave the Florida-born singer his only major US pop hit. Astoundingly, Whitman's version of the 25-year-old Paul Whiteman winner and its B side, 'China Doll', reached the UK Top 20 in 1955.

PATTI PAGE
YOU BELONG TO ME ♪
Mercury

▲ 9
🔟 8
—/250

America's most popular female artist of 1952 added to her hit tally with a reading of this much recorded country song. The track could be found on the B side of Page's chart-topping 'I Went To Your Wedding'.

HILLTOPPERS
TRYING
Dot

▲ 7
🔟 1
—/250

Three students from the Western Kentucky College teamed with a former graduate, Billy Vaughn, to record a song that the latter had penned to suit lead singer Jimmy Sacca's strong expressive voice. After a slow start, this almost a cappella track (recorded in the college's auditorium) climbed up the chart. It also reached the UK hit parade when it was finally released there in 1956. A later instrumental interpretation by Vaughn in 1958 made the US Top 100.

UNITED KINGDOM
September 1952

BING CROSBY
ISLE OF INNISFREE
Brunswick

▲ 3
🔟 1
169/250

Three years after taking the Irish song 'Galway Bay' up the transatlantic charts, 'Der Bingle' clocked up his first official UK chart entry with another paean to the Emerald Isle. Incidentally, in the US the earlier hit was re-released on the B side of this track.

UNITED STATES
October 1952

MILLS BROTHERS
GLOW WORM ♪
Decca

▲ 2
🔟 3•
115/250

Brothers Herbert, Harry and Donald together with father John gave the world many memorable recordings, including 'Dinah' (1932), 'Paper Doll' (1943) and their interpretation of this turn-of-the-century German song with English lyrics by Johnny Mercer. Later in the decade, the quartet tried to adapt to rock'n'roll; they appeared in the film *The Big Beat* and bravely covered The Silhouettes' doo-wop classic 'Get A Job'.

JOHNNY STANDLEY
IT'S IN THE BOOK
(PARTS 1 & 2)
Capitol

▲ 1
🔟 1•
68/250

Johnny Standley was among the few one-hit wonders in the early 1950s. The actor/singer, who toured with Horace Heidt's band, put his name in the record books when this self-composed parody of a fundamentalist preacher powered its way to the top. Part one is a monologue based on 'Little Bo Peep' (complete with canned laughter), while Heidt & His Musical Knights joined him on the hand-clapping revivalist-styled B side. Standley's follow-up, 'Clap Your Hands', and later tracks like 'Rock & Roll Must Go' went nowhere.

UNITED KINGDOM
October 1952

GUY MITCHELL
FEET UP
Columbia

▲ 2
⑩ 1
164/250

recent London Palladium shows had been very successful, enjoyed a higher chart placing in the UK with this fun-filled diaper ditty.

Surely only Bob Merrill would compose a song about the joys of changing a baby? Mitchell, whose

---

UNITED STATES
November 1952

JONI JAMES
WHY DON'T YOU
BELIEVE ME
MGM

▲ 1
⑩ 1
46/250

It was third time lucky for the Chicago-born ex-dancer (real name Joan Carmello Babbo), whose first two MGM releases made few ripples. James' original version of the memorable ballad, written by her orchestra leader Lew Douglas, beat stiff opposition from Patti Page. Coincidentally, the last release from both Page and James, 'You Belong To Me', had lost out to Jo Stafford's rush-released rendition. It is believed that Joni paid for the recording session that yielded this gold disc.

EDDIE FISHER
OUTSIDE OF HEAVEN
RCA

▲ 10
⑩ 9
—/250

His time in the army had no effect on Fisher's fantastic career – he ended 1952 with a double-

sided Top 10 entry (coupling 'Lady Of Spain'). Celebrated songsmiths Sammy Gallop and Chester Conn composed the powerful lost-love ballad, which flew to No 1 in the UK.

MARIO LANZA
BECAUSE YOU'RE MINE
RCA

▲ 7
⑩ 4•
—/250

One of the world's finest operatic tenors' last major transatlantic success came with the title song from the fourth of his seven starring movies. Lanza's death in Rome at the age of 38 in 1959 is still shrouded with mystery, but there's no disputing the fact that during the vocalist's short but spectacular career he sold many millions of singles and albums, and was equally popular on both sides of the Atlantic.

EDDIE FISHER
LADY OF SPAIN
RCA

Leading British composer Tolchard Evans penned this lively ode to a Spanish señorita, which had introduced leading British orchestra leader Ray Noble to the US public in 1931. As always heart-throb Fisher was joined on his single by Hugo Winterhalter's top-notch orchestra.

VERA LYNN
YOURS
London

A re-recording of her 1941 UK best-seller quickly returned the 'Sweetheart of our GI's in England'

(as the American press called her) to the US Top 10. The song, which started out in Cuba as 'Quierme Mucho', could be found on the B side of 'Homing Waltz' in the UK.

PEARL BAILEY
TAKES TWO TO TANGO
Coral

This critically acclaimed vocalist had the top-selling single of her long and successful career with an Al Hoffman and Dick Manning-penned tango tune, which also sold well by another jazz celebrity, Louis Armstrong. The Virginia-born ex-big-band vocalist is probably best remembered for her roles in such films as *Carmen Jones*, *St Louis Blues* and *Porgy And Bess*.

UNITED KINGDOM
November 1952

AL MARTINO
HERE IN MY HEART
Capitol

See US entry (May).

JO STAFFORD
YOU BELONG TO ME
Columbia

See US entry (August).

NAT 'KING' COLE
SOMEWHERE ALONG THE WAY
Capitol

See US entry (August).

ROSEMARY CLOONEY
HALF AS MUCH
Columbia

See US entry (July).

FRANKIE LAINE
HIGH NOON
Columbia

See US entry (August).

VERA LYNN
FORGET ME NOT
Decca

The UK's bestselling female artist of 1952 was not only the sole British vocalist in the first-ever Top 10, but she had three separate entries. On this memorable Johnny Johnston composition Vera was joined by his vocal group, The Johnston Singers.

DORIS DAY & FRANKIE LAINE
SUGARBUSH
Columbia

See US entry (August).

RAY MARTIN & HIS ORCHESTRA
BLUE TANGO
Columbia

▲ 8
⑩ 1
—/250

The only instrumental in the first UK chart came from an orchestra fronted by a Vienna-born composer and arranger who had spent the last 15 years living in Britain. Martin, who formed the BBC Northern Variety Orchestra and hosted the long-running radio show *Melody From The Sky*, now headed Columbia Records' A&R team. His was the top-selling British version of Leroy Anderson's US No 1 hit.

MARIO LANZA
BECAUSE YOU'RE MINE
HMV

▲ 3
⑩ 1•
87/250

See US entry.

AL MARTINO
TAKE MY HEART
Capitol

▲ 9
⑩ 2
—/250

America's most successful new singer of 1952 was quickly signed by Capitol, who rush-released this track in June 1952 to combat a cover by Toni Arden. It soon joined his chart debut 'Here In My Heart' (which was cut on the same session) in both the US and UK Top 20s.

DORIS DAY
MY LOVE AND DEVOTION
Columbia

▲ 10
⑩ 2
—/250

In the UK, the photogenic film star lifted her version of this Milton Carson composition above those of local heavyweights Teddy Johnson and Jimmy Young. However, in the US Perry Como's rendition ignited more interest.

UNITED STATES
December 1952

JO STAFFORD
KEEP IT A SECRET
Columbia

▲ 6
⑩ 5
—/250

As Patti Page's recording of Jessie Mae Robinson's 'I Went To Your Wedding' slipped from No 1, it was joined in the Top 10 by this other noteworthy Robinson composition. Simultaneously, Slim Whitman's version climbed the country chart. No longer was Robinson a secret outside R&B circles.

PERRY COMO
DON'T LET THE STARS GET IN YOUR EYES
RCA

▲ 1
⑩ 7
33/250

This irresistible country song gave the popular personality his seventh No 1 in seven years and his first official UK chart topper. It was the most successful C&W composition of the time, with Top

10 entries by composer Slim Willet as well as Red Foley, Ray Price and Skeets McDonald.

JIMMY BOYD
I SAW MOMMY KISSING SANTA CLAUS
Columbia

▲ 1
⑩ 1
170/250

After UK labels rejected his Christmas novelty, composer Tommie Connor took it to the US, where it was recorded by this 12-year-old from Mississippi. Boyd's interpretation sold 700,000 in just ten days, and a year later it became a major UK hit for the student from the Hollywood Professional School For Children. Boyd's later unsuccessful seasonal singles included 'Santa Got Stuck Up The Chimney' and the US-only singles 'I Saw Mommy Do The Mambo', 'A Kiss For Christmas' and 'Reindeer Rock'.

DON HOWARD
OH HAPPY DAY
Essex

▲ 4
🔟 1•
—/250

Some critics could not believe that such a 'horrible record' could hit – but the 17-year-old Ohio student (born Don Howard Koplow) proved them wrong. He penned the happy lyric to a folk-styled song that had been written as a girl's camp sing-along, and it was first released on the tiny Triple A label. Despite its simplicity and his far from perfect vocal, it outsold versions by hit makers Lawrence Welk and the Four Knights. However, few people heard Howard's follow-up recording, 'Listen To My Song'.

SPIKE JONES & HIS
CITY SLICKERS
I SAW MOMMY KISSING
SANTA CLAUS
RCA

▲ 7
🔟 1•
—/250

With seasonal smashes like 'All I Want For Christmas (Is My Two Front Teeth)' and 'Rudolph

The Red-Nosed Reindeer' behind him, it was only natural that the zany performer and his music-murdering City Slickers would vandalize Jimmy Boyd's bestseller. The California combo, whose touring show had been known as The Musical Depreciation Revue, gave it their usual 'anything goes' treatment. The vocal on the track was handled by trumpet virtuoso George Rock.

TERESA BREWER
TILL I WALTZ AGAIN WITH YOU
Coral

▲ 1
🔟 2
29/250

The second most successful single of 1953 kept the one-time child protégé in the top spot for five weeks. She was backed on the potent pop ditty by the Jack Pleis Orchestra.

UNITED KINGDOM
December 1952

KAY STARR
COMES A-LONG A-LOVE
Capitol

▲ 1
🔟 1
84/250

Despite a relatively poor showing Stateside, the effervescent vocalist took this bouncy Al Sherman song to the very top in the UK. Interestingly, an advertisement for the record described Starr as 'at her rockin' best'.

BING CROSBY & JANE WYMAN
ZING A LITTLE ZONG
Brunswick

▲ 10
🔟 2
—/250

Actress Wyman (one-time wife of future President Ronald Reagan) sang this cute novelty number in

the film *Just For You* with her co-star Crosby. The Harry Warren and Leo Robin song was nominated for an Academy Award.

MANTOVANI & HIS ORCHESTRA
WHITE CHRISTMAS
Decca

▲ 6
🔟 1
—/250

Irving Berlin's perennial hit revisited the UK Top 10 thanks to a string-laden treatment by Britain's most popular orchestra. It was included on his album *Christmas Carols*, which reached the US Top 20 on four different occasions and earned Mantovani another gold disc.

NAT 'KING' COLE
BECAUSE YOU'RE MINE
Capitol

On both sides of the Atlantic, Mario Lanza's original recording of this film theme outsold all other versions. However, there was still room on both charts for singer/pianist Cole's unique treatment.

JOHNNIE RAY
FAITH CAN MOVE
MOUNTAINS
Columbia

If anything, the 'Prince of Wails' had a more loyal fan following in the UK than in his homeland. Despite stiff competition from Jimmy Young and Nat 'King' Cole, this unsuccessful US single returned Ray to the Top 10.

BING CROSBY
SILENT NIGHT
Brunswick

No one has sold more Christmas records than Crosby, whose 'White Christmas' single has topped 30 million copies and whose LP *Merry Christmas* has been a bestseller every year since 1945. Among his other Yuletide classics is this treatment of the universally loved early nineteenth-century German carol.

LOUIS ARMSTRONG
TAKES TWO TO TANGO
Brunswick

Few entertainers in the twentieth century have been as internationally popular as 'Satchmo'. Not only does he have the longest chart span of any artist in the US (1926–1988), Armstrong is also the oldest artist to top the singles chart on either side of the Atlantic. In his homeland, Armstrong's recording of the tango finished behind Pearl Bailey's. However, British audiences preferred the jazz giant's distinctive treatment and the novelty rendition by Hermoine Gingold and TV personality Gilbert Harding.

TONY BRENT
WALKIN' TO MISSOURI
Columbia

Soon after songs about mockingbirds and sparrows had flown up the chart, this Indian-born vocalist (real name Reginald Bretagne) clicked with his second single, an ode about a poor little robin who couldn't afford to fly to Missouri. The bouncy little novelty was written by Bob Merrill, and in the US, Sammy Kaye's Orchestra (with Tony Russo's vocals) walked away with all the honours.

MAX BYGRAVES
COWPUNCHER'S
CANTATA
HMV

Arguably, this all-round entertainer from London was the last of the true British music hall stars. The multi-faceted performer chalked up the first of his 11 Top 20 entries in the decade with a medley which parodied western songs like 'Mule Train', 'Riders In The Sky' and 'Cry Of The Wild Goose'. It was an unusual concept, but as Bygraves' character in the very popular radio series *Educating Archie* often remarked, it was a 'good idea, son'.

UNITED STATES
January 1953

GAYLORDS
TELL ME YOU'RE MINE
Mercury

▲ 3
🔟 1
135/250

Ronnie Vincent (aka Ronnie Gaylord) fronted the Detroit trio, whose name raised a few eyebrows in later decades. The first of their hits was a revival of a pre-war Italian song, 'Per Un Bacio D'Amor', to which Ronnie had added English lyrics.

JONI JAMES
HAVE YOU HEARD
MGM

▲ 5
🔟 2
—/250

Both sides of the 23-year-old vocalist's second successive million seller reached the Top 20 (the coupling was 'Wishing Ring'). The Duprees steered the song, written by James' musical director Lew Douglas, back into the Top 20 in 1963.

KAREN CHANDLER
HOLD ME, THRILL ME, KISS ME
Coral

▲ 7
🔟 1•
—/250

Three years after her UK hits as Eve Young, the singer from Idaho had her only major US smash with a captivating song that composer Harry Noble released a year before as 'Hold Me'. The number returned to the US Top 10 by Mel Carter in 1965, and reached the UK Top 20 in 1994 by Gloria Estefan.

UNITED KINGDOM
January 1953

EDDIE FISHER
OUTSIDE OF HEAVEN
HMV

▲ 1
🔟 1
70/250

See US entry (November 1952).

WINIFRED ATWELL
BRITANNIA RAG
Decca

▲ 5
🔟 1
—/250

Trinidad-born honky tonk/boogie woogie pianist Winifred Atwell was one of the biggest-selling recording artists in the UK during the 1950s. The popular entertainer followed her first major hit, 'Black and White Rag', with this composition which she had written especially for Queen Elizabeth II's first Royal Variety Show.

TONY BRENT
MAKE IT SOON
Columbia

▲ 9
🔟 2•
—/250

Although he never appeared in the US with Tex Beneke's Band (as was claimed at the time) Brent had sung with the Ambrose and Cyril Stapleton Bands in the UK in the early 1950s. He followed this French song with another five Top 20 entries. Brent, who arguably could handle a beat ballad better than any other British singer of the era, subsequently relocated to Australia.

PERRY COMO
DON'T LET THE STARS
GET IN YOUR EYES
HMV

```
▲ 1
⑩ 1
33/250
```

See US entry (December 1952).

AL MARTINO
NOW
Capitol

```
▲ 3
⑩ 3
171/250
```

This one-time winner of Arthur Godfrey's *Talent Scouts* show had his third UK Top 10 entry in two months, with a single that failed to show on the US bestsellers. It outsold local cuts by such UK headliners as Joe Loss and Dick James.

MILLS BROTHERS
GLOW WORM
Brunswick

```
▲ 10
⑩ 1•
—/250
```

See US Entry (October 1952).

UNITED STATES
February 1953

JULIUS LA ROSA
ANYWHERE I WANDER
Cadence

```
▲ 4
⑩ 1
—/250
```

Fifteen months after he became a regular on the top-rated *Arthur Godfrey & Friends* show, La Rosa had his first hit with a Frank Loesser composition which had come from fellow Brooklyn-born entertainer Danny Kaye's film *Hans Christian Andersen*. Eight months later, La Rosa was fired live on air from that successful TV show for reportedly lacking humility.

PATTI PAGE
THE DOGGIE IN THE
WINDOW
Mercury

```
▲ 1
⑩ 9
17/250
```

Bob Merrill composed the universally known novelty number that gave 'The Singing Rage' her only transatlantic Top 20 entry (due to label problems, many of Page's earlier Mercury hits were not released in the UK at the time). Interestingly, very few people noticed when her sequel record, 'Arfie, The Doggie In The Window', was for sale.

KAY STARR
SIDE BY SIDE
Capitol

```
▲ 8
⑩ 4
—/250
```

The consistently successful singer's rousing rendition of a perennially popular singalong song from the late 1920s returned her to the transatlantic Top 10.

NAT 'KING' COLE
PRETEND
Capitol

```
▲ 3
⑩ 4
159/250
```

Along with such gems as 'Too Young', 'Nature Boy' and 'Mona Lisa', this optimistic ode is one of the influential entertainer's best-loved records. It was given a rock treatment by Carl Mann in 1959, and returned to the UK Top 10 in 1981 recorded by Alvin Stardust.

FRANKIE LAINE
I BELIEVE
Columbia

▲ 2
⑩ 7
104/250

No record has spent more weeks at the top of the UK chart than the 18 scored by Laine's version of this semi-religious big ballad. The much acclaimed song was initially written for inclusion in Jane Froman's TV show *US Canteen*. Subsequently, revivals by both The Bachelors (1964) and Robson & Jerome (1995) were also huge UK hits.

UNITED KINGDOM
February 1953

EDDIE FISHER
EVERYTHING I HAVE IS YOURS
HMV

▲ 8
⑩ 2
—/250

After the success of 'Lady Of Spain', the melodic vocalist revived another Tolchard Evans tune from the 1930s. The romantic song was also featured (sung by Monica Lewis) in the 1952 film of the same name.

GUY MITCHELL
SHE WEARS RED FEATHERS
Columbia

▲ 1
⑩ 2
39/250

Mitchell's first official UK No 1 hit was another bouncy Bob Merrill novelty number. The song was about a London banker who brought home a hula hula girl who lived on 'just coco-nuts and fish from the sea'.

ART & DOTTY TODD
BROKEN WINGS
HMV

▲ 6
⑩ 1•
—/250

Despite stiff opposition from British headliners The Stargazers and Dickie Valentine (who apparently recorded it first), this married couple from New Jersey reached the UK Top 10 with the original version of a song that did not take off in the US. The duo's highest-ranking hit in their homeland was 'Chanson d'Amour (Song Of Love)' in 1958, which reportedly sold over a million.

DANNY KAYE
WONDERFUL COPENHAGEN
Brunswick

▲ 5
⑩ 1•
—/250

One of the year's most successful films was the musical *Hans Christian Andersen*, starring the internationally acclaimed singer/actor and entertainer Danny Kaye (born David Kaminsky). On the single, the consistently enjoyable performer coupled two of the movie's best-known tracks, 'Wonderful Copenhagen' and 'Anywhere I Wander' (which was a US hit for Julius La Rosa).

UNITED STATES

March 1953

JONI JAMES
YOUR CHEATIN' HEART
MGM

▲ 7
🔟 3
—/250

Both sides of Hank Williams' first posthumous single were covered by a handful of pop artists. The top-selling crossover hit came from one of the legendary singer/songwriter's biggest fans, his label-mate Joni James, whose interpretation of this country classic added another gold record to her collection.

PERRY COMO
WILD HORSES
RCA

▲ 7
🔟 8
—/250

While other second-generation crooners were making little headway on the chart, it seemed that a team of wild horses couldn't keep Como away. His latest runaway success was based on a nineteenth-century work called 'Wilder Reiter'.

FRANKIE LAINE & JIMMY BOYD
TELL ME A STORY
Columbia

▲ 4
🔟 8
—/250

Forty-year-old Laine helped 13-year-old Boyd achieve his second and last chart entry. The novelty song was composed by Terry Gilkyson, who had penned Laine's earlier hit 'The Cry Of The Wild Goose'. It was coupled with 'The Little Boy And The Old Man'.

UNITED KINGDOM

March 1953

STARGAZERS
BROKEN WINGS
Decca

▲ 1
🔟 1
96/250

Dick Rowe, later known as the 'man who turned down The Beatles' produced the most successful British vocal group of the 1950s, The Stargazers. Formed in 1949, the mixed quintet were fronted by Marie Benson when they took their version of Art & Dotty Todd's US release to the top – it was the first single by a UK act to reach No 1.

LITA ROZA
(HOW MUCH IS) THAT DOGGIE IN THE WINDOW
Decca

▲ 1
🔟 1•
93/250

Ted Heath's popular vocalist reached No 1 with a cute canine novelty that Patti Page had taken to the top in the US. Interestingly, Roza thought so little of the song that she refused to sing it on stage. The entertainer, who was voted the UK's No 1 Female Singer in the *NME* Poll of 1955, sold few records in the late 1950s, despite appearances on TV shows such as *6-5 Special* and *Oh, Boy*!

DICKIE VALENTINE
ALL THE TIME AND
EVERYWHERE
Decca

▲ 9
⑩ 1
—/250

UK's most popular home-grown heart-throb hit with a Bob Merrill song that Mindy Carson had cut first in the US.

In the mid-1950s no other British male vocalist was as successful as Londoner Valentine (born Richard Brice). The one-time child actor first found musical fame when he joined Ted Heath's Band as a teenager in the late 1940s. After his version of 'Broken Wings' flew into the Top 20, the

PATTI PAGE
(HOW MUCH IS) THAT
DOGGIE IN THE WINDOW
Oriole

▲ 9
⑩ 1•
—/250

See US Entry (February).

UNITED STATES
April 1953

PERCY FAITH & HIS ORCHESTRA (& FELICIA SANDERS)
SONG FROM *MOULIN ROUGE* (WHERE IS YOUR HEART)
Columbia

▲ 1
⑩ 2
7/250

Over two million copies of this treatment of the melodic film theme were sold in the US. Vocal chores on the easy-on-the-ear ballad were handled by black songstress Felicia Sanders. It topped the chart for ten weeks and was the year's biggest hit. Faith's orchestra returned to the top in 1960 with another film theme, 'A Summer Place'.

LES BAXTER & HIS ORCHESTRA
APRIL IN PORTUGAL
Capitol

▲ 2
⑩ 2
118/250

As you might have guessed, the infectious instrumental originated in Portugal where it was

known as 'Coimbra'. Vocal versions of the song (with English lyrics by Jimmy Kennedy) by Vic Damone and Tony Martin also sold well.

RICHARD HAYMAN & HIS ORCHESTRA
RUBY
Mercury

▲ 3
⑩ 1•
175/250

Harmonica-playing Hayman and his orchestra made their first appearance in the US chart with this recording of the popular Mitchell Parish-penned film theme. Massachusetts-born Hayman, a long-time conductor for the noted Boston Pops Orchestra, was soon joined in the US Top 20 by the vastly different newcomers, Bill Haley & The Comets.

UNITED KINGDOM
April 1953

JOHNSTON BROTHERS
OH HAPPY DAY
Decca

▲ 4
⑩ 1
—/250

After scoring as a songwriter ('Homing Waltz') and vocal arranger ('Auf Weidersehn Sweetheart'), Johnny Johnston took his (unrelated) quartet up the UK lists with their recording of Don Howard's US hit. It was coupled with Eddie Fisher's charter, 'Downhearted'.

FRANK CHACKSFIELD'S TUNESMITHS
LITTLE RED MONKEY
Parlophone

▲ 10
⑩ 1
—/250

This bouncy ditty was composed by clavioline player Jack Jordan, who was featured on the hit by the orchestra leader/arranger from Sussex. Rosemary Clooney, Rose Murphy, Mel Blanc and The Harmonicats were among the American artists who later recorded vocal versions of the popular children's song.

JOHNNIE RAY
SOMEBODY STOLE MY GAL
Philips

▲ 6
⑩ 2
—/250

With the aim of repeating the US success of 'Walkin' My Baby Back Home', Ray revisited bandleader Ted Weems' back catalogue. His rousing rendition of the up-tempo singalong

standard, on which he was again joined by the Buddy Cole Quartet, returned him to the UK Top 10 once more.

FRANKIE LAINE
I BELIEVE
Philips

▲ 1
⑩ 2
1/250

See US entry (February).

GUY MITCHELL
PRETTY LITTLE BLACK EYED SUSIE
Columbia

▲ 2
⑩ 3
168/250

In the US, this track was on the B side of Mitchell's minor hit, 'She Wears Red Feathers'. However, in the UK, the catchy hand-clapper was released as the follow-up single and it joined 'Feathers' in the Top 3.

KAY STARR
SIDE BY SIDE
Capitol

▲ 7
⑩ 2
—/250

See US entry (February).

NAT 'KING' COLE
PRETEND
Capitol

▲ 2
⑩ 3
100/250

See US entry (February).

UNITED STATES
May 1953

SILVANA MANGANO
ANNA
MGM

▲ 6
⑩ 1•
—/250

The noted Italian actress found herself listed among the bestsellers, even though vocal chores on the track were actually handled by Flo Sandons. 'Anna', also known as 'El Negro Zambon', was the title song of a film produced by Mangano's husband, Dino De Laurentiis, in which she took the role of a nun.

PERRY COMO
SAY YOU'RE MINE AGAIN
RCA

▲ 5
⑩ 9
—/250

A group called The Three Dots & Ginny first recorded the song that quickly returned the romantic balladeer to the heights. Como was joined by The Ramblers, who had already supported him on his recent No 1, 'Don't Let The Stars Get In Your Eyes'.

RED BUTTONS
THE HO HO SONG
Columbia

▲ 10
⑩ 1•
—/250

One of America's favourite funny men (who was born Aaron Schwatt in New York) took both sides of his only chart record into the Top 20. The other side of the novelty, 'Strange Things Are Happening (Ho Ho, Hee Hee, Ha Ha)' was in reality simply part two of the A side. Elliot Lawrence & His Orchestra backed vaudeville veteran Buttons on both the tracks.

EDDIE FISHER
I'M WALKING BEHIND YOU
RCA

▲ 1
⑩ 11
53/250

Soon after debuting successfully at the London Palladium, this dynamic vocalist clocked up his first official transatlantic No 1 with a British-composed 'you-married-the-wrong-man' ode. Before the decade ended, Fisher married and divorced film stars Debbie Reynolds and Elizabeth Taylor, followed a few years later by actress/singer Connie Stevens.

UNITED KINGDOM
May 1953

EDDIE FISHER
DOWNHEARTED
HMV

▲ 3
⑩ 3
151/250

Among the popular performer's five UK Top 10 entries in 1953 was this sad song from the pen of chart regular Bob Hilliard. Back in his homeland, it became Fisher's fourteenth Top 20 entry of the decade.

FRANKIE LAINE & JIMMY BOYD
TELL ME A STORY
Philips

▲ 5
⑩ 3
216/250

See US entry (March).

BILLY COTTON & HIS BAND
IN A GOLDEN COACH
Decca

▲ 3
⑩ 1
229/250

At the time, you couldn't turn on the Light Programme (the UK's only pop music radio station) without hearing someone singing this Coronation classic. In the charts, the version recorded by cockney Cotton and his popular band led the procession.

EDDIE FISHER
I'M WALKING BEHIND YOU
HMV

▲ 1
⑩ 4
59/250

See US entry.

MURIEL SMITH
HOLD ME THRILL ME KISS ME
Philips

▲ 3
⑩ 1•
114/250

In the US, the timeless tune earned Karen Chandler a gold record. In the UK, however, despite her earlier successes under the name Eve Young, Chandler's rendition trailed behind Smith's cover. It was to be the only notable bestseller by the American-born and UK-based singer/actress, who starred in the London productions of both *South Pacific* and *The King and I* . In fact, Smith dubbed Juanita Hall's vocals in the record-breaking film version of *South Pacific*.

FRANK CHACKSFIELD & HIS ORCHESTRA
LIMELIGHT
Decca

▲ 2
⑩ 2
68/250

Orchestra leader Chacksfield was one of the top-selling British recording artists in the US in the mid-1950s. His 40 piece orchestra's interpretation of the Charlie Chaplin-composed film theme was the biggest-selling version of the much recorded song on both sides of the Atlantic.

MANTOVANI & HIS ORCHESTRA
MOULIN ROUGE
Decca

▲ 1
⑩ 2
32/250

'Monty', as the orchestra leader was popularly known, returned to the transatlantic Top 20 with the title song from a film in which José Ferrer played painter Toulouse Lautrec. Penned by French classical composer Georges Auric, the memorable melody had originally been called ' Le Long De La Seine'.

UNITED STATES
June 1953

**FRANK CHACKSFIELD
& HIS ORCHESTRA**
TERRY'S THEME FROM
LIMELIGHT
London

▲ 6
⑩ 1
—/250

See UK entry (May).

**LES BAXTER &
HIS ORCHESTRA**
RUBY
Capitol

▲ 9
⑩ 3
—/250

Both Baxter's and Richard Hayman's orchestras clicked with the theme song from the King Vidor film *Ruby Gentry*, which starred Jennifer Jones and Charlton Heston. This rendition featured harmonica virtuoso Danny Welton.

PERRY COMO
NO OTHER LOVE
RCA

▲ 2
⑩ 10
113/250

This show-stopping song from Rodgers & Hammerstein's current musical *Me And Juliet*

(starring 'Davy Crockett' hit maker Bill Hayes) earned the one-time barber another gold record. 'No Other Love' was based on the writer's instrumental 'Beneath The Southern Cross' (from the 1952 TV documentary *Victory At Sea*).

**LES PAUL &
MARY FORD**
VAYA CON DIOS
Capitol

▲ 1
⑩ 9
1/250

No single had a better US chart history in the 1950s than this popular pair's version of the moving semi-religious ballad. Britain's Paddy Roberts composed the B side, 'Johnny (Is The Boy For Me)', which also picked up a lot of jukebox plays.

UNITED KINGDOM
June 1953

WINIFRED ATWELL
CORONATION RAG
Decca

▲ 5
⑩ 2
—/250

As Coronation fever gripped Great Britain, the Queen of the Ivories took her self-penned regal rag

up the chart. It was played on Atwell's lucky 'other piano' – an old honky tonk keyboard which cost her just £2.50, and which she had insured for £1,000!

DICKIE VALENTINE
IN A GOLDEN COACH
Decca

```
▲ 7
⑩ 2
—/250
```

A record three million TV viewers watched the Coronation in the UK, and as a souvenir many bought versions of the timely tune composed by Harry Leon, best known for writing Gracie Fields' theme song, 'Sally'.

RON GOODWIN & HIS ORCHESTRA
TERRY'S THEME FROM
LIMELIGHT
Parlophone

```
▲ 3
⑩ 1•
101/250
```

At times this George Martin-produced recording of the popular film theme joined Frank Chacksfield's version in the UK Top 3. The Devon-born conductor/arranger and composer, who had previously worked with the bands of Geraldo, Ted Heath and Stanley Black, is best-known in the US for his 1957 hit 'Swinging Sweethearts' (called 'Skiffling Strings' in the UK).

UNITED STATES
July 1953

AMES BROTHERS
YOU YOU YOU
RCA

```
▲ 2
⑩ 5
67/250
```

One of the year's catchiest and most played songs originated from Germany. The clean-cut quartet were backed on their million seller by Hugo Winterhalter's distinguished orchestra.

HILLTOPPERS
PS I LOVE YOU
Dot

```
▲ 4
⑩ 2
197/250
```

Before Kentucky-born lead singer Jimmy Sacca was drafted, the US' leading vocal group of 1953 recorded a stockpile of songs. Among them were a revival of a Gordon Jenkins and Johnny Mercer composition from 1934 and its B side, 'I'd Rather Die Young (Than Grow Old Without You)', both of which reached the Top 20.

KAY STARR
HALF A PHOTOGRAPH
Capitol

```
▲ 10
⑩ 5
—/250
```

This Bob Russell-penned tearjerker quickly reinstated the husky voiced vocalist in the Top 20. It was soon joined by the B side, 'Allez-Vous-En', from the new Cole Porter musical, *Can Can*.

UNITED KINGDOM
July 1953

AL MARTINO
RACHEL
Capitol

▲ 10
🔟 4
—/250

The Italian-American balladeer continued his string of consecutive UK Top 10 entries with this minor US hit. As usual, he was backed on the track by the Monty Kelly Orchestra.

TED HEATH & HIS MUSIC
HOT TODDY
Decca

▲ 6
🔟 1
—/250

An infectious instrumental that composer Ralph Flanagan had escorted up the US hit parade kept Heath's acclaimed entourage 'hot' in Britain. Later

in the year, his versatile band ventured into rock territory when they covered Bill Haley's first hit, 'Crazy Man Crazy'.

DORIS DAY & JOHNNIE RAY
LET'S WALK THAT-A-WAY
Philips

▲ 4
🔟 3
183/250

Four years after she and Frank Sinatra recorded 'Let's Take An Old-Fashioned Walk', Day and Ray teamed on a similarly themed duet. The wholesome boy-meets-girl song, which stiffed Stateside, came from the pens of Twomey, Wise and Weisman, the writers of many subsequent Elvis tracks.

UNITED STATES
August 1953

EDDIE FISHER
WITH THESE HANDS
RCA

▲ 8
🔟 12
—/250

In 1951, this masterful Benny Davis and Abner Silver big ballad headed the UK sheet music charts, and versions by Lee Lawrence and Nelson Eddy & Jo Stafford sold well. In the US, however, it took Fisher's unique handling to turn it into a hit.

PEE WEE HUNT & HIS ORCHESTRA
OH!
Capitol

▲ 3
🔟 1•
133/250

Five years after singer/trombonist Hunt headed

the charts with a tongue-in-cheek revival of 'Twelfth Street Rag', his orchestra returned to the big league with an update of a song that Ted Lewis & His Band made famous in 1920. Ohio-born Hunt, who had been playing professionally since the late 1920s, was one of the leading lights of the dixieland revival.

EARTHA KITT
C'EST SI BON (IT'S SO GOOD)
RCA

▲ 8
🔟 1
—/250

South Carolina-born Kitt first came to the public's attention via her appearance in the Broadway show, *New Faces of 1952* (which was subsequently turned into a film). She first charted with an Anglo-French love song that had been a mid-table hit for Danny Kaye and Johnny Desmond three years earlier. The seductive vocalist was backed on the record by the Henri Rene Orchestra.

RUSTY DRAPER
GAMBLER'S GUITAR
Mercury

After his pop-oriented version of the country No 1 'No Help Wanted' introduced him to the Top 20, this Jim Lowe composition also proved lucky for the man from Missouri, who was voted Best New Artist of 1953. Unusually, the record entered the country chart after it had become a pop hit – a feat previously accomplished only by Bing Crosby and Patti Page.

JUNE VALLI
CRYING IN THE CHAPEL
RCA

One of the most recorded songs of the era proved to be the vehicle that transported Valli into the Top

10 for the only time. The New Yorker, whose earlier singles had included unsuccessful covers of 'Cry', and 'Why Don't You Believe Me', was another singer who first came to the public's attention via Arthur Godfrey's *Talent Scouts* show.

DARRELL GLENN
CRYING IN THE CHAPEL
Valley

Texas songwriter Artie Glenn wrote this semi-religious ballad for his 16-year-old son Darrell and, despite stiff opposition, this original version reached the Top 10 on both the country and pop charts. The song was also big by The Orioles, whose rendition is sometimes cited as the first rock'n'roll hit. Although Darrell never returned to the winner's circle, he had releases on a handful of labels and was later active as a producer and recording engineer.

UNITED KINGDOM
August 1953

JUNE HUTTON
SAY YOU'RE MINE AGAIN
Capitol

A song that Perry Como had earlier taken into the US Top 10 gave the ex-big-band vocalist her sole UK hit. Hutton, who had replaced Jo Stafford in The Pied Pipers, was the half-sister of photogenic 1930s/1940s bandleader Ina Ray Hutton. On this track and the B side, the popular 'Song From *Moulin Rouge*', she was supported by husband Axel Stordahl's orchestra.

NAT 'KING' COLE
CAN'T I
Capitol

Billy May's celebrated orchestra supported the smooth-sounding baritone on this noteworthy track, which enjoyed a higher chart profile in the UK than it achieved in his homeland. Its US coupling was the title song from Cole's first movie, *Blue Gardenia*.

JIMMY YOUNG
ETERNALLY
Decca

▲ 8
⑩ 1
—/250

This vocal version of 'Terry's Theme From *Limelight*' now joined the two instrumental interpretations in the UK Top 10. Lyrics for the song, which charted in the US by Vic Damone, were composed by Geoffrey Parsons.

GISELE MACKENZIE
SEVEN LONELY DAYS
Capitol

▲ 6
⑩ 1•
—/250

In the US, the Canadian vocalist's (born Gisele LeFleche) version of the compelling Earl Shuman composition lost a chart battle with Georgia Gibbs. However, in the UK her recording (which was coupled with the popular 'Till I Waltz Again With You') beat a big field, which included such local headliners as Lita Roza, Jean Campbell and June Whitfield.

GUY MITCHELL
LOOK AT THAT GIRL
Philips

▲ 1
⑩ 4
27/250

By the end of 1953, Mitchell's magic seemed to have worn thin in the US. Nevertheless, he was still one of the biggest-selling artists in the UK – this meritorious Johnnie Ray-styled Bob Merrill song gave him his second No 1 in six months.

UNITED STATES
September 1953

RAY ANTHONY &
HIS ORCHESTRA
DRAGNET
Capitol

▲ 3
⑩ 1
240/250

The theme from America's most popular TV cops show was the Cleveland-based trumpet-tooting bandleader's (born Raymond Antonini) biggest hit. The ex-member of both Glenn Miller and Jimmy Dorsey's Bands also took this version of the theme from the Jack Webb series into the UK Top 10. Soon afterwards, humorist Stan Freberg's wonderful Dragnet spoof, 'St George and The Dragonet', topped the US chart.

REX ALLEN
CRYING IN THE CHAPEL
Decca

▲ 10
⑩ 1•
—/250

One of the most popular western movie stars of the 1950s joined three other recording artists in the Top 20 with his country interpretation of this happy tear-tale – it was the first time that four acts had hit with the same song since 'Tennessee Waltz'. The Arizona Cowboy (which, coincidentally, was the title of Allen's first feature film) was later to handle the narrations for literally dozens of Disney films. 'Crying In The Chapel' returned to top the UK charts in 1965 recorded by Elvis Presley.

FRANK CHACKSFIELD
& HIS ORCHESTRA
EBB TIDE
London

▲ 2
⑩ 2•
108/250

See UK entry (February 1954).

JULIUS LA ROSA
EH CUMPARI
Cadence

▲ 2
⑩ 2•
142/250

This happy-go-lucky opus was adapted from an old Italian folk song by musical director Archie Bleyer (who also owned Cadence Records) and La Rosa, who sang it in Italian. Although the youthful entertainer never revisited the Top 10, he stored up several more Top 40 entries during the early years of rock, and in the 1970s hosted a successful radio show in New York.

JONI JAMES
MY LOVE, MY LOVE
MGM

▲ 10
⑩ 4
—/250

James' future husband, arranger/conductor Nick

Acquaviva, co-wrote the transatlantically popular singer's seventh US Top 20 entry in less than a year. She was joined on the track by Jack Halloran's Choir.

UNITED KINGDOM
September 1953

FRANKIE LAINE
WHERE THE WIND
BLOWS
Philips

▲ 2
⑩ 4
155/250

In 1953, no artist spent longer in the UK chart than the strong-voiced American vocalist, who held the top spot for a record-shattering 27 weeks. Among his UK-only bestsellers was this Terry Gilkyson song, which had backing vocals that may have influenced later John Leyton hits.

NAT 'KING' COLE
MOTHER NATURE AND
FATHER TIME
Capitol

▲ 7
⑩ 5
—/250

A track that was not released in the US continued the romantic song stylist's run of UK hits. It easily outsold local covers by such noted recording artists as Dick James, Victor Sylvester and Dickie Valentine (who was accompanied by Ted Heath's Orchestra).

DEAN MARTIN
KISS
Capitol

▲ 5
⑩ 1
—/250

In 1946, this romantic crooner teamed with comedian Jerry Lewis; three years later they made the first of their 16 films together, and before long the relaxed balladeer had become a frequent chart visitor on both sides of the Atlantic. Even though the song from Joseph Cotton and Marilyn Monroe's movie *Niagara* made few ripples in the US, it gave Dino his first official UK hit.

UNITED STATES
October 1953

STAN FREBERG
ST GEORGE AND THE
DRAGONET
Capitol

▲ 1
⑩ 1•
86/250

As Ray Anthony's 'Dragnet' dropped, this hilarious Sgt Joe Friday-styled monologue and its similar coupling, 'Little Blue Riding Hood', shot up the charts – the single selling a reported 400,000 in its first week. Freberg was backed by the orchestra of Walter Schumann, who composed the *Dragnet* theme which both tracks utilized. No sooner had they slipped out of the Top 20 than Freberg's 'Christmas Dragnet' took their place. Freberg, whose subsequent rock'n'roll satires became legendary, went on later to have a brilliant career in advertising.

TONY BENNETT
RAGS TO RICHES
Columbia

▲ 1
⑩ 3
26/250

This dynamic vocalist, whose own rags-to-riches story started with an appearance on Arthur Godfrey's *Talent Scouts* show, scored his third US No 1. The full-bodied Richard Adler and Jerry Ross song was also a major R&B hit for Billy Ward & The Dominoes, featuring newcomer Jackie Wilson.

TERESA BREWER
RICOCHET
Coral

▲ 4
⑩ 3
191/250

Soon after making her big-screen debut in *Those Redheads From Seattle* with Guy Mitchell, the youthful veteran's assertive interpretation of a top-drawer pop song shot Brewer back into the transatlantic lists. The B side 'Too Young To Tango' was penned by later hit maker Sheb Wooley.

EDDIE FISHER
MANY TIMES
RCA

▲ 7
⑩13
—/250

No male entertainer in the first half of the decade had a better US track record than the singer who first charted in the company of the Marlin Sisters in 1948. This particular hit was heard many times on Fisher's regular 15 minute TV series.

UNITED KINGDOM
October 1953

DAVID WHITFIELD
BRIDGE OF SIGHS
Decca

▲ 9
⑩ 1
—/250

A couple of years after winning on Hughie Green's popular Radio Luxembourg talent show, *Opportunity Knocks*, this old-school operatic-styled tenor had the first of many UK bestsellers with his third single. The powerful vocalist from Hull hit with a song penned by one of Britain's finest composers, Billy Reid. In the US, the superior ballad was covered unsuccessfully by Georgia Gibbs.

WINIFRED ATWELL
FLIRTATION WALTZ
Decca

▲ 10
⑩ 3
—/250

Another noted pianist, Joe 'Mr Piano' Henderson, co-wrote the infectious instrumental that gave the one-time child protégé her third Top 10 entry of the year.

FRANKIE LAINE
HEY JOE!
Philips

▲ 1
⑩ 5
99/250

Boudleaux Bryant, who later found fame as the composer of many Everly Brothers hits, penned the country foot-tapper that quickly reinstalled Laine at the top. The song had been a US country No 1 earlier in 1953 by Carl Smith.

MANTOVANI & HIS ORCHESTRA
SWEDISH RHAPSODY
Decca

▲ 2
⑩ 3•
102/250

After successfully recording Percy Faith's hit 'Moulin Rouge', the acclaimed British orchestra scored with this unmistakable interpretation of Faith's B side. During the late 1950s alone Mantovani's orchestra visited the US Top 20 LP chart on 13 occasions, earned a handful of gold albums and sold out concerts across America. When *Film Encores* headed the US LPs in 1959 it was one of their six entries in the Top 30. The orchestra remained top record sellers into the 1970s.

DAVID WHITFIELD
ANSWER ME
Decca

▲ 1
⑩ 2
83/250

Six months after Frankie Laine's rendition of 'I Believe' left his on the starting line, Whitfield's recording of 'Answer Me' beat Laine's original version to the top in the UK.

FRANKIE LAINE
ANSWER ME
Philips

▲ 1
⑩ 6
11/250

Laine's third UK No 1 of 1953 joined his two other recent releases in the Top 5. Surprisingly, in the US Nat 'King' Cole scooped all the honours with the intense and dramatic semi-religious ballad a few months later.

DIANA DECKER
POPPA PICCOLINO
Columbia

▲ 2
⑩ 1•
175/250

'Papaveri E Papere' was the original Italian title of this jolly song about an organ grinder and his monkey, which many British children found under the tree on Christmas Day 1953. American-born, UK-based movie actress Decker then tried unsuccessfully to repeat the winning formula with 'I'm A Little Christmas Cracker', 'Do You Love Old Santa Claus' and other parent-related offerings such as 'Oh My Papa' and 'Mama Mia'. Her last Columbia records were as a vocalist with producer Norrie Paramor's Big Ben Banjo Band.

UNITED STATES
November 1953

PERRY COMO
YOU ALONE (SOLO TU)
RCA

▲ 10
⑩ 11
—/250

Como rounded off a great year with a double-sided Top 20 entry (the coupling was 'Pa-Paya Mama'). Composer Al Stillman also had a good year, having earlier written the transatlantic smash 'I Believe'.

DEAN MARTIN
THAT'S AMORE
Capitol

▲ 2
⑩ 1
102/250

On both sides of the Atlantic, the popular singer/actor reached the runner-up position with an Italian-American opus that came from the Martin & Lewis movie *The Caddy*. Interestingly, Martin almost turned down the song, which also returned him to the UK chart in 1996.

UNITED KINGDOM
November 1953

GUY MITCHELL
CHICKA BOOM
Philips

| ▲ 4 |
| ⑩ 5 |
| 186/250 |

An infectious song taken from his debut film *Those Redheads From Seattle* (a 3D movie which co-starred Teresa Brewer) added to the one-time rodeo rider's enviable UK hit collection.

LES PAUL & MARY FORD
VAYA CON DIOS
Capitol

| ▲ 7 |
| ⑩ 1• |
| —/250 |

See US entry (June).

EDDIE FISHER
WISH YOU WERE HERE
HMV

| ▲ 8 |
| ⑩ 5 |
| —/250 |

See US entry (August 1952).

JIMMY BOYD
I SAW MOMMY KISSING SANTA CLAUS
Columbia

| ▲ 3 |
| ⑩ 2• |
| —/250 |

See US entry (December 1952).

TED HEATH & HIS MUSIC
DRAGNET
Decca

| ▲ 9 |
| ⑩ 2 |
| —/250 |

This poll-winning Britsh band joined Ray Anthony in the UK Top 10 with their interpretation of a memorable TV theme, which had first been released by the R&B combo, Johnny Moore's Three Blazers.

UNITED STATES
December 1953

PATTI PAGE
CHANGING PARTNERS
Mercury

| ▲ 4 |
| ⑩ 10 |
| 184/250 |

Soon after being voted Female Singer of the Year for the second successive time, Page proved the voting DJs right when her rendering of the extremely popular ballroom floor-filler easily outsold those by Kay Starr and Dinah Shore.

EDDIE CALVERT
OH, MEIN PAPA
Essex

| ▲ 9 |
| ⑩ 1• |
| —/250 |

See UK entry.

EARTHA KITT
SANTA BABY
RCA

| ▲ 4 |
| ⑩ 2• |
| —/250 |

One of the decade's most distinctive performers had her highest-ranked hit with this sultry seasonal opus. A year later, Kitt's new version tagged '(This Year's) Santa Baby' found its way into far fewer Christmas stockings.

EDDIE FISHER
OH! MY PA-PA
RCA

▲ 1
🔟 14
23/250

According to RCA, a record 300,000 copies of this single were sold in the US in the first three days. It was an English-written vocal version of a moving Swiss song (from the 1948 musical *Fireworks*) that British trumpeter Eddie Calvert also took into the transatlantic Top 10.

TONY BENNETT
STRANGER IN PARADISE
Columbia

▲ 2
🔟 4
154/250

Even though a handful of versions of the show-stopping song from the hit musical *Kismet* charted on both sides of the Atlantic, none outsold Bennett's intense interpretation. As usual, he was supported by Percy Faith's Orchestra.

UNITED KINGDOM
December 1953

RAY ANTHONY & HIS ORCHESTRA
DRAGNET
Capitol

▲ 7
🔟 1•
—/250

See US entry (September).

WINIFRED ATWELL
LET'S HAVE A PARTY
Philips

▲ 2
🔟 4
69/250

Over a million copies were sold around the world of Atwell's second single on Philips. It was a honky tonk piano medley which included such well-known party favourites as 'If You Knew Susie', 'Knees Up Mother Brown' and 'Boomps-a-Daisy'.

RAY MARTIN & HIS ORCHESTRA
SWEDISH RHAPSODY
Columbia

▲ 4
🔟 2•
—/250

In Christmas week 1953, 'Answer Me' hogged the top two spots in the UK and 'Swedish Rhapsody' held positions 4 and 5. Even though Mantovani's version initially outsold all other recordings, it was

Martin's late rendition that now led the pack. Rock'n'roll never appealed to Martin, who left his position as Columbia Records' music director in 1957 and moved to the US, and subsequently to South Africa.

BEVERLEY SISTERS
I SAW MOMMY KISSING SANTA CLAUS
Philips

▲ 6
🔟 1
—/250

The UK's most popular female vocal group of the 1950s consisted of Joy Beverley (later married to England soccer captain Billy Wright) and her twin sisters, Teddie and Babs. The identically dressed, close-harmony trio from London, who recorded many of the early 1950's most successful songs, joined Jimmy Boyd in the Top 10 with their treatment of the British-penned Christmas classic. They were the only British vocal group to reach the US Top 100 in the 1950s, thanks to the 400,000 selling 'Greensleeves' in 1957.

LEE LAWRENCE
CRYING IN THE CHAPEL
Decca

▲ 7
⑩ 1•
—/250

In the UK, where it received few BBC plays, the much recorded American song only scored by operatic pop vocalist Lawrence (born Leon Siroto in Lancashire), who had been recording since the late 1940s. After a brief chart return with 'Suddenly There's A Valley', he unsuccessfully climbed on the rock'n'roll bandwagon with a surprisingly good version of 'Don't Nobody Move' and the spoof 'Rock'n'Roll Opera'. In 1957, Lawrence relocated to the US, where he worked the club circuit until his death in 1961.

JOAN REGAN
RICOCHET
Decca

▲ 8
⑩ 1
—/250

For her first two releases, the photogenic Essex-born vocalist covered songs released in the US by Teresa Brewer. Regan's rendition of 'Till I Waltz Again With You' narrowly missed the chart, while the follow-up, 'Ricochet', shot into the Top 10. She was joined on the recording by Ronnie Aldrich & The Squadronaires.

EDDIE CALVERT
OH MEIN PAPA
Columbia

▲ 1
⑩ 1
7/250

After several years in the bands of Billy Ternent and Geraldo, this trumpeter from Preston, Lancashire, formed his own band at the end of the 1940s. Calvert recorded briefly for Melodisc in 1951 before joining Norrie Paramor's stable of artists at Columbia. He not only held the No 1 spot in the UK for nine weeks, but also reached the US Top 10 with this interpretation of a standout Swiss song which earned 'the man with the golden trumpet' a golden disc.

UNITED STATES
January 1954

FOUR ACES
STRANGER IN PARADISE
Decca

▲ 5
🔟 4
—/250

After a relatively slow sales period, the influential close-harmony team returned to the Top 10 with this successful show song. For copyright reasons, the group were not allowed to sing it on their British tour, but that did not stop it reaching the UK Top 10 a year later, following the show's arrival in Britain.

TONY MARTIN
STRANGER IN PARADISE
RCA

▲ 10
🔟 7
—/250

Chart regular Martin, who was married to film star Cyd Charisse, had one of the top-selling transatlantic treatments of the very popular musical song, which borrowed its melody from classical composer Borodin.

DORIS DAY
SECRET LOVE
Columbia

▲ 1
🔟 5
60/250

Numerous R&B and country singers covered the Academy Award-winning ballad from Day's box office smash *Calamity Jane*. Among the varied artists who had success with this love song over the years are Slim Whitman, The Moonglows, Kathy Kirby, Billy Stewart and Freddy Fender.

ANDY GRIFFITH
WHAT IS WAS, WAS
FOOTBALL
Capitol

▲ 9
🔟 1•
—/250

One of US' best-loved performers first came to the public's attention via this double-sided comedy monologue, on which he was billed as Deacon Andy Griffith. The self-penned single was picked up by Capitol from a small label in Griffith's home state, South Carolina. The record's success led to a starring role in the film *A Face In The Crowd* and to his own very popular TV series. Griffith, who was immortalized in the 1994 country hit 'Elvis And Andy', finally debuted in the album chart in 1996!

FOUR ACES
THE GANG THAT SANG
'HEART OF MY HEART'
Decca

▲ 8
🔟 5
—/250

The US' No 1 vocal group of 1954 had their 'barber shop quartet' roots showing on this retro-sounding singalong. An all-star version teaming Don Cornell, Johnny Desmond and Alan Dale also reached the US Top 20.

UNITED KINGDOM

January 1954

DAVID WHITFIELD
RAGS TO RICHES
Decca

▲ 3
⑩ 3
202/250

Many pop pundits had considered Whitfield's operatic vocal style too dated to appeal to the masses. Nevertheless, in true rags-to-riches fashion he proved them wrong, and his treatment of Tony Bennett's US No 1 was Whitfield's third Top 10 single in three months.

FRANKIE LAINE
BLOWING WILD
Philips

▲ 2
⑩ 7
139/250

He may have passed his sales peak in the US, but in the UK heart-throb Laine could do no wrong. This punchy interpretation of the theme from a Gary Cooper movie only narrowly missed the top spot. In the US, it was simply the B side of the overlooked single 'Answer Me'.

GUY MITCHELL
CLOUD LUCKY SEVEN
Philips

▲ 2
⑩ 6
116/250

For the second time in eight months, the B side of a minor Mitchell hit in the US was successfully released as a separate single in the UK. It only narrowly missed the summit and was his sixth UK Top 5 entry in 12 months.

EDDIE FISHER
OH! MY PA-PA
HMV

▲ 9
⑩ 6
—/250

See US entry (December 1953).

OBERNKIRCHEN CHILDREN'S CHOIR
HAPPY WANDERER
Parlophone

▲ 2
⑩ 1•
61/250

On both sides of the Atlantic people sang this tune's happy 'Val-De Ri, Val-De Ra' refrain while imagining that they were wandering through breathtaking mountain scenery with knapsacks on their backs. In the UK, the German song (originally called 'Der Frohliche Wanderer') was most popular sung by a children's choir from the German town of Obernkirchen, whose youthful version strode ahead of those recorded by local hit makers like The Stargazers, The Beverley Sisters and Diana Decker.

DEAN MARTIN
THAT'S AMORE
Capitol

▲ 2
⑩ 2
163/250

See US Entry (November 1953).

KEN MACKINTOSH & HIS BAND
THE CREEP
HMV

▲ 10
⑩ 1•
—/250

Yorkshire-born saxophonist Mackintosh fronted one of the UK's most popular dance bands. On trombonist Don Lang's suggestion, they wrote this song for a new teenage dance called The Creep. The Teddy boy-targeted track, which was initially planned as a B side, attracted many covers on both sides of the Atlantic. Mackintosh's band were frequently seen on late 1950s pop shows, although by then the demand for their big-band sound had all but disappeared.

UNITED STATES
February 1954

GAYLORDS
FROM THE VINE CAME
THE GRAPE
Mercury

▲ 8
⑩ 2
—/250

This group, who first met at the University of Detroit, had the highest-ranking rendition of a song that The Hilltoppers also took into the Top 20. The George Annis orchestra backed them on the record.

JO STAFFORD
MAKE LOVE TO ME!
Columbia

▲ 1
⑩ 6•
54/250

Few females sold more records than Stafford in the 1950s. The unique, vibrato-free vocalist had her last million seller with a suggestive song based on 'Tin Roof Blues' – a jazz instrumental written and originally recorded in the early 1920s by The New Orleans Rhythm Kings. Like most releases by her contemporaries, demand for Stafford's singles decreased with the rise of rock, and she slipped into semi-retirement by the 1960s.

GEORGIE SHAW
TILL WE TWO ARE ONE
Decca

▲ 8
⑩ 1•
—/250

Whoever selected Shaw's songs had an ear for a hit. Not only did his previous single, 'Let Me Go Devil', top the bestsellers a year later as 'Let Me Go Lover', but the B side of this hit, 'Honeycomb', headed the lists in 1957 (when Shaw's reissued single was easily outsold by Jimmie Rodgers' revival). Regular chart visitor Tom Glazer composed the ballad that gave the Eddie Fisher-influenced singer his biggest seller.

HILLTOPPERS
TILL THEN
Dot

▲ 10
⑩ 3•
—/250

A standout ballad that the Mills Brothers clicked with in the 1940s returned this popular quartet to the heights in the 1950s, and in the 1960s it gave a third vocal quartet, The Classics, their only Top 20 entry.

FOUR KNIGHTS
I GET SO LONELY
Capitol

▲ 3
⑩ 1•
140/250

This one-time gospel quartet from North Carolina, who were voted Top New Group of 1951, first came to the public's attention via appearances on the Arthur Godfrey and Red Skelton shows. There is little doubt that this instantly memorable opus inspired 'Sh-Boom' and so indirectly launched a thousand doo-wop groups. The transatlantic Top 10 entry, sometimes known as 'Oh Baby Mine', was inspired by the traditional tune 'Gently Down The Stream' and its composer, Pat Ballard, also penned another of 1954's biggest songs, 'Mr Sandman'.

FRANK SINATRA
YOUNG-AT-HEART
Capitol

▲ 2
⑩ 1
123/250

New Jersey-born Sinatra, who is regarded by many as the greatest vocalist of the century, sang with the Harry James and Tommy Dorsey Bands before he embarked on his amazingly successful solo career in 1942. Sinatra's biggest hit since 'Five Minutes More' (1946) was a captivating pre-war melody (originally called 'Moonbeam') to which Carolyn Leigh had added lyrics. Later that year, the song was used in a movie of the same name starring Sinatra and Doris Day.

UNITED KINGDOM
February 1954

BONNIE LOU
TENNESSEE WIG WALK
Parlophone

▲ 4
⑩ 1•
232/250

A few months after the Illinois native had the US country hit version of 'Seven Lonely Days', she strolled into the UK Top 10 with for the only time with this bouncy country dance song. The singer, who has been called the first female rockabilly performer, was a regular on the *Midwestern Hayride*. Subsequent singles, including the similar 'Tennessee Mambo' and 'Tennessee Polka', failed to ignite interest. Her only US pop Top 40 entry was 'Daddy-O' (backed by The Harmonaires) in 1955.

FRANK CHACKSFIELD & HIS ORCHESTRA
EBB TIDE
Decca

▲ 9
⑩ 3•
—/250

For the first time in the decade, two British recordings were simultaneously in the US Top 10 and, interestingly, both were instrumentals. Alongside Eddie Calvert's tearjerking trumpet track was this smooth orchestral version of a standout ballad which was first cut by its composer, harpist Robert Maxwell. Chacksfield, who was credited with discovering the UK's first rock star, Tommy Steele, sold over 20 million records in his career.

JOSE FERRER & ROSEMARY CLOONEY
WOMAN (UH-HUH)/MAN
Philips

▲ 7
⑩ 1•
—/250

Noted Puerto Rican film star Ferrer (born José Vincente Ferrer y Centron) and his equally famous wife took one side of the single each to enlighten us about the opposite sex. British record buyers showed more interest in the enterprise than their American cousins.

NORMAN WISDOM
DON'T LAUGH AT ME
Columbia

▲ 3
⑩ 1•
141/250

The UK's most famous film funny man in the 1950s composed this 'tears-of-a-clown' ballad, which he released in late 1952, soon after his similarly themed 'Heart Of A Clown'. Wisdom's theme song sold few copies until it was included in his first film, *Trouble in Store*. The Londoner, who has kept the UK laughing for over four decades, also reached the Top 20 in 1957 with 'Wisdom Of A Fool' which, despite its title, was not written especially for him.

GUY MITCHELL
CUFF OF MY SHIRT
Philips

▲ 9
⑩ 7
—/250

Few singer/writer pairings were more fruitful in the 1950s than that of Guy Mitchell and Bob Merrill. Although it made little noise Stateside, the last of their numerous UK hits together easily outsold local covers by top-line vocalists Frankie Vaughan and Dennis Lotis.

TED HEATH & HIS MUSIC
SKIN DEEP
Decca

▲ 9
⑩ 3
—/250

This was one of the most requested tunes at Heath's successful Sunday Night Swing Sessions at the London Palladium. It was composed by jazz drummer Louis Bellson, whose version with the Duke Ellington Orchestra also charted in the UK.

DAVID WHITFIELD
THE BOOK
Decca

▲ 5
⑩ 4
233/250

In the 1954 *NME* poll, only Dickie Valentine and Dennis Lotis had more votes than Whitfield in the

British Male Vocalist category. The first of his three Top 10 entries that year was written by one of the UK's finest pop songsmiths, Paddy Roberts.

STARGAZERS
I SEE THE MOON
Decca

▲ 1
⑩ 2
26/250

Inter-racial American act The Mariners had earlier recorded the novelty song that took the UK's most popular vocal group to the top for the second time in a year. It was coupled with their treatment of Julius La Rosa's party hit 'Eh, Cumpari'.

UNITED STATES
March 1954

PATTI PAGE
CROSS OVER THE BRIDGE
Mercury

▲ 3
⑩ 11
182/250

Bennie Benjamin and George Weiss, who had penned her breakthrough single 'Confess', composed the jaunty jewel which quickly transported Page back to the top end of the chart.

PERRY COMO
WANTED
RCA

▲ 1
⑩ 12
16/250

Veteran vocalist/songwriter Jack Fulton penned this lilting love lament, which headed the pop list for two months. A made-for-Britain version recorded by Al Martino ran neck and neck with Como's cut in the UK.

NAT 'KING' COLE
ANSWER ME, MY LOVE
Capitol

▲ 6
⑩ 5
—/250

In the UK, both Frankie Laine and David Whitfield topped the chart with renditions of this powerful semi-religious ballad. In the US, however, it was Cole's classy cut that enjoyed the most sales.

UNITED KINGDOM
March 1954

DUKE ELLINGTON & HIS ORCHESTRA
SKIN DEEP
Philips

▲ 7
⑩ 1•
—/250

Few, if any, American composers are held in as high esteem as Duke Ellington, who headed his own inimitable band for 50 years. Among the legendary entertainer's best-known works are 'Caravan', 'Don't Get Around Much Anymore', 'Mood Indigo', 'Satin Doll', 'Sophisticated Lady', and 'Take The A Train'. Ellington's only hit single of the decade was a double-sided treatment of 'Skin Deep' which featured the composer, drummer Louis Bellson.

KAY STARR
CHANGING PARTNERS
Capitol

▲ 4
⑩ 3
177/250

Patti Page outsold Starr with her performance of this impressive Joe Darion and Larry Coleman composition in the US. However, in the UK, they changed places.

BING CROSBY
CHANGING PARTNERS
Brunswick

▲ 9
⑩ 4
—/250

This very popular song also returned the king of the casual crooners to the heights, after a relatively quiet sales period. It was coupled with his interpretation of 'Y'All Come', a knee-slapper that has since become a country classic.

ALMA COGAN
BELL BOTTOM BLUES
HMV

▲ 4
⑩ 1
—/250

Although Alma Cogan was the most successful British girl singer of the 1950s, the first of a dozen Top 20 entries came only with her eighteenth release, a song about an absent sailor boyfriend which was co-written by Hal David (who subsequently penned a string of hits with Burt Bacharach). Teresa Brewer had previously taken the bouncy opus into the US Top 20, but her version was not released in the UK at the time.

FRANKIE LAINE
GRANADA
Philips

▲ 9
⑩ 8
—/250

This celebrated Mexican classic from 1932 was given a typical Laine workout and the resulting record added to his formidable list of UK hits. Seven years later Frank Sinatra's version also graced the UK Top 20.

UNITED STATES
April 1954

EDDIE FISHER
A GIRL, A GIRL (ZOOM-BA DI ALLI NELLA)
RCA

▲ 7
⑩ 15
—/250

The US' most successful recording artist of the year had another double-sided Top 20 entry; the Benjamin & Weiss winner was coupled with the title song from the Italian film *Anema E Core*. Fisher's accompanist, Harry Askt (previously with Fisher's idol, Al Jolson), co-wrote the English lyrics, 'With All My Heart And Soul'.

TONY MARTIN
HERE
RCA

▲ 7
⑩ 8•
—/250

Dorcas Cochran, who penned Martin's 1951 top seller 'I Get Ideas', also helped write the polished

performer's last major US hit, the melody of which was based on 'Caro Nome' which came from Verdi's operetta *Rigoletto*.

AMES BROTHERS
THE MAN WITH THE BANJO
RCA

▲ 7
⑩ 6
—/250

Music publisher Robert Mellin, composer of the group's top-selling 'You You You', also co-wrote this toe-tapper for the singers who had been discovered by another of the century's top independent publishers, Al Gallico.

UNITED KINGDOM
April 1954

DORIS DAY
SECRET LOVE
Philips

▲ 1
⑩ 4
3/250

See US entry (January).

JOHNNIE RAY
SUCH A NIGHT
Philips

▲ 1
⑩ 4
55/250

Radio stations on both sides of the Atlantic banned Ray's recording of the Lincoln Chase-composed song that The Drifters had taken into the R&B Top 5. Despite only attracting so-so sales Stateside, it

gave the 'Nabob of Sob' another British chart topper.

FRANKIE LAINE
THE KID'S LAST FIGHT
Philips

▲ 3
⑩ 9
210/250

Prolific songsmith Bob Merrill composed the heavyweight hit maker's eighth UK Top 10 entry in a year. Like the majority of Laine's singles, this tale, about a boxer who won his bout but died of fever, ranked higher in the UK than in the US.

NAT 'KING' COLE
TENDERLY
Capitol

▲ 10
⑩ 6
—/250

Billboard's 1953 DJ poll voted this romantic Walter Gross and Jack Lawrence ballad their second favourite song of all time. A year later, Cole's flawless interpretation of it earned him a UK-only hit.

RUBY WRIGHT
BIMBO
Parlophone

▲ 7
⑩ 1•
—/250

In the US, Jim Reeves released the children's novelty as a follow-up to his chart-topping country hit, 'Mexican Joe'. In the UK, however, it was Indiana-born Wright who charted with it. In 1959, the singer also had the UK hit version of Tommy Dee's Buddy Holly tribute record, 'Three Stars'. Perhaps surprisingly, neither of Wright's UK hits sold well in her homeland.

GUY MITCHELL
DIME AND A DOLLAR
Philips

▲ 8
⑩ 8
—/250

Although he had rarely been out of the UK bestsellers since 1951, this was the singer's last big money spinner for almost three years. The song was penned by Jay Livingston and Ray Evans and was featured in the film *Red Garters*, which starred Mitchell and Rosemary Clooney.

UNITED STATES
May 1954

KITTY KALLEN
LITTLE THINGS MEAN A LOT
Decca

▲ 1
⑩ 2
9/250

Before she scored a transatlantic No 1 with this melodic love ballad, the Philadelphia-born vocalist had sung with the renowned bands of Jimmy Dorsey, Jack Teagarden, Artie Shaw and Harry James – in fact, Kallen was the singer on the latter's 1945 No 1, 'It's Been A Long, Long Time'. Her biggest hit was penned by DJ Carl Stutz and journalist Edith Lindemann, and she was supported on the chart topper by the Jack Pleis Orchestra, who also played on the No 2 single from the Four Aces.

KAY STARR
IF YOU LOVE ME (REALLY LOVE ME)
Capitol

▲ 4
⑩ 7
222/250

Starr's winning performance of this moving French ballad was joined in the Top 10 by its B side, 'The Man Upstairs'. The song had originally been recorded by its co-writer Edith Piaf in 1949 as 'Hyme A L'Amour'.

KAY STARR
THE MAN UPSTAIRS
Capitol

▲ 7
⑩ 6
—/250

A semi-religious song, which bore some resemblance to Starr's earlier 'Half A Photograph', helped the blues-influenced vocalist to achieve her only double-sided Top 10 entry.

FRANK WEIR WITH HIS SAXOPHONE, CHORUS & ORCHESTRA
THE HAPPY WANDERER
London

▲ 4
⑩ 1•
209/250

In the UK, the soprano sax-playing British orchestra leader's treatment of the cheerful backpacker's anthem trailed behind the Obernkirchen Children's Choir version. Nonetheless, it was the biggest-selling version in the US – in fact, no British recording fared better in America that year. 'The Happy Wanderer' was also the London-based veteran's only bestseller – although his orchestra backed Vera Lynn on her UK hit 'My Son My Son' later that year.

FOUR ACES
THREE COINS IN THE
FOUNTAIN
Decca

▲ 2
⑩ 6
166/250

This Philadelphia-based foursome's interpretation of the Academy Award-winning song was placed higher in the US than Frank Sinatra's rendition. Across the Atlantic the result was reversed.

UNITED KINGDOM
May 1954

JO STAFFORD
MAKE LOVE TO ME!
Philips

▲ 8
⑩ 2•
—/250

See US entry (February).

BILLY COTTON & HIS BAND
FRIENDS AND
NEIGHBOURS
Decca

▲ 3
⑩ 2•
194/250

It seemed as if the whole of Britain was whistling the cheerful cockney refrain that proved to be the last big hit for an entertainer who, perhaps more than anyone else, personified British popular music in the early 1950s. Max Bygraves, Max Miller and its composer Malcolm Lockyer also released renditions of this successful singalong song.

JOAN REGAN
SOMEONE ELSE'S ROSES
Decca

▲ 5
⑩ 2
—/250

Milton Carson, who composed the 1952 hit 'My Love And Devotion', also penned the popular British performer's second successive Top 10 entry. Both of these Carson compositions had originally been recorded by Doris Day.

MAX BYGRAVES
HEART OF MY HEART
HMV

▲ 7
⑩ 2
—/250

The popular Tanner Sisters (who supported Buddy Holly on his 1958 UK tour) joined the cockney comedian/singer on this reworking of the singalong standard.

UNITED STATES
June 1954

ARCHIE BLEYER
HERNANDO'S HIDEAWAY
Cadence

▲ 2
⑩ 1•
169/250

Although best known as the founder of Cadence Records, and the person who discovered the Everly Brothers, The Chordettes and Andy Williams, New Yorker Bleyer had several hits in his own right. Arthur Godfrey's long-time musical arranger's biggest seller was a castanet-led show stopper from the Broadway musical *The Pajama Game*. Bleyer wed Janet Ertel from The Chordettes (whose daughter, Jacquelyn, married Phil Everly), and he retired in the mid-1960s.

FRANK SINATRA
THREE COINS IN THE FOUNTAIN
Capitol

▲ 7
⑩ 2
—/250

Top composers Sammy Cahn and Jule Styne wrote this award-winning song for a Clifton Webb and Dorothy McGuire movie of the same name. Thanks in part to Nelson Riddle's outstanding arrangement, Sinatra's interpretation reached the Top 10 and went all the way to No 1 in the UK.

HENRI RENE & HIS MUSETTE ORCHESTRA
THE HAPPY WANDERER
RCA

▲ 8
⑩ 2•
—/250

As *Billboard* noted that 'Teens now demand music with a beat', Alan Freed's stage shows attracted thousands and Bill Haley's 'Rock Around The Clock' only narrowly missed the chart. Nonetheless, it was business as usual in the Top 10, which welcomed conductor/arranger Rene's version of the jolly hiking hit from Germany (where he was raised). 'The Happy Wanderer' was the biggest seller for the orchestra, which had previously supported many chart regulars including Tony Martin, Dinah Shore and Eartha Kitt.

CREW-CUTS
CRAZY 'BOUT YOU, BABY
Mercury

▲ 8
⑩ 1
—/250

Soon after The Four Knights scored with 'I Get So Lonely', this youthful white Canadian quartet opened their chart account with a self-composed ditty written along similar lines. The Toronto foursome were renamed (they were originally tagged The Canadaires) and helped along the path to fame by top Cleveland DJ Bill Randle. The group, who received a lot of press criticism over their habit of covering R&B records, were proud to say that 'We put barbershop harmony into the pop field'.

UNITED KINGDOM
June 1954

FOUR KNIGHTS
I GET SO LONELY
Capitol

▲ 5
⑩ 1•
—/250

See US Entry (February).

PERRY COMO
WANTED
HMV

▲ 4
⑩ 2
200/250

See US entry (March).

DAVID WHITFIELD
CARA MIA
Decca

▲ 1
⑩ 5
4/250

After a handful of UK-only hits, the big-voiced British vocalist reached the transatlantic Top 10 with his second UK No 1. The song, which sold over three million copies worldwide, was written by Decca executive Bunny Lewis and Mantovani (whose orchestra backed Whitfield). It was the

first US gold disc earned by a British male vocalist. In 1965 Jay & The Americans returned 'Cara Mia' to the US Top 10.

PERRY COMO
IDLE GOSSIP
HMV

▲ 3
⑩ 3
135/250

Even though it was not released as a single in his homeland, the casual crooner from Canonsburg (Pennsylvania) had a major UK hit with this tender love tale.

AL MARTINO
WANTED
Capitol

▲ 4
⑩ 5
173/250

In the US, the public were turning a deaf ear to many Martino waxings. However, in the UK his popularity was such that this made-for-Britain recording of a Jack Fulton ballad sold as well as Perry Como's US chart-topping treatment.

UNITED STATES
July 1954

CREW-CUTS
SH-BOOM
Mercury

▲ 1
⑩ 2
25/250

At the outset, the Canadian quartet did not want to record the song that many consider to be 'the first rock'n'roll hit'. Nevertheless, their treatment of the R&B charter by The Chords went all the way to No 1, and started a rush of pop and country artists covering R&B hits. Incidentally, on the week it

entered the Top 10 Elvis Presley cut his debut disc, a revival of R&B stomper 'That's All Right'.

GAYLORDS
THE LITTLE SHOEMAKER
Mercury

▲ 2
⑩ 3•
149/250

The trio's treatment of a French tune that Petula Clark had clicked with in the UK gave them their last notable hit. As on the group's previous Top 10 entries, they sang the foot-tapper partly in Italian. Lead singer Ronnie Gaylord left in 1954 and neither he nor The Gaylords returned to the heights, even though they climbed on the R&B/rock bandwagon by covering songs like 'Mambo Rock', 'Pledging My Love' and ' My Babe'.

FOUR TUNES
I UNDERSTAND JUST HOW YOU FEEL
Jubilee

Numbered among the pioneers of doo-wop (as it was later called) were this New York vocal group whose roots went back to The Ink Spots. Six months after reaching the pop Top 20 with a distinctive up-tempo 'r'-rolling rendition of Irving Berlin's 'Marie', they reappeared with a tender ballad penned by member Pat Best (also composer of the standard 'I Love You For Sentimental Reasons'). 'I Understand' also charted by June Valli, and was revived successfully in 1961 by The G-Clefs and in 1964 by Freddie & The Dreamers.

CHORDS
SH-BOOM
CAT

A self-penned novelty, cut as the B side of their rendition of Patti Page's 'Cross Over The Bridge', inspired the formation of hundreds of doo-wop groups and started a string of R&B hits in the US Top 10 that has never ended. A cover by The Crew-Cuts (on Page's label Mercury) topped the chart, and a parody by Stan Freberg sold well and instigated a much publicized feud with The Chords. The group, who soon changed their name to The Chordcats and then The Sh-Booms, were never able to repeat this success.

HUGO WINTERHALTER & HIS ORCHESTRA
THE LITTLE SHOEMAKER
RCA

This was not the sole version of the toe-tapper from France to march up the US charts; it followed hot on the heels of The Gaylords' treatment of the children's novelty tune. Another RCA hit maker, Eddie Fisher, can be heard leading the chorus.

ROSEMARY CLOONEY
HEY THERE
Columbia

One of the year's most recorded songs came from the smash Broadway musical, *The Pajama Game*, which starred John Raitt (Bonnie's father). A year further on, Clooney and Johnnie Ray both took the outstanding Mozart-based ballad into the UK Top 5.

KITTY KALLEN
IN THE CHAPEL IN THE MOONLIGHT
Decca

Hillbilly writer Billy Hill composed this timeless love song, which Shep Fields & His Rippling Rhythm Orchestra had taken to No. 1 in 1936. Kallen's sensitive interpretation restored it to the bestsellers' list and outpaced a cover by R&B hit makers The Orioles. The vocalist, who headlined at the London Palladium for two weeks in 1955, returned briefly to the US Top 10 eight years later with 'My Coloring Book'.

UNITED KINGDOM
July 1954

KITTY KALLEN
LITTLE THINGS MEAN
A LOT
Brunswick

▲ 1
⑩ 1•
37/250

See US entry (May).

PETULA CLARK
THE LITTLE SHOEMAKER
Polygon

▲ 7
⑩ 1
—/250

When aged 12, Petula had been the youngest star at the VE Day celebrations in Trafalgar Square. By the time she started recording in 1949, she had appeared in several films, hosted her own radio show and become one of the UK's first TV stars. Clark's first hit was a French children's novelty originally entitled 'Le Petite Cordonnier'. The

lyric was by John Turner, who helped with the new English lyrics to 'Auf Wiederseh'n Sweetheart' for another war time star, Vera Lynn.

FRANK SINATRA
THREE COINS IN THE
FOUNTAIN
Capitol

▲ 1
⑩ 1
41/250

See US entry (June).

FOUR ACES
THREE COINS IN THE
FOUNTAIN
Brunswick

▲ 5
⑩ 1
—/250

See US entry (May).

UNITED STATES
August 1954

McGUIRE SISTERS
GOODNIGHT,
SWEETHEART,
GOODNIGHT
Coral

▲ 8
⑩ 1
—/250

Sisters Phyllis, Dorothy and Christine McGuire from Ohio were the most popular female vocal group in the US during the mid-1950s. The trio were winners on Arthur Godfrey's *Talent Scouts* in 1952 and soon replaced The Chordettes on his daytime show (where they stayed for six years). The talented harmony vocalists' first hit came with their sixth single, a cover of an R&B ballad originally performed by its composers, The Spaniels. Its

success confirmed that pop versions of R&B songs could sell in vast quantites.

LES PAUL &
MARY FORD
I'M A FOOL TO CARE
Capitol

▲ 10
⑩ 10
—/250

Like their earlier hit 'Tennessee Waltz', this song first appeared in the country field in 1948. A Fats Domino-cloned version of the Ted Daffan composition narrowly missed the Top 20 by Joe Barry in 1961.

VICTOR YOUNG & HIS SINGING STRINGS
THE HIGH AND THE MIGHTY
Decca

▲ 6
⑩ 2•
—/250

This talented composer and conductor from Chicago had one of the top-selling recordings of the high-flying Ned Washington and Dimitri Tiomkin film title theme. Young died in 1956, shortly before his compositions 'Around The World' and 'When I Fall In Love' added to his hit tally for the decade.

LES BAXTER & HIS ORCHESTRA
THE HIGH AND THE MIGHTY
Capitol

▲ 6
⑩ 4
—/250

One of the most prolific film score writers of the twentieth century also hit the heights with his orchestra's version of the title theme from John Wayne's popular plane-in-peril movie.

LEROY HOLMES & HIS ORCHESTRA
THE HIGH AND THE MIGHTY
MGM

▲ 9
⑩ 1•
—/250

Rounding out the trio of Top 10 versions of the much recorded film theme was the one by MGM Records' musical director Leroy Holmes & His Orchestra (with whistling provided by Fred Lowry). The Pittsburgh-born conductor, who had earlier worked as an arranger for the bands of Harry James and Vincent Lopez, backed many of MGM's recording artists in the 1950s.

ROSEMARY CLOONEY
THIS OLE HOUSE
Columbia

▲ 1
⑩ 5
52/250

Amazingly, this version of Stuart Hamblen's self-penned country hit replaced the other side, 'Hey There', at the top of the US charts. The rousing knee-slapper also reached the summit in the UK, as did a rockin' 1981 rendition by Shakin' Stevens.

UNITED KINGDOM
August 1954

WINIFRED ATWELL
THE STORY OF THREE LOVES
Philips

▲ 9
⑩ 5
—/250

Her training as a classical pianist held Atwell in good stead when it came to recording her version of Rachmaninoff's '18th Variation On A Theme By Paganini'. The music, which was heard in the Kirk Douglas film of the same name, was a hit in the US by harmonica virtuoso Jerry Murad.

FRANKIE LAINE
MY FRIEND
Philips

▲ 3
⑩ 10
130/250

Ervin Drake and Jimmy Shirl, who composed

Laine's earlier semi-religious chart topper 'I Believe', also penned this paean to his best friend, God. Laine's rendition was a big crowd-pleaser during the punchy performer's sellout UK tour.

DORIS DAY
THE BLACK HILLS OF DAKOTA
Philips

▲ 7
⑩ 5
—/250

Few could argue that Sammy Fain and Paul Francis Webster's score for *Calamity Jane* was not one of the finest of the decade. Apart from 'Secret Love', it included this winning western ballad, which followed the former up the UK list.

UNITED STATES
September 1954

RALPH MARTERIE & HIS ORCHESTRA
SKOKIAAN
Mercury

▲ 3
⑩ 1•
217/250

Bill Haley & The Comets may have reached the Top 20 bestsellers in 1953 with 'Crazy Man Crazy', but it was Marterie's version that garnered more airplay. The Italian-born bandleader and trumpet player, who is credited with selling over a million copies of both 'Pretend' and 'Caravan' in 1953, had his only Top 10 entry with a treatment of this South African instrumental. Coincidentally, Haley's 1959 revival of 'Skokiaan' was to be the rock'n'roll legend's last hit.

FOUR LADS
SKOKIAAN (SOUTH AFRICAN SONG)
Columbia

▲ 7
⑩ 1
—/250

These ex-choir boys from Toronto (who attended the same school as The Crew-Cuts) joined Columbia in 1951. They first came to the public's attention as backing vocalists behind Johnnie Ray, and subsequently scored bestsellers of their own with tracks like 'Istanbul' and 'Gilly Gilly Ossenfeffer'. The quartet's vocal version of the big African hit (named after a Zulu drink) reached the Top 20 alongside Ralph Marterie's interpretation and the original by Rhodesia's Bulawaya Sweet Rhythms Band, which had sold 175,000 copies in South Africa.

EDDIE FISHER
I NEED YOU NOW
RCA

▲ 1
⑩ 16
50/250

This superior Jimmie Crane and Al Jacobs song increased Fisher's gold disc collection and sent him to No 1 for the third time in just over a year. Simultaneously, the writers' composition 'Hurt' reached the R&B Top 10 by another favourite of female fans, Roy Hamilton.

DON CORNELL
HOLD MY HAND
Coral

▲ 5
⑩ 4
—/250

Even though it was banned by the BBC (for mentioning 'the Kingdom of Heaven'!), this song from the 'teenager loves older man' movie *Susan Slept Here* topped the UK chart. Curiously, it easily outsold several lyrically doctored (amended to 'the wonder of Heaven') British covers.

UNITED KINGDOM
September 1954

DON CORNELL
HOLD MY HAND
Vogue

▲ 1
⑩ 1•
23/250

See US entry.

NAT 'KING' COLE
SMILE
Capitol

▲ 2
⑩ 7
119/250

British-born silent comedy legend Charlie Chaplin composed this melody for his 1936 film *Modern Times*. Cole's unforgettable performance added to his long list of transatlantic winners. Chaplin fan Michael Jackson included 'Smile' on the multi-platinum *History* album in 1995.

MAX BYGRAVES
GILLY GILLY
OSSENFEFFER
KATZENELLEN BOGEN
BY THE SEA
HMV

▲ 7
⑩ 3
—/250

Surely the most oddly titled hit of the era was written by supreme novelty songsmiths Al Hoffman and Dick Manning, and taken into the US charts earlier by The Four Lads. Forty years after Bygraves' bestseller, children can still be heard singing 'There's a tiny house....'.

UNITED STATES
October 1954

DORIS DAY
IF I GIVE MY HEART TO
YOU
Columbia

▲ 4
⑩ 6
247/250

Denise Lor had the original version of this wistful ballad on the Majar label. However, it was the fresh-faced film star's interpretation on the major Columbia label that registered the most sales.

BILL HALEY & HIS COMETS
SHAKE, RATTLE AND
ROLL
Decca

▲ 7
⑩ 1
—/250

A month before DJ Alan Freed re-christened his radio programme *The Rock & Roll Show* and introduced that phrase into the general language, Haley hit the Top 10 for the first time with a lyrically toned-down cover of the current Joe Turner R&B charter. The record also rocketed the ground-breaking Philadelphia band into the UK Top 10, and in doing so helped launch rock'n'roll on both sides of the Atlantic.

PERRY COMO
PAPA LOVES MAMBO
RCA

▲ 4
⑩ 13
226/250

Days after singing the national anthem at the World Series, the consistently successful singer scored with one of the biggest mambo hits. The song, which label-mates the Ames Brothers previously rejected, was written by regular chart makers Al Hoffman and Dick Manning.

DAVID WHITFIELD
CARA MIA
London

▲ 10
⑩ 1•
—/250

See UK entry (June).

UNITED KINGDOM

October 1954

AL MARTINO
THE STORY OF TINA
Capitol

▲ 10
⑩ 6
—/250

Despite some stiff opposition from British newcomer Ronnie Harris, this Stateside song stylist added another UK-only hit to his collection with a Greek ballad that started out as 'Dio Prasina Matia'. It was, however, the vocalist's last UK Top 10 entry until 1973. Curiously, in the US, Martino's most successful spell came during the beat boom period of the mid-1960s.

DEAN MARTIN
SWAY
Capitol

▲ 6
⑩ 3
—/250

Norman Gimbel added the English lyric to the Mexican song 'Quien Sera', which took the unmistakable vocalist back into the US and UK hit parades. Six years later fellow Italian American Bobby Rydell returned the dance-floor-filler to the transatlantic Top 20.

DORIS DAY
IF I GIVE MY HEART
TO YOU
Philips

▲ 4
⑩ 6
241/250

See US entry.

VERA LYNN
MY SON MY SON
Decca

▲ 1
⑩ 4•
80/250

Dame Vera Lynn (a title bestowed by the Queen in 1975) is one of few entertainers who can truthfully be called 'legends in their lifetime'. In the UK she is held in great esteem, even by millions of people who are too young to remember the war. Her last Top 10 single was a stirring Eddie Calvert composition and a natural follow-up to his 'Oh Mein Papa'.

ROSEMARY CLOONEY
THIS OLE HOUSE
Philips

▲ 1
⑩ 3
78/250

See US entry (August).

BILLIE ANTHONY
THIS OLD HOUSE
Columbia

▲ 4
⑩ 1•
211/250

Like numerous British singers of the era, many of the songs that Glasgow-born Anthony (real name Philomena Brown) recorded were cover versions. Billie's one hit came with her rendition of Rosemary Clooney's No 1. The Scottish singer's interpretation so impressed the composer, Stuart Hamblen, that he personally tried to get work for her in the US. Among Billie's other less rewarding releases were renditions of 'Ricochet', 'Bell Bottom Blues', 'Make Love To Me', 'Teach Me Tonight', 'Tweedle Dee', 'Sweet Old Fashioned Girl' and 'Lay Down Your Arms'.

FRANKIE LAINE
THERE MUST BE A
REASON
Philips

▲ 9
⑩ 11
—/250

Thousands of screaming teenagers greeted the 41-year-old superstar during his much publicized UK tour, and many more bought Laine's version of this Benny Davis composition. In the US, the B side, 'Someday', sold better.

FRANKIE LAINE
RAIN RAIN RAIN
Philips

▲ 8
⑩ 12
—/250

As Laine-mania (as it could have been called) swept through the UK, his rendition of this rousing

song became the vocalist's sixth Top 10 entry of the year. The Four Lads provided vocal accompaniment on the track, which came from a gospel album the two acts recorded together.

JOAN REGAN
IF I GIVE MY HEART TO
YOU
Decca

▲ 3
⑩ 3
224/250

The glamorous entertainer, whose voice inspired comparisons with Vera Lynn, pipped Doris Day at the post with her interpretation of the enchanting love song. It was soon joined in the Top 20 by another Jimmie Crane and Al Jacobs composition, 'I Need You Now' (by Eddie Fisher).

UNITED STATES
November 1954

DE CASTRO SISTERS
TEACH ME TONIGHT
Abbott

▲ 3
⑩ 1•
185/250

On both sides of the Atlantic, Cuban-born Babette, Cherie and Peggy De Castro had the biggest-selling version of the Sammy Cahn composition. The flamboyant trio's treatment of the semi-suggestive song outsold Janet Brace's original recording and other covers by regular hit makers Jo Stafford, Nat 'King' Cole and Dinah Washington. In 1959, the sisters' cha cha update of 'Teach Me Tonight' was a minor US success.

CHORDETTES
MR SANDMAN
Cadence

▲ 1
⑩ 1
28/250

Five years after becoming regular performers on Arthur Godfrey's show, the female vocal group from Wisconsin topped the US charts for seven

weeks with their second Cadence release. Label owner Archie Bleyer, who had been Arthur Godfrey's musical director, produced the track that gave the one-time barbershop quartet their first bestseller on either side of the Atlantic. The catchy Pat Ballard composition was first recorded by Vaughn Monroe on the B side of his hit 'They Were Doin' The Mambo'.

ROSEMARY CLOONEY
MAMBO ITALIANO
Columbia

▲ 10
⑩ 6•
—/250

In the mid-1950s, the record industry was as excited about mambo music as about rock'n'roll, and many thought that the former had the most potential. Bob Merrill composed this pop/mambo novelty, which became Clooney's second successive UK No 1. In the US, the ABC network banned it because 'it did not reach standards of good taste'.

UNITED KINGDOM
November 1954

BILLY ECKSTINE
NO ONE BUT YOU
MGM

▲ 3
⑩ 1
125/250

Not long after being presented with an award for selling ten million singles on MGM, the unique American vocalist scored a UK-only success with a song from the Lana Turner film *The Flame And The Flesh*.

DAVID WHITFIELD
SANTO NATALE
Decca

▲ 2
⑩ 6
182/250

Noteworthy American tunesmiths Dick Manning and Al Hoffman composed the ballad that made it

six UK Top 10 entries in a year for Whitfield. The seasonal song also reached the US Top 40.

WINIFRED ATWELL
LET'S HAVE ANOTHER PARTY
Philips

▲ 1
⑩ 6
90/250

Another Christmas meant another medley hit by the popular pianist. This party-targeted single, which sold over a million worldwide, included renditions of 'Bye Bye Blackbird', 'Nellie Dean' and 'Sheik Of Araby'.

UNITED STATES
December 1954

EDDIE FISHER
COUNT YOUR BLESSINGS (INSTEAD OF SHEEP)
RCA

▲ 5
⑩17
—/250

This memorable Irving Berlin lullaby from Bing Crosby's movie *White Christmas* ended another great year for the singer Berlin called 'the closest thing I've heard to Al Jolson'. Incidentally, one of the year's biggest Christmas novelty songs was called 'I Want Eddie Fisher For Christmas'.

JOAN WEBER
LET ME GO, LOVER
Columbia

▲ 1
⑩ 1•
88/250

When a vocalist was needed to sing the theme for a Studio One play about music business corruption, Mitch Miller chose this pregnant 18-year-old housewife because her 'five and dime voice' would not distract viewers. The record sold 500,000 in two weeks and rocketed the new mother from New Jersey to the top. It was to be her only hit, and sadly within 18 months she had lost both contract and husband. Little more was heard of Weber until her death was reported in 1981.

AMES BROTHERS
THE NAUGHTY LADY OF
SHADY LANE
RCA

▲ 3
⑩ 7•
218/250

RCA claimed to have sold 309,748 copies of this bouncy novelty in only ten days, which gave the brothers their only transatlantic Top 10 entry. Like others, the group lost sales due to the rise of rock, even though RCA told teenagers 'You ain't heard rock'n'roll until you've dug the Ames Brothers'. Lead singer Ed Ames had a handful of solo hits after the quartet disbanded in the early 1960s.

FOUR ACES
MR SANDMAN
Decca

▲ 10
⑩ 7
—/250

At the end of 1954, an avalanche of artists on both sides of the Atlantic were asking favours of the sandman. In the US, this rendition was pipped at the post by The Chordettes, while in the UK Dickie Valentine's version crossed more counters.

FONTANE SISTERS
HEARTS OF STONE
Dot

▲ 1
⑩ 3
94/250

In 1950, New Jersey natives Marge, Bea & Geri Fontane (born Rosse) were voted Most Promising Vocal Group. At the time they had a few good sellers in their own right and notched up a couple of Top 10 entries with Perry Como. After a couple of relatively quiet years, the trio scored with several covers of R&B hits; the first and biggest of these had originally been recorded by The Jewels and also reached the pop Top 20 by another R&B act, The Charms.

UNITED KINGDOM

December 1954

RONNIE HILTON
I STILL BELIEVE
HMV

▲ 3
⑩ 1
188/250

As the first half of the decade ended, two balladeers from Hull climbed up the UK Top 10: David Whitfield and newcomer Ronnie Hilton. Both sides of the latter's second single reached the Top 20. His treatment of the Billy Reid song outperformed versions by chart regular Al Martino and fellow newcomer Ronnie Harris. The high-flying flip, 'Veni Vidi Vici', had earlier been cut in the US by The Gaylords.

BIG BEN BANJO BAND
LET'S GET TOGETHER
NO 1
Columbia

▲ 6
⑩ 1•
—/250

Columbia Records' A&R head Norrie Paramor was Big Ben, the leader of the session band that strummed their way up the charts with a medley of minstrel favourites. Included were such Jolson gems as 'Swanee', 'April Showers' and 'Rock-a-Bye Your Baby'. Big Ben also clocked up another Top 20 entry with the similarly styled 'Let's Get Together Again' a year later.

DICKIE VALENTINE
FINGER OF SUSPICION
Decca

▲ 1
⑩ 3
49/250

There was a definite suspicion that the UK's No 1 teen heart-throb had covered American Jane Froman's version of the song. However, Valentine adamantly denied this accusation, claiming that he recorded his chart topper (backing vocals from The Stargazers) before Froman.

RUBY MURRAY
HEARTBEAT
Columbia

▲ 3
⑩ 1
145/250

The words 'overnight sensation' could have been coined to describe the meteoric rise of the Belfast-born vocalist who, just three months after making her chart debut, had five singles simultaneously in the Top 20. The 19-year-old, who replaced Joan Regan on the top-rated TV series *Quite Contrary*, first hit with her second Columbia single, a song that had also been recorded by US hit maker Karen Chandler (aka Eve Young) and popular British singer Lita Roza.

UNITED STATES
January 1955

TERESA BREWER
LET ME GO, LOVER!
Coral

▲ 8
🔟 4
—/250

A rewrite of the 1953 temperance song 'Let Me Go Devil' became one of the most recorded tunes of 1955, and returned this bill-topping female singer to the transatlantic Top 10.

SARAH VAUGHAN
MAKE YOURSELF
COMFORTABLE
Mercury

▲ 8
🔟 1
—/250

When outstanding female vocalists are discussed, you can be sure that the name Sarah Vaughan will be mentioned. The acclaimed song stylist, who sung with the bands of Earl Hines, Billy Eckstine and Dizzy Gillespie in the 1940s, had one of her biggest sellers with this Bob Merrill composition. Among the other songs associated with the multi-award-winning singer are 'Nature Boy', 'Whatever Lola Wants' and the duet 'Passing Strangers' with Billy Eckstine.

McGUIRE SISTERS
SINCERELY
Coral

▲ 1
🔟 2
45/250

For six weeks the vocal trio's smooth rendition of The Moonglows' self-composed R&B charter led the bestsellers. The coupling, a cover of the DeJohn Sisters hit 'No More', was also successful on both sides of the Atlantic.

BILLY VAUGHN & HIS ORCHESTRA
MELODY OF LOVE
Dot

▲ 2
🔟 1
141/250

After leaving The Hilltoppers, the talented arranger/conductor became Dot Records' musical director, and his orchestra backed regular hit makers the Fontane Sisters, Gale Storm and Pat Boone, as well as recording successfully in their own right. Vaughn's distinctive-sounding outfit had the biggest-selling revival of a 50-year-old song, which also charted by the Four Aces, David Carroll's Orchestra and Frank Sinatra. An advert for the hit heralded it as 'The Waltz of the Century'.

JAYE P. MORGAN
THAT'S ALL I WANT
FROM YOU
RCA

▲ 5
🔟 1•
—/250

According to her press release, the husky vocalist was born Mary Martin in a log cabin in Colorado and early in life joined the Morgan Family Variety Troupe. During Morgan's late teens she sang with Frank DeVol's band and made her first solo records in 1953 on Derby. The singer (named after a famous American industrialist) was a frequent Top 100 entrant and was often seen on TV programmes like *The Robert Q Lewis Show* and *Stop The Music*. Hugo Winterhalter's Orchestra provided the backing on Morgan's biggest hit.

DEJOHN SISTERS
(MY BABY DON'T LOVE
ME) NO MORE
Epic

▲ 8
🔟 1•
—/250

Suddenly there was a glut of girl groups all over the US chart. The latest female team to break through were the DeJohn Sisters (Julie and Dux DeGiovanni) from Bill Haley's hometown of Chester, Pennsylvania. Following a handful of unsuccessful singles, they made the grade with one of their own compositions, which outsold a cover by the McGuire Sisters. Sadly for these sisters, there were to be no more big hits.

UNITED KINGDOM
January 1955

ROSEMARY CLOONEY
MAMBO ITALIANO
Philips

▲ 1
🔟 4
62/250

See US entry (November 1954).

DICKIE VALENTINE
MR SANDMAN
Decca

▲ 5
🔟 4
—/250

In the year that America's prestigious *Cash Box* magazine listed him among the 20 Most Promising Male Vocalists, one of Britain's most celebrated solo singers had the biggest UK hit with the much recorded Pat Ballard composition.

BILL HALEY & HIS COMETS
SHAKE, RATTLE AND ROLL
Brunswick

▲ 4
🔟 1
227/250

See US Entry (October 1954).

ALMA COGAN
I CAN'T TELL A WALTZ FROM A TANGO
HMV

▲ 6
🔟 2
—/250

The 'girl with the giggle in her voice' danced up the UK chart with a Hoffman & Manning novelty that

Patti Page had previously recorded on the B side of 'The Mama Doll Song'.

FOUR ACES
MR SANDMAN
Brunswick

▲ 9
🔟 2
—/250

See US entry (December 1954).

RUBY MURRAY
SOFTLY SOFTLY
Columbia

▲ 1
🔟 2
28/250

Leading British composer Paddy Roberts co-wrote the gentle ballad that took the teenage singing sensation to the top for the only time. The tune, which became Murray's theme song, was covered in the US by Jaye P. Morgan and Guy Lombardo.

TENNESSEE ERNIE FORD
GIVE ME YOUR WORD
Capitol

▲ 1
🔟 1
9/250

Thanks initially to repeated plays on AFN (American Forces Network), the B side of Ford's Top 10 country hit 'River Of No Return' returned him to the top of the UK chart. Interestingly, they flipped it over because 'it was a novelty to hear a cowboy singing a plush ballad'.

UNITED STATES
February 1955

PENGUINS
EARTH ANGEL
(WILL YOU BE MINE)
Dootone

▲ 8
🔟 1•
—/250

R&B was the fastest-growing musical style and doo-wop (as it was later termed) was its fastest-growing sub-genre. The most successful doo-wop track ever was recorded cheaply in a garage and was first released as the B side of The Penguins' second single. When it hit, lawsuits flew everywhere, and litigation over the correct composers and the group's contract harmed their future career. The influential 'Earth Angel' has sold well for over 40 years and is now said to have passed the ten million mark.

PERRY COMO
KO KO MO
(I LOVE YOU SO)
RCA

▲ 4
🔟 14
—/250

Gene & Eunice's self-penned R&B smash was turned into a major pop hit by one of the few early 1950s stars who withstood the onslaught of rock'n'roll. When his daughter heard it she exclaimed, 'It's not you, daddy!'.

GEORGIA GIBBS
TWEEDLE DEE
Mercury

▲ 3
🔟 2
187/250

This carefully cloned cover of a Lavern Baker hit so incensed the R&B singer that she tried (unsuccessfully) to sue Gibbs for stealing her vocal and instrumental arrangement. In early 1957, after Gibbs also cut her 'Tra La La', Baker insured herself for $125,000 with Gibbs as the beneficiary 'in case her death deprived Gibbs of the chance to copy her songs'.

CREW-CUTS
KO KO MO
(I LOVE YOU SO)
Mercury

▲ 10
🔟 3
—/250

Even though their previous three singles failed to chart, the celebrated Canadian vocal team had a double-sided Top 10 entry when they returned to covering R&B hits. On this side the group recorded a Gene & Eunice song with which Perry Como fared even better.

JOHNNY MADDOX
THE CRAZY OTTO
(MEDLEY)
Dot

▲ 2
🔟 1•
162/250

'Ivory Rag', 'Play A Simple Melody' and 'When You Wore A Tulip' were all part of the medley that gave the Tennessee honky tonk pianist his only major hit. It was a lively cover of a top-selling German single by pianist Crazy Otto (born Fritz Schulz-Reichel), who soon afterwards had a No 1 US LP with an eponymous album. Maddox, a former child protégé, could not repeat the winning formula, although he tried with tracks like 'Johnny's Medley' and 'Rock & Roll Medley'.

DAVID CARROLL & HIS ORCHESTRA
MELODY OF LOVE
Mercury

▲ 9
🔟 1•
—/250

Mercury Records' noted arranger and conductor Carroll (born Nick Schrier in Chicago) and his orchestra backed chart regulars The Crew-Cuts, The Gaylords, Rusty Draper and Georgia Gibbs before notching up a hit of their own with a revival of a 50-year-old standard. Incidentally, its success came at a time when surveys showed that 45 RPM singles now outsold 78s in the US.

CREW-CUTS
EARTH ANGEL
Mercury

▲ 8
⑩ 4
—/250

In the week after the flip side, 'Ko Ko Mo', charted, the beaty barbershop quartet's version of this top-drawer doo-wop ballad joined The Penguins' original recording in the Top 10. The track was also their only UK Top 10 entry.

UNITED KINGDOM
February 1955

AMES BROTHERS
THE NAUGHTY LADY OF
SHADY LANE
HMV

▲ 6
⑩ 1•
—/250

See US entry (December 1954).

DEAN MARTIN
NAUGHTY LADY OF
SHADY LANE
Capitol

▲ 5
⑩ 4
—/250

UK record buyers bought as many copies of the celebrated crooner's version of the Tepper & Bennett novelty number as they did of the Ames Brothers' US hit treatment. For the uninitiated, the naughty lady in question was only a few days old!

TERESA BREWER
LET ME GO, LOVER!
Vogue/Coral

▲ 9
⑩ 1
—/250

See US entry (January).

RUBY MURRAY
HAPPY DAYS AND
LONELY NIGHTS
Columbia

▲ 6
⑩ 3
—/250

No artist spent longer in the UK chart in 1955 than Murray, whose version of the well-known 1920s song joined two of her previous singles in the Top 6 – a truly staggering feat that no other female singer has ever equalled.

UNITED STATES
March 1955

BILL HAYES
THE BALLAD OF DAVY
CROCKETT
Cadence

▲ 1
⑩ 1•
42/250

Three versions of the title song from the box office smash *Davy Crockett* reached the Top 20 on both sides of the Atlantic, with Hayes' sole hit leading the way. The singer, who was born (on a mountain top?) in Illinois, had been a regular performer on TV's *Show Of Stars* since 1951. Among his earlier records were overlooked treatments of 'Charmaine', 'Too Young' and 'High Noon', and later cuts included 'The Ballad Of James Dean' and 'The Legend Of Wyatt Earp'.

JONI JAMES
HOW IMPORTANT CAN
IT BE
MGM

MGM's bestselling female singer visited the Top 10 for the last time with a Benjamin & Weiss ballad that also sold well by Sarah Vaughan. Despite frequent appearances on Dick Clark's shows, Joni was not really accepted by rock fans and retired in the early 1960s. Incidentally, MGM's leading lass during the rock era, Connie Francis, was described at first as 'a cross between Joni James and Gale Storm'.

FESS PARKER
BALLAD OF DAVY
CROCKETT
Columbia

In the year that Disneyland opened, Walt Disney had one of his biggest hits with *Davy Crockett* – a film that inspired children worldwide to don coonskin caps. The movie's star was Texas-born Parker, whose treatment of the theme came a close

second to Bill Hayes' recording. In 1957, Parker's version of 'Wringle Wrangle' (which also was composed by George Bruns and Tom Blackburn) from another of the actor's Disney westerns, *Westward Ho The Wagons*, fared better than Hayes' cover. Parker subsequently starred in the 1960s TV series *Daniel Boone*.

COWBOY CHURCH
SUNDAY SCHOOL
OPEN UP YOUR HEART
(AND LET THE
SUNSHINE IN)
Decca

Stuart Hamblen, who composed the 1954 million seller 'This Ole House', penned and produced this unusual don't-let-the-devil-win ditty, which was supposedly sung by a Sunday school choir. A *Billboard* reviewer said of the track, 'I have never heard a record with so much simplicity and warmth'. Lead voice on the number is a youngster called Carole Sue – although some claim that she is actually an adult female whose voice has been speeded up. Later less successful singles from the entourage included 'Don't Send Those Kids To Sunday School'.

UNITED KINGDOM
March 1955

DAVID WHITFIELD
BEYOND THE STARS
Decca

▲ 8
🔟 7
—/250

The British entertainer, voted third Most Promising Male Vocalist in the US by *Cash Box*, added to his portfolio of UK hits with another Mantovani and Bunny Lewis composition. The writers had earlier been responsible for the balladeer's transatlantic million seller 'Cara Mia'.

DEAN MARTIN
LET ME GO, LOVER!
Capitol

▲ 3
🔟 5
247/250

It appears that Martin cut both Joan Weber's US No 1 and the other side, the Ames Brothers' hit 'The Naughty Lady Of Shady Lane', especially for the UK market. If so, it was a wise move, as his recordings out-performed the original versions.

NAT 'KING' COLE
A BLOSSOM FELL
Capitol

▲ 3
⑩ 8
237/250

See US entry (May).

RAY BURNS
MOBILE
Columbia

▲ 4
⑩ 1•
248/250

British song stylist Burns, who recorded with Ambrose's Orchestra in 1949, was a member of Cyril Stapleton's very popular Show Band when his cover of Julius La Rosa's single charted. By August 1955, when Burns scored his second and last Top 20 entry, 'That's How A Love Song Was Born', he had already gone solo. The rise of rock hurried the end of the vocalist's career and later releases like 'Condemned For Life (With a Rock And Roll Wife)' created little interest.

RUBY MURRAY
LET ME GO, LOVER!
Columbia

▲ 5
⑩ 4
—/250

Record buyers in the UK could not get enough of the shy nasal-voiced vocalist, whose distinctive version of the US No 1 song joined the other side, 'Happy Days And Lonely Nights', in the Top 10.

EDDIE FISHER
WEDDING BELLS
HMV

▲ 5
⑩ 7
—/250

Just before he married film star Debbie Reynolds, the American heart-throb released a matrimonial melody that had first surfaced in Germany as 'Hochzeitsglocken'. In his homeland, the B side, 'A Man Chases A Girl (Until She Catches Him)', made a bigger chart dent.

JOHNNY BRANDON
TOMORROW
Polygon

▲ 8
⑩ 1•
—/250

In 1955, Londoner Brandon (and The Phantoms) reached the UK Top 20 with both this self-penned singalong and another British composition, 'Don't Worry'. Soon afterwards, the one-time BFN (British Forces Network) DJ relocated to the US to try to make the grade there. His US releases on MGM and King were well received by critics but sold relatively few copies. When he first returned to the UK in 1956 coaches of fans reportedly met him at the airport, but, like many of the singer's contemporaries, rock'n'roll turned the 'Tomorrow' star into yesterday's news.

DICKIE VALENTINE
A BLOSSOM FELL
Decca

▲ 9
⑩ 5
—/250

Soon after starring at one of the earliest pop music shows held at the Royal Albert Hall, Valentine's version of the topnotch British ballad joined Nat 'King' Cole's cut in the Top 10.

RUBY MURRAY
IF ANYONE FINDS THIS
I LOVE YOU
Columbia

▲ 4
⑩ 5
—/250

As she celebrated her twentieth birthday, the Irish chart sensation collected another hit with a moving treatment of an orphan's ode which Kay Starr had cut Stateside. Miss Murray was joined on the record by Anne Warren.

UNITED STATES
April 1955

TENNESSEE ERNIE FORD
BALLAD OF DAVY CROCKETT
Capitol

▲ 6
⑩ 2
—/250

On both sides of the Atlantic this treatment of the very popular film theme came a close second to Bill Hayes' recording. Also in 1955, the deep-voiced vocalist, who, like Crockett, was born in Tennessee, launched a very successful TV series in his homeland.

PEREZ PRADO & HIS ORCHESTRA
CHERRY PINK AND APPLE BLOSSOM WHITE
RCA

▲ 1
⑩ 1
8/250

The Cuban-born organist and bandleader, who was known as 'El Rey De Mambo' ('The King Of Mambo'), topped the transatlantic charts with his treatment of an instrumental that started life as 'Cerisier Rose Et Pommer Blanc' in France in 1950. The pioneering mambo outfit first cut the track in 1951, but it was their later re-recording that was heard in the Jane Russell/Jayne Mansfield film *Underwater!* The new version, which featured trumpeter Billy Regis, headed the US list for an amazing ten weeks.

GEORGIA GIBBS
DANCE WITH ME HENRY (WALLFLOWER)
Mercury

▲ 2
⑩ 3•
168/250

A year after 'Work With Me Annie' topped the R&B charts by The Midnighters, a rewrite, 'The Wallflower (Roll With Me Henry)' by Etta James, followed suit. Soon after that, 'her nibs Miss Gibbs' took a cleaned-up version of the latter into the Top 10 alongside her 'Tweedle Dee', although it was the last trip to the heights of the hit parade for the 34-year-old, who had been singing professionally for 20 years.

LES BAXTER & HIS CHORUS & ORCHESTRA
UNCHAINED MELODY
Capitol

▲ 2
⑩ 5
121/250

Three versions of the theme from the Chester Morris movie *Unchained* reached the US Top 10 simultaneously, with the biggest-selling treatment coming from one of the top orchestras of the decade. The song later turned gold again for the Righteous Brothers (1965 and 1990) and Robson & Jerome (1995).

AL HIBBLER
UNCHAINED MELODY
Decca

▲ 5
⑩ 1
—/250

In the US, the most successful vocal version of the extremely popular film theme was by Hibbler, a unique vocalist whose style straddled the line between jazz, pop and R&B. Although he was no rocker and nudging 40, the blind ex-Duke Ellington Band vocalist was also accepted by rock'n'roll audiences, and as the single climbed Hibbler was starring in an Alan Freed rock'n'roll tour on the East Coast.

NAT 'KING' COLE
DARLING JE VOUS AIME BEAUCOUP
Capitol

▲ 10
⑩ 6
—/250

Back in 1936, the bilingual love ballad was heard in the film *Love And Hisses*, a vehicle for celebrated columnist and commentator Walter Winchell. Before the inimitable Cole made it his own, it had been the theme song for World War II star Hildegarde.

UNITED KINGDOM
April 1955

PEREZ PRADO & HIS ORCHESTRA
CHERRY PINK AND APPLE BLOSSOM WHITE
HMV

▲ 1
⑩ 1
54/250

See US entry.

JOAN REGAN
PRIZE OF GOLD
Decca

▲ 6
⑩ 4
—/250

The title song from Richard Widmark and Mai Zetterling's film *Prize Of Gold* was Regan's last Top 10 entry for four years. Later in the year, her version of the similarly titled 'Croce Di Oro' ('Cross Of Gold') took the vocalist into the US Top 100 for the only time.

DEAN MARTIN
UNDER THE BRIDGES OF PARIS
Capitol

▲ 6
⑩ 6
—/250

Surprisingly, the appeal of this melodic French song failed to cross the Atlantic. Nonetheless, over the channel in the UK, American vocalists Martin and Eartha Kitt both rushed recordings of it into the Top 10.

RONNIE HILTON
A BLOSSOM FELL
HMV

▲ 10
⑩ 2
—/250

The third version of the popular ballad to reach the UK Top 10 was by a song stylist who had been born Adrian Hill, and originally appeared with his brothers in a group called The Singing Hills.

EDDIE CALVERT
CHERRY PINK AND APPLE BLOSSOM WHITE
Columbia

▲ 1
⑩ 2
24/250

Even though 'Oh Mein Papa' sold almost three million copies, the British trumpeter's next half dozen releases (including his hit composition 'My Son My Son') were relatively poor sellers. However, Calvert's treatment of the film theme followed Perez Prado's original version into the top spot in the UK.

DORIS DAY
READY WILLING AND ABLE
Philips

▲ 7
⑩ 7
—/250

As the vivacious performer made her UK stage debut, she charted with a song taken from her latest movie, *Young At Heart* (co-starring Frank Sinatra). In the US, the soundtrack album cracked the Top 20, but the single was unable to grab many sales.

TONY BENNETT
STRANGER IN PARADISE
Philips

▲ 1
⑩ 1•
71/250

See US entry (December 1953).

EARTHA KITT
UNDER THE BRIDGES OF PARIS
HMV

▲ 7
⑩ 1•
—/250

'Sous Les Ponts De Paris' was the original French title of the song that earned the slinky nightclub singer with a unique vocal style her first UK bestseller, while in the US it had been the B side of the Christmas hit, 'Santa Baby'. Kitt, who first found fame in Paris at the dawn of the decade, returned to the UK charts in both the 1980s and 1990s.

CREW-CUTS
EARTH ANGEL
Mercury

▲ 4
🔟 1•
144/250

See US entry (February).

TONY MARTIN
STRANGER IN PARADISE
HMV

▲ 6
🔟 1
—/250

See US Entry (January 1954).

UNITED STATES
May 1955

ROY HAMILTON
UNCHAINED MELODY
Epic

▲ 9
🔟 1•
—/250

Hamilton was the R&B find of 1954. Before this crossover hit he had R&B smashes with 'You'll Never Walk Alone', 'If I Loved You', 'Ebb Tide' and 'Hurt' and frequently headlined rock'n'roll and R&B package shows, where adoring fans mobbed him. Bad health brought temporary retirement in 1956, and, although a 1957 return was successful, the Georgia-born singer never reached the same heights. The influential performer, who described his style as 'a mix of Gospel, pop and classical music with a touch of R&B', died from a stroke aged 40 in 1969.

ART MOONEY & HIS ORCHESTRA
HONEY-BABE
MGM

▲ 6
🔟 1•
—/250

In the late 1940s, the bandleader from Massachusetts was seldom away from the chart thanks to singalong versions of standards like 'I'm Looking Over A Four Leaf Clover' and 'Baby Face'. After a few relatively quiet years, his orchestra were featured on two Top 10 hits in 1955; the first was their treatment of this marching song from the Van Heflin film *Battle Cry*. Mooney's later attempts at rock'n'roll, such as 'Rock And Roll Tumbleweed',

'I Played The Fool' and 'Tutti Frutti' (with vocalist Ocie Smith), garnered few sales.

NAT 'KING' COLE
A BLOSSOM FELL/IF I MAY
Capitol

▲ 2
🔟 7
148/250

Three months before it debuted in the US, Cole's interpretation of the noteworthy British ballad had outsold local heart-throb Dickie Valentine's recording in the UK. The American coupling, 'If I May', came from the prolific pen of R&B songsmith Rose Marie McCoy.

BILL HALEY & HIS COMETS
ROCK AROUND THE CLOCK
Decca

▲ 1
🔟 2
14/250

Take a song written by an old timer that sold few copies when released previously by another act, and ensure that it has a title which has been used unsuccessfully on more than one occasion. For good measure, include a guitar solo lifted from one of the artist's earlier flops, spend only a little time on the recording and release it on a B side. It doesn't sound like the recipe for a hit, but these ingredients produced this 25 million seller which influenced the rest of twentieth-century music

UNITED KINGDOM
May 1955

INK SPOTS
MELODY OF LOVE
Parlophone

▲ 10
🔟 1•
—/250

Despite stiff opposition from currently popular vocal teams the McGuire Sisters, the Four Aces and the Beverley Sisters, the No 1 male group of the 1940s had the UK hit version of Billy Vaughn's US million-selling instrumental. The group on the track were actually an Ink Spots spin-off formed by ex-member Charlie Fuqua (whose nephew Harvey fronted The Moonglows). For the record, the original foursome's hits included the No 1s 'I'm Making Believe' (1944), 'The Gypsy' (1946) and 'To Each His Own' (1946).

JOHNNIE RAY
IF YOU BELIEVE
Philips

▲ 7
🔟 5
—/250

For his film debut, the hearing-aid wearing, hysteria-inducing teen idol appeared in the all-star Cinemascope production *There's No Business Like Show Business*. The single from the film coupled this Irving Berlin composition with one of the writer's earliest successes, 'Alexander's Ragtime Band'.

AL HIBBLER
UNCHAINED MELODY
Brunswick

▲ 2
🔟 1•
113/250

See US entry (April).

JIMMY YOUNG
UNCHAINED MELODY
Decca

▲ 1
🔟 2
45/250

Four recordings of the unforgettable melody reached the UK chart, with the British balladeer's rendition ranking higher than any of the three American versions.

FOUR ACES
STRANGER IN PARADISE
Brunswick

▲ 6
🔟 3
—/250

See US entry (January 1954).

LES BAXTER
& HIS CHORUS
& ORCHESTRA
UNCHAINED MELODY
Capitol

▲ 10
🔟 1•
—/250

See US entry (April).

UNITED STATES
June 1955

FRANK SINATRA
LEARNIN' THE BLUES
Capitol

▲ 2
🔟 3
155/250

The singer they call 'The Voice' reached runner-up spot on both sides of the Atlantic with this swinging side. Although in his fortieth year, Sinatra was as popular as he had been in the 1940s, when the first teeny boppers screamed and swooned over him.

McGUIRE SISTERS
SOMETHING'S GOTTA GIVE
Coral

▲ 6
🔟 3
—/250

For the first time, the popular sister act clicked with a non-R&B cover; it was a Johnny Mercer-penned song from Fred Astaire's film *Daddy Longlegs*. The B side, 'Rhythm 'N' Blues', also got its fair share of sales and jukebox spins.

UNITED KINGDOM
June 1955

ALMA COGAN
DREAMBOAT
HMV

▲ 1
🔟 3
73/250

The only English female to top the UK charts in the 1950s was this always stunningly attired artist. The song that took the lively and very popular performer there had previously been recorded in the US by both the Paulette Sisters and the Five DeMarco Sisters.

ROSEMARY CLOONEY
WHERE WILL THE DIMPLE BE
Philips

▲ 6
🔟 5
—/250

Even though she was still only in her twenties and had just been voted the US' Top Female Artist,

Clooney's days as a big record seller were over in America. The US audience even overlooked this cuter-than-cute Bob Merrill composition. After many personal problems, the popular entertainer made a successful showbiz comeback and is still selling out concerts and picking up Grammy nominations in the 1990s.

UNITED STATES
July 1955

SOMETHIN' SMITH & THE REDHEADS
IT'S A SIN TO TELL A LIE
Epic

While other major labels scrambled to climb on board the rock'n'roll and R&B bandwagons, Columbia showed little interest and continued to release easy-on-the-ear singles like this revival of Fats Waller's 1936 chart topper. The male vocal/instrumental trio consisted of guitarist Smith, pianist Saul Striks and violinist Major Short, the first-named being yet another previous winner on Arthur Godfrey's *Talent Scouts* show. Despite later appearances on Dick Clark's TV shows, the critically acclaimed trio proved to be one-hit wonders.

GISELE MACKENZIE
HARD TO GET
X

A standout song that was introduced on the NBC TV show *Justice* gave the Canadian star of *Your Hit Parade* her highest-ranked hit. Despite many more TV appearances over the next decade, Mackenzie's first release on RCA's X label was the vocalist's last Top 40 entry.

SAMMY DAVIS JR
SOMETHING'S GOTTA GIVE
Decca

One of the century's finest entertainers learned his trade while in the popular Will Mastin Trio (with his father and uncle) between 1940 and 1954. The multi-talented performer was an instant solo success and *Cash Box* voted him Most Promising Male Vocalist of 1955. Not only did the New Yorker's stylish treatment of the film tune join the McGuire Sisters' interpretation in the Top 10, but the B side, the title song from the film *Love Me Or Leave Me*, also reached the Top 20.

PAT BOONE
AIN'T THAT A SHAME
Dot

After three small sellers on Republic Records, the Florida-born teen idol debuted in the Top 20 with his treatment of The Charms' R&B hit 'Two Hearts', a song he disliked. Boone was also unenthusiastic about covering this Fats Domino R&B No 1, not least because the title was grammatically incorrect. Interestingly, on the B side was a revival of father-in-law Red Foley's 1949 country No 1 'Tennessee Saturday Night'. In the UK, where Domino's recording was not released at the time, Boone's version was also a bestseller.

UNITED KINGDOM
July 1955

DICKIE VALENTINE
I WONDER
Decca

▲ 4
⑩ 6
221/250

For the second time in six months, the UK's No 1 male vocalist won a chart battle with American Jane Froman. 'I Wonder' was a semi-religious ballad that bore a resemblance to her earlier record 'I Believe' (a No 1 hit for Frankie Laine).

RUBY MURRAY
EVERMORE
Columbia

▲ 3
⑩ 6
138/250

Paddy Roberts, who composed Murray's No 1 'Softy Softly', also penned the song that gave the UK's bestselling singles artist of 1955 her sixth Top 10 entry in seven months.

FRANKIE LAINE
COOL WATER
Philips

▲ 2
⑩ 13
89/250

This acclaimed western composition could have been written especially for the robust performer. However, it had been penned back in 1941 by Bob Nolan for his group The Sons Of The Pioneers. In the US, Vaughn Monroe (supported by The Sons Of The Pioneers) achieved the highest-ranking rendition in 1948.

SLIM WHITMAN
ROSE MARIE
London

▲ 1
⑩ 1
6/250

Three years after scoring his biggest US hit with a song from the operetta *Rose Marie*, the country performer spent a record-breaking 11 consecutive weeks at the top of the UK chart with that show's title song. The single, which had been a US country Top 10 entry a year before, sold over 750,000 copies in the UK alone.

MALCOLM VAUGHAN
EVERY DAY OF MY LIFE
HMV

▲ 5
⑩ 1
234/250

When producer Wally Ridley watched up-and-coming comedy duo Earle & Vaughan, he was most impressed by Welshman Vaughan's impression of Mario Lanza and offered him a solo recording contract. For his first single the one-time child actor covered David Whitfield's 'Mama', but it was the B side, a version of Denise Lor's 'Every Day Of My Life', that started off the vocalist's string of chart hits.

DAVID WHITFIELD
EV'RYWHERE
Decca

▲ 3
⑩ 8
107/250

Thanks to Whitfield's top-selling version, the winner of the first Ivor Novello award for Most Popular Song of the Year was 'Ev'rywhere', which had been composed in the mid-1930s by Tolchard Evans. It was covered unsuccessfully in the US by Tony Martin.

UNITED STATES
August 1955

MITCH MILLER & HIS ORCHESTRA & CHORUS
THE YELLOW ROSE OF TEXAS
Columbia

▲ 1
🔟 2
34/250

Top Cleveland DJ Bill Randle tipped off Miller about the commercial potential of this old Civil War song – originally known as 'Gallant Hood Of Texas' (after General John B. Hood). The noted A&R man agreed, and his recording of the old confederate marching tune topped the US chart and almost repeated the feat in the UK.

LES PAUL & MARY FORD
HUMMINGBIRD
Capitol

▲ 8
🔟 11•
—/250

Guitar pioneer Paul and wife Mary's last significant seller was a cover of a noteworthy number penned and originally recorded by Don & Lou Robertson (the latter one of the popular 1940s group, the Dinning Sisters). Many later rock stars acknowledged a great debt to the influential guitar wizard, who was inducted into the Rock and Roll Hall of Fame in 1988. It is therefore ironic that it was rock'n'roll that helped curtail his successful recording career.

BOYD BENNETT & HIS ROCKETS
SEVENTEEN
King

▲ 5
🔟 1•
—/250

Were the Rockets influenced by The Comets or vice versa? Either way, both acts had been rocking since the early 1950s. In the US, Muscle Shoals-born Bennett had a chart battle over his composition 'Seventeen' with the Fontane Sisters, while in the UK he just out-pointed Frankie Vaughan (who also covered his follow-up, 'My Boy Flat Top'). Interestingly, the track, which King did not want

to release, features Bennett's vocal and not band member Big Moe, as is often presumed.

CHUCK MILLER
THE HOUSE OF BLUE LIGHTS
Mercury

▲ 9
🔟 1•
—/250

Scat-singing boogie pianist Miller's revival of Freddie Slack and Don Raye's 1946 smash sounded right for these Bill Haley and Boyd Bennett times. It was the biggest hit for the California showman, who had recorded earlier with little success on Capitol. His subsequent rock-related releases, including covers of 'Plaything', 'Bye Bye Love' and another stomping Don Raye song, 'Down The Road A Piece', failed to light up the chart.

JOHNNY DESMOND
THE YELLOW ROSE OF TEXAS
Coral

▲ 6
🔟 1•
—/250

The veteran vocalist, who had sung with the bands of Bob Crosby, Gene Krupa and Glenn Miller, scored his first solo Top 20 bestseller in early 1955 with 'Play Me Hearts And Flowers'. After Desmond's (born Giovanni Desimons in Detroit) next three singles stiffed, producer Dick Jacobs decided quickly to cover Mitch Miller's runaway smash and the result earned the star of radio's top-rated *Breakfast Club* his highest-placed hit.

CHUCK BERRY
MAYBELLENE
Chess

▲ 5
🔟 1
—/250

As usual, this fast, moving R&B hit was covered by a handful of pop acts; unusually, though, none of those versions could touch the sales of the original. Berry first called his hot-rod rocker 'Ida Mae' but the title was changed, partly because it drew attention to the fact that it owed something to 'Ida Red' (especially Cowboy Copas' 1946 interpretation). Interestingly, Berry himself had imagined that this ground-breaking track would be the B side to the bluesy 'Wee Wee Hours'.

UNITED KINGDOM
August 1955

FRANKIE LAINE
STRANGE LADY IN TOWN
Philips

▲ 6
⑩ 14
—/250

Once again, Laine scored in the UK with a western movie theme that sold relatively poorly in his homeland. In the US, the title song from a Greer Garson and Dana Andrews film was found on the B side of the small-selling 'Cool Water'.

FRANK SINATRA
LEARNIN' THE BLUES
Capitol

▲ 2
⑩ 2
143/250

See US entry (June).

SLIM WHITMAN
INDIAN LOVE CALL
London American

▲ 7
⑩ 2
—/250

See US entry (September 1952).

CATERINA VALENTE
THE BREEZE AND I
Polydor

▲ 5
⑩ 1•
245/250

Chances are that Paris-born Valente is the only hit maker who can boast that her mother was a world-famous clown. Be that as it may, the multi-lingual singer/dancer and one-time circus performer was one of Europe's most popular vocalists in the late 1950s. She reached the Top 20 in both the UK and US with a revival of a Cuban song (originally called 'Andalucia') that both Jimmy Dorsey and Xavier Cugat (featuring vocalist Dinah Shore) had found success with in 1940.

UNITED STATES
September 1955

FOUR LADS
MOMENTS TO REMEMBER
Columbia

▲ 3
⑩ 2
127/250

American radio DJs could not get enough of the Canadian quartet's clean-cut harmony style, and in the mid-1950s no vocal group received more airplay. The memorable ballad was penned by Al Stillman, whose 'The Breeze And I' was simultaneously scoring in the UK.

CREW-CUTS
GUM DROP
Mercury

Shortly after their cover of The Charms' single 'Two Hearts' failed to chart, the crew-cutted Canadian quartet clicked with a version of another Charms' track, 'Gum Drop'. As the record climbed, the popular foursome toured the UK, where they were met by many female fans sporting similar hair styles (known as Crew-sader cuts). The group, who helped popularize R&B material, folded in 1963 with nine Top 20 entries behind them.

FONTANE SISTERS
SEVENTEEN
Dot

Few artists recorded as many covers of R&B and rock songs as the close-harmony trio, who achieved six Top 20 entries in the decade. Apart from their treatment of this Boyd Bennett number, they also cut such noted songs as 'Adorable', 'Rock Love', 'Daddy-O', 'Rollin' Stone', 'Eddie My Love' and 'I'm In Love Again'. When record buyers developed a taste for original versions, the sisters' sales slumped.

LES BAXTER & HIS ORCHESTRA
WAKE THE TOWN AND TELL THE PEOPLE
Capitol

Vocal team The Notables joined Baxter's orchestra on the Sammy Gallup and Jerry Livingston-composed follow-up to the chart topping 'Unchained Melody'.

FOUR ACES
LOVE IS A MANY-SPLENDOURED THING
Decca

This Academy Award-winning song (from the William Holden movie of the same name) was an ideal vehicle for the early 1950s most successful male quartet, but when thousands of new vocal groups arrived on the scene in the mid- and late 1950s the Aces got lost in the shuffle. In future years several different line-ups toured the US, and in the 1990s original lead singer Al Alberts sued a Disney-backed Four Aces for $9 million.

ROGER WILLIAMS
AUTUMN LEAVES
Kapp

Multi-instrumentalist and one-time child protégé Williams (born Louis Weertz in Omaha) was another artist who could thank Arthur Godfrey's *Talent Scouts* show for setting him on the road to fame. For his second Kapp single he revived a much recorded 1950s song, which had started out in France as 'Les Feuilles Mortes'. It was the third instrumental No 1 of the year, and formed the launch pad for one of the most successful American pianists of all time.

PERRY COMO
TINA MARIE
RCA

Both Como and supreme songwriter Bob Merrill were able to adapt to the changing music scene in the 1950s, as this up-tempo teen-targeted track clearly showed.

UNITED KINGDOM
September 1955

EDDIE CALVERT
JOHN AND JULIE
Columbia

Soon after his treatment of 'Stranger In Paradise' reached the Top 20, the talented trumpeter returned to the Top 10 with the theme from an enchanting British children's film.

STARGAZERS
CLOSE THE DOOR
Decca

In the year that they were again voted the UK's Best Vocal Group by *NME* readers, The Stargazers clocked up another Top 10 entry with an infectious novelty number that Jim Lowe had recorded earlier in the US.

JIMMY YOUNG
THE MAN FROM LARAMIE
Decca

The title theme from James Stewart's latest western movie failed to chart by both Al Martino and James Brown (the actor – not Soul Brother No 1) in the US. However, in the UK it helped this popular performer to become the first British recording artist to score two No 1 hits with successive singles.

SAMMY DAVIS JR
LOVE ME OR LEAVE ME
Brunswick

Davis was an all-round entertainer with few, if any equals and, alongside fellow Rat Pack members Frank Sinatra and Dean Martin, he became one of the world's top performers. His first UK hit came shortly after the album *Starring Sammy Davis Jr* headed the US chart and 'That Old Black Magic' had taken him back into the US singles Top 20.

CYRIL STAPLETON & HIS ORCHESTRA
BLUE STAR
Decca

Things were moving in Britain: the first commercial TV station had been launched and rock'n'roll was first mentioned in *NME*. Simultaneously, bandleader Stapleton signed a new TV deal with the BBC and his easy-on-the-ear interpretation of the theme from the US TV series *Medic* became his biggest UK hit. Vocal chores on the track were handled by one-time Eric Winstone Band singer Julie Dawn. In 1959, Stapleton's version of 'The Children's Marching Song' was a US Top 20 entry.

UNITED STATES
October 1955

BILLY VAUGHN & HIS ORCHESTRA & CHORUS
THE SHIFTING, WHISPERING SANDS (PARTS 1 & 2)
Dot

Ken Nordene handled the narrative on the left-field western opus which also reached the UK Top 20. Similar follow-ups, 'Little Boy Blue' and 'The Ship That Never Sailed', never anchored in the Top 40.

DON CORNELL
THE BIBLE TELLS ME SO
Coral

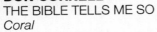

An argument with the Archbishop of Canterbury (head of the Church of England) about this single could not get the BBC to lift their ban on the country gospel song, which harmed its UK progress. The arrival of rock'n'roll did not unduly worry Cornell, who covered records by Buddy Holly, Eddie Cochran, Lonnie Donegan and The Moonglows, and even released an album entitled *For Teenagers Only*. However, as it turned out there was no room on the bandwagon for the popular club entertainer.

CHEERS
BLACK DENIM TROUSERS
Capitol

Actor Bert Convy was part of this trio assembled by songwriters/producers Jerry Leiber & Mike Stoller. They raced up the chart with a ditty about the death of a biker, the release of which coincided with James Dean's fatal crash. The record had a rock feel even though the group's vocal was only slightly more revolutionary than that of Vaughn Monroe and Edith Piaf, who covered it. The trio, whose follow-up, 'Chicken', dealt with a 'chicken' hot-rod race, were voted second Most Promising Vocal Group by US DJs.

RUSTY DRAPER
THE SHIFTING, WHISPERING SANDS
Mercury

Soon after Draper's treatment of 'Seventeen' reached No 18, he chalked up the biggest hit of his career with a million-selling version of a monologue that was also riding high by Billy Vaughn. It was one of six Top 20 entries during the decade for a pop/country performer who usually relied on carefully chosen covers of other artists' records.

PLATTERS
ONLY YOU
Mercury

The most successful black group of the 1950s released six singles on King and built up a formidable West Coast following before making their chart debut. Manager Buck Ram signed them to Mercury as part of a deal that also took his high-flying act The Penguins there. The Platters' Mercury debut was a re-recording of 'Only You', a Ram song that King had refused to release. It lay dormant for three months before rocketing up the hit parade, leaving a collection of cover versions trailing in its wake.

AL HIBBLER
HE
Decca

Englishman Richard Mullen ('My September Love') co-wrote this dramatic ballad, which, like the distinctive baritone's previous hit, 'Unchained Melody', was revived successfully in the 1960s by the Righteous Brothers. Before taking a musical back seat, the unique vocalist had one more Top 20 entry, 'After The Lights Go Down' in 1956. Also that year the veteran was named third Most Outstanding New Male Vocalist behind Elvis and Pat Boone!

UNITED KINGDOM
October 1955

MITCH MILLER & HIS ORCHESTRA & CHORUS
YELLOW ROSE OF TEXAS
Philips

▲ 2
⑩ 1•
142/250

See US Entry (August).

ROSEMARY CLOONEY
HEY THERE
Philips

▲ 4
⑩ 6•
—/250

See US entry (July 1954).

BILL HALEY & HIS COMETS
ROCK AROUND THE CLOCK
Brunswick

▲ 1
⑩ 2
2/250

See US entry (May 1955).

JOHNNIE RAY
HEY THERE
Philips

▲ 5
⑩ 6
—/250

In the US, his distinctive interpretation of the much recorded ballad was the B side of Ray's mid-table hit 'Hernando's Hideaway' (also from *The Pajama Game)'*. However, in the UK, where he was still amazingly popular, the track ran neck-and-neck with a version recorded by label-mate Rosemary Clooney.

JOHNSTON BROTHERS
HERNANDO'S HIDEAWAY
Decca

▲ 1
⑩ 2
85/250

As the Johnston Brothers' spirited recording of his castanets-clicking classic from *The Pajama Game* moved into top spot in the UK, 29-year-old composer Jerry Ross died of leukaemia. Another of his compositions, 'Hey There', stood at No 5.

UNITED STATES
November 1955

TENNESSEE ERNIE FORD
SIXTEEN TONS
Capitol

▲ 1
⑩ 3•
30/250

An unprecedented 600,000 copies of this finger-snapping single were sold in nine days in the US and it was a transatlantic No 1 (despite a BBC ban for mentioning St Peter!). The coal-mining song had originally been recorded by its composer Merle Travis in 1947. In the late 1950s, Ford scored with several top-selling gospel albums, including

Hymns (the first LP by a solo artist to be certified gold). He died in 1991 – following a meal at the White House.

GALE STORM
I HEAR YOU KNOCKING
Dot

▲ 3
⑩ 1
196/250

Fats Domino's songwriting partner, Dave Bartholomew, penned this punchy pounder and his band played on the original version by R&B

performer Smiley Lewis. The pop hit was by the Texas-born (real name Josephine Cottle) star of TV's popular *My Little Margie* series and it was the first of a handful of Top 20 entries for the singer/actress, who had earlier appeared in such diverse movies as *Tom Brown's Schooldays* and *The Texas Rangers*. A 1970 recording of the song by Dave Edmunds was a transatlantic Top 10 entry.

PAT BOONE
AT MY FRONT DOOR
(CRAZY LITTLE MAMA)
Dot

▲ 8
⑩ 2
—/250

At a time when Elvis signed for RCA, his late 1950s arch rival returned to the Top 10 with a bouncy R&B number, which also reached the pop Top 20 by its composers The El Dorados.

UNITED KINGDOM
November 1955

RUBY MURRAY
I'LL COME WHEN YOU
CALL
Columbia

▲ 6
⑩ 7
—/250

In less than 12 months the distinctive young Irish vocalist had racked up an unprecedented run of UK hits, hosted a TV series and topped the bill at the Palladium. She ended a sensational year with her seventh Top 10 entry in a row.

WINIFRED ATWELL
LET'S HAVE A DING DONG
Decca

▲ 3
⑩ 7
213/250

The UK's most popular pianist had her biggest hit of the year with another party medley. This time it included such singalong standards as 'Happy Days Are Here Again', 'Oh You Beautiful Doll' and 'Ain't She Sweet'.

JOHNNIE RAY
SONG OF THE DREAMER
Philips

▲ 10
⑩ 7
—/250

Billy Brooks cut the song first for the US R&B market, while Eddie Fisher's later interpretation lifted it into the pop Top 20. In the UK, however, it was Ray's impassioned performance that nabbed the vast majority of sales.

FOUR ACES
LOVE IS A MANY-
SPLENDOURED THING
Brunswick

▲ 2
⑩ 4•
127/250

See US entry (September).

PAT BOONE
AIN'T THAT A SHAME
London American

▲ 7
⑩ 1
—/250

See US entry (July).

STARGAZERS
TWENTY TINY FINGERS
Decca

▲ 4
⑩ 4•
242/250

Top American tunesmiths Tepper & Bennett penned the cute novelty that lightheartedly looked at the arrival of twins. The song, which featured the group's new lead singer Eula Parker, had been recorded earlier in the US by Art Mooney's Orchestra (with The Cloverleafs). Despite later tracks like 'Rockin' And Rollin'' and 'She Likes To Rock', it was to be the award-winning act's last Top 20 hit.

UNITED STATES
December 1955

FRANK SINATRA
LOVE AND MARRIAGE
Capitol

▲ 6
⑩ 4
—/250

This transatlantic hit is generally regarded as the first song made successful by television. The bouncy Sammy Cahn and Jimmy Can Heusen composition was introduced by Sinatra on NBC's musical adaptation of Thornton Wilder's *Our Town* – which was modestly billed as 'the greatest TV show ever produced'.

DEAN MARTIN
MEMORIES ARE MADE OF THIS
Capitol

▲ 1
⑩ 2
49/250

Soon after he and partner Jerry Lewis split up acrimoniously, Martin had his only transatlantic No 1 with a memorable hook-filled hit penned by vocal group The Easy Riders, who also helped out on backing vocals.

DREAM WEAVERS
IT'S ALMOST TOMORROW
Decca

▲ 8
⑩ 1•
—/250

As 1955 ended, Elvis signed to RCA, R&B was heard on Ed Sullivan's TV show, Alan Freed's stage shows broke box office records and the first rock film, *Rock'n'Roll Revue*, was released. Rock may have been on a roll, but there was still room for this classy ballad performed by a septet from Florida. Members Wade Buff and Gene Adkinson penned the song in 1952 and financed the recording themselves. Many critics were surprised when the 'cheap-sounding' track sold a million and topped the UK chart.

BARRY GORDON
NUTTIN' FOR CHRISTMAS
MGM

▲ 6
⑩ 1•
—/250

In the year that such children's favourites as Disneyland and McDonald's opened, the last chart newcomer was seven-year-old Barry from Massachusetts, whose cute treatment of Tepper & Bennett's novelty number sold over two million copies. The boy, who had appeared on Ted Mack's *Original Amateur Hour* when he was just three years old, was backed on the track by the Art Mooney Orchestra. His future releases, including 'Rock Around Mother Goose' and 'Rock Little Children', sold relatively few.

UNITED KINGDOM
December 1955

DICKIE VALENTINE
CHRISTMAS ALPHABET
Decca

▲ 1
⑩ 7
94/250

This cute and catchy Buddy Kaye-composed Christmas novelty gave Valentine the year's biggest seasonal hit, and left the McGuire Sisters' earlier version out in the cold. Coincidentally, the singer's brother, David, later managed Cliff Richard, who revived the song in 1991.

MAX BYGRAVES
MEET ME ON THE CORNER
HMV

▲ 2
⑩ 4
178/250

Top British songwriter Paddy Roberts' catchy composition would have given the ever-popular performer his only No 1 hit if not for 'Rock Around The Clock'.

PETULA CLARK
SUDDENLY THERE'S A VALLEY
Nixa

▲ 7
⑩ 2
—/250

One-time child protégé Petula had the biggest-selling UK hit with a song that Gogi Grant and Jo Stafford found success with in the US.

DAVID WHITFIELD
WHEN YOU LOSE THE ONE YOU LOVE
Decca

▲ 7
⑩ 9
—/250

Even though his previous two singles failed to chart, the internationally known British vocalist returned with this outstanding big ballad. The record also dented the US bestsellers after his two successive appearances on Ed Sullivan's TV show.

FRANKIE LAINE
HAWKEYE
Philips

▲ 7
⑩15
—/250

Producer Mitch Miller often said 'thank God for the British', since on numerous occasions they made hits out of his American misses. This Boudleaux Bryant (composer of Laine's earlier success 'Hey Joe') number was one such example.

JOHNSTON BROTHERS
JOIN IN AND SING AGAIN
Decca

▲ 9
⑩ 3•
—/250

'Jingle King' Johnny Johnston's most successful recording group (he was also in The Keynotes) had their final Top 10 entry with a medley that included 'Charleston', 'Margie' and 'Sheik Of Araby'. Earlier in the year, US music polls named the quartet among the top vocal groups – a feat no other British act achieved until the 1960s.

ALMA COGAN
NEVER DO A TANGO WITH AN ESKIMO
HMV

▲ 6
⑩ 4•
—/250

Although the Tommie Connor-composed novelty was the Sussex-born singer's last Top 10 entry, she stored up a further ten UK Top 40 singles before the decade ended. Despite her sales slumping in the 1960s, Cogan remained a popular performer and often made the headlines – if only for her extravagant parties, which many celebrities, including The Beatles, attended. Sadly, this effervescent songstress died of cancer in 1966, aged only 34.

UNITED STATES
January 1956

PLATTERS
THE GREAT PRETENDER
Mercury

▲ 2
⑩ 2
152/250

Crossover R&B hits were no longer unusual, and many black artists and their producers targeted records at both the pop and R&B markets. One such act was The Platters, whose follow-up to 'Only You' joined that smash single at the top end of both the R&B and pop charts. Surprisingly, the group did not want to record 'The Great Pretender' as they considered it 'too hillbilly'.

DON CHERRY
BAND OF GOLD
Columbia

▲ 5
⑩ 2•
—/250

Kit Carson (aka Liza Morrow) first recorded this song, which had been written a couple of years earlier by Englishman Jack Taylor and US newspaper man Bob Musel. The single that earned Cherry his only gold disc was the first hit Ray Conniff arranged at Columbia. The balladeer's later releases, including the similarly titled 'Hair Of Gold', proved less fruitful. Cherry split the rest of his life (he died in 1995) between singing and golf – he was very proficient at both.

KAY STARR
ROCK AND ROLL WALTZ
RCA

▲ 1
⑩ 8•
89/250

Unexpectedly, the first transatlantic No 1 to include the words 'rock and roll' was by a non-rock artist, whose biggest hits were behind her. Nonetheless, many teenagers were among the 350,000 who snapped up copies within the first four days. The song came from the pen of Roy Alfred, composer of the earlier R&B/pop smash 'The Hucklebuck'. The influential vocalist became one of the first American artists to record a British rock number, when she cut Eden Kane's 'Well I Ask You' in 1961.

NELSON RIDDLE & HIS ORCHESTRA
LISBON ANTIGUA
Capitol

▲ 1
⑩ 1•
48/250

Few would disagree that New Jersey-native Nelson was one of the most respected and in-demand arrangers of the century. Before this 30-year-old Portuguese instrumental (originally titled 'Lisboa Antigua') gave him a surprise chart topper, the Capitol Records musical director had made a name for himself via his outstanding work with singers like Nat 'King' Cole, Frank Sinatra and Ella Mae Morse. In later years, the one-time trombonist with the Tommy Dorsey and Bob Crosby Bands worked with scores of MOR superstars.

EDDIE FISHER
DUNGAREE DOLL
RCA

▲ 8
⑩ 18
—/250

As rock's influence spread, RCA announced that 'Eddie Fisher sang 'slow rock and roll'. Nevertheless, his spirited cover of the Rock Brothers' 'Seventeen'-styled song was about as close as this vocalist came to proving his rock'n'roll credentials. Interestingly, Fisher was actually younger than pioneer rockers Bill Haley, Chuck Berry and Boyd Bennett.

BILL HALEY & HIS COMETS
SEE YOU LATER, ALLIGATOR
Decca

▲ 6
⑩ 3•
—/250

When Fats Domino rejected this catchy rocker, white R&B singer/songwriter Bobby Charles released it himself. His recording was quickly covered by Roy Hall and then by Haley, who took it into the transatlantic Top 10. The kiss-curled 'King of Rock' received a gold disc for it on the Arthur Godfrey TV show.

UNITED KINGDOM
January 1956

BILL HALEY & HIS COMETS
ROCK-A-BEATIN' BOOGIE
Brunswick

▲ 4
⑩ 3
—/250

Two years after The Treniers had first cut this song, composer Haley's own version joined 'Rock Around The Clock' in the UK Top 5. It was one of an unprecedented nine UK hits in 1956 for the act whose shows were breaking box office records across the US.

TENNESSEE ERNIE FORD
SIXTEEN TONS
Capitol

▲ 1
⑩ 2
76/250

See US entry (November 1955).

BILL HAYES
THE BALLAD OF DAVY CROCKETT
London American

▲ 2
⑩ 1•
201/250

See US entry (March 1955).

FRANK SINATRA
LOVE AND MARRIAGE
Capitol

▲ 3
⑩ 3
243/250

See US entry (December 1955).

TENNESSEE ERNIE FORD
THE BALLAD OF DAVY CROCKETT
Capitol

▲ 3
⑩ 3•
—/250

See US entry (April 1955).

FRANK SINATRA
THE TENDER TRAP
Capitol

▲ 2
⑩ 4
198/250

Soon after being voted Top Male Singer by *NME* readers (an award presented to him by Ruby Murray), 'Ol' Blue Eyes' took the title song from his latest film into the runner-up slot.

LONNIE DONEGAN
ROCK ISLAND LINE
Decca

▲ 8
⑩ 1
—/250

Scottish-born Donegan's brand of skiffle, a 'do-it yourself' folk/blues that had first been played at US 'rent parties' in the late 1920s, altered the course of British music. This frantic washboard-driven version of Leadbelly's 'Rock Island Line' was recorded by Donegan while still the banjo player of Chris Barber's Jazz Band for their 1954 LP *New Orleans Joys*. To everyone's surprise, it was released as a single, steamed into the transatlantic Top 10, and within months scores of skiffle groups had sprung up in every British town.

FRANKIE LAINE
SIXTEEN TONS
Philips

▲ 10
⑩ 16
—/250

This made-for-Britain cover of the US' most popular song continued Laine's staggering run of UK bestsellers. Like his early hits 'Mule Train' and 'The Cry Of The Wild Goose' it had originally been recorded by Tennessee Ernie Ford.

UNITED STATES
February 1956

FOUR LADS
NO, NOT MUCH!
Columbia

▲ 4
⑩ 3
236/250

As their recording of Al Stillman and Robert Allen's 'Moments To Remember' slid down the Top 20, the popular foursome returned to the chart with another notable composition penned by the same writers.

LES BAXTER &
HIS ORCHESTRA &
CHORUS
THE POOR PEOPLE
OF PARIS
Capitol

▲ 1
⑩ 7•
57/250

Their instrumental interpretation of Edith Piaf's 1954 French release 'La Goulante Du Pauvre Jean' gave the orchestra a second No 1 in less than a year. It inspired such answer records as 'The Rich People of Brooklyn' and 'The Rich People Of Hollywood'. Baxter's ground-breaking *Taboo!* album (released simultaneously with the single) earned him the name 'The Godfather of Exotica' during the space-age bachelor-pad music craze of the mid-1990s. He died soon after his belated return to the spotlight in 1996.

PAT BOONE
I'LL BE HOME
Dot

▲ 6
⑩ 3
—/250

Amazingly, Boone had four cover versions simultaneously in the Top 100. The most successful was his treatment of The Flamingos' 'I'll Be Home' (a sequel to their earlier 'Please Come Back Home'). The flip, Little Richard's 'Tutti Frutti', also cracked the Top 20. In the UK, the A side headed the chart for five weeks.

UNITED KINGDOM
February 1956

EVE BOSWELL
PICKIN' A CHICKEN
Parlophone

▲ 9
⑩ 1•
—/250

When this Hungarian-born singer came to the UK from South Africa in 1949, she joined Geraldo's Orchestra (singing on several of their records) and was with them until 1951. As a soloist, Boswell is best remembered for 'Sugarbush' in 1952 and 'Pickin' A Chicken'. She discovered the latter in South Africa and the prolific Paddy Roberts added English lyrics. It was one of three singles in the Top 20 produced by Parlophone's new A&R head, George Martin. In the US, Jim Reeves covered the novelty number.

GARY MILLER
ROBIN HOOD
Nixa

▲ 10
⑩ 1•
—/250

Not long after his 'Yellow Rose Of Texas' bloomed in the Top 20, the balladeer from Blackpool (born Neville Williams) had the biggest version of this well-loved TV theme. In the late 1950s Miller racked up four UK Top 20 singles, and although his treatments of 'Garden of Eden' and 'The Story Of My Life' were beaten by others, they possessed a zest lacking on most British records. The singer, who toured with Buddy Holly in 1958, was one of the UK's better beat ballad vocalists of the era.

DEAN MARTIN
MEMORIES ARE MADE OF THIS
Capitol

▲ 1
🔟 7
47/250

See US entry (December 1955).

LOU BUSCH & HIS ORCHESTRA & CHORUS
ZAMBESI
Capitol

▲ 2
🔟 1•
121/250

Soon after the African tune 'Skokiaan' had become a big US hit, the popular American honky tonk pianist (aka Joe 'Fingers' Carr) had a UK-only smash with another catchy instrumental from that continent. Later in the year, Busch made his final trip up the transatlantic charts with 'Portuguese Washerwoman'. 'Zambesi' returned to the UK Top 20 by The Piranhas in 1982.

HILLTOPPERS
ONLY YOU
London American

▲ 3
🔟 1•
109/250

A timely cover of this Platters hit gave the quartet the ninth of their ten US Top 20 entries and their first UK chart entry (initially, The Platters' version was not available in Britain). The group, who wore college sweaters, white bucks and beanies, were another victim of rock'n'roll. Member Billy Vaughn had many more hits as an orchestra leader and producer though, and, with various personnel changes, The Hilltoppers continued performing into the 1970s.

DREAM WEAVERS
IT'S ALMOST TOMORROW
Brunswick

▲ 1
🔟 1•
44/250

See US entry (December 1955).

KAY STARR
ROCK AND ROLL WALTZ
HMV

▲ 1
🔟 4•
58/250

See US entry (January).

DON CHERRY
BAND OF GOLD
Philips

▲ 6
🔟 1•
—/250

See US entry (January).

NAT 'KING' COLE
DREAMS CAN TELL A LIE
Capitol

▲ 10
🔟 9
—/250

For the second time in a year, the perennially popular performer outsold local star Dickie Valentine with a recording of a song composed by British trio Howard Barnes, Harold Cornelius and Dominic John. Unlike his previous hit, 'A Blossom Fell', the single was not released in the US.

UNITED STATES

March 1956

DICK HYMAN TRIO
MORITAT
(A THEME FROM *THE THREEPENNY OPERA*)
MGM

Almost 30 years after Kurt Weill composed the theme, this multi-talented New York jazz pianist/arranger/conductor/composer turned it into gold. The recording was the highest ranked of six chart versions, beating such established artists as Lawrence Welk, Billy Vaughn, Les Paul and the similarly named Richard Hayman. The trio, fronted by a one-time member of Benny Goodman, Percy Faith and Mitch Miller's Bands, were voted Most Promising Instrumental Group of 1955 in *Cash Box*. Bobby Darin's 1959 vocal version ('Mack The Knife') also sold over a million copies.

TEENAGERS FEATURING FRANKIE LYMON
WHY DO FOOLS FALL IN LOVE
Gee

Although not the first schoolboy-led group, the New York quintet fronted by 13-year-old Lymon were the most successful and have influenced countless other male and female acts (for instance, both Diana Ross and Madonna give much credit to Lymon). Despite several pop covers, their self-penned debut disc sold a million in the US and was the first R&B single to top the UK chart. Interestingly, Frankie's younger brother Lewis Lymon, and his band The Teenchords, recorded a sequel, 'I Found Out Why'.

PERRY COMO
HOT DIGGITY
(DOG ZIGGITY BOOM)
RCA

This was one of the year's bounciest, happiest transatlantic hits, whose melody was based on Chabrier's 'Espana Rhapsody'. It was coupled with 'Juke Box Baby', a teen-slanted toe-tapper with a lyric crammed full of current rock titles.

CARL PERKINS
BLUE SUEDE SHOES
Sun

This sharp-dressed cat's anthem was the first record ever to enter the pop, country and R&B charts. Many acts have covered Carl's bona fide classic but only Elvis' version came close. The rockabilly legend, who described his music as 'a country man's song with a black man's rhythm', has remained a popular live artist and is held in great esteem by many later rock giants. The Beatles are among the Tennessee star's fans and they recorded Perkins' compositions 'Honey Don't', 'Matchbox' and 'Everybody's Trying To Be My Baby'.

ELVIS PRESLEY
HEARTBREAK HOTEL
RCA

A week after his last Sun single, 'I Forgot To Remember To Forget', slipped from the top of the country chart, Presley's sixth RCA release (the first five being re-issues of Sun tracks), took over at No 1. It was not, however, an overnight hit. In fact, the track, which RCA were not keen on, struggled until Elvis was seen singing it on national TV. In the UK, where it received bad reviews, few radio plays and no TV, it only narrowly missed the No 1 position.

UNITED KINGDOM
March 1956

EDMUND HOCKRIDGE
YOUNG AND FOOLISH
Nixa

▲ 10
🔟 1•
—/250

Canadian actor/singer Hockridge settled in the UK in 1951, and starred in the London productions of such winning shows as *Carousel, Guys And Dolls, Can Can* and *The Pajama Game*. The strong-voiced baritone was very popular in the UK during the 1950s and appeared in six Royal Variety Shows. His biggest-selling single came from the musical *Plain And Fancy* and Hockridge's version left recordings by such stalwarts as Jo Stafford, Dean Martin and the McGuire Sisters way behind in the sales stakes.

DAVE KING
MEMORIES ARE MADE OF THIS
Decca

▲ 5
🔟 1•
250/250

Middlesex-born King was one of the UK's most popular comedians and TV show hosts of the 1950s, who vocally came from the Crosby-Como school of relaxed crooners. The biggest of his three Top 20 entries was a cover of Dean Martin's hit which, at times, was the only record by a British performer in the Top 10. The easy-going entertainer, who for a season was Perry Como's summer replacement on US TV, subsequently became a respected character actor, appearing in such programmes as *Coronation Street*.

BILL HALEY & HIS COMETS
SEE YOU LATER ALLIGATOR
Brunswick

▲ 7
🔟 4
105/250

See US entry (January).

JIMMY PARKINSON
THE GREAT PRETENDER
Columbia

▲ 9
🔟 1•
—/250

A return trip to Britain was the prize this Sydney native won in an Australian talent competition. While in the UK, Parkinson convinced Cyril Stapleton to let him sing with the BBC Show Band, which led to a deal with Columbia. For his second single he covered a Platters track that was not being released in the UK (their label had no outlet then). The song was a big hit for Parkinson, and six months later for The Platters. In spring 1957, Parkinson decided to complete his return journey.

WINIFRED ATWELL
POOR PEOPLE OF PARIS
Decca

▲ 1
🔟 8
57/250

After the French song 'Le Goulant Du Pauvre Jean' ('The Ballad Of Poor John') was wrongly heard as 'Le Goulant De Pauvre Gens' ('The Ballad of Poor People') it was re-christened 'Poor People Of Paris'. Incidentally, Atwell refused to plug her UK No 1 on Ed Sullivan's US TV show, when the proposed eight-minute slot was cut to less than two.

JIMMY YOUNG
CHAIN GANG
Decca

▲ 9
🔟 4
—/250

The entertainer who outsold all other British male vocalists in 1955 registered another UK bestseller with a cover of a song that jazz performer Bobby Scott (composer of 'A Taste Of Honey') had taken into the US Top 20.

DICK HYMAN TRIO
THEME FROM *THE THREEPENNY OPERA*
MGM

▲ 9
🔟 1•
—/250

See US entry.

UNITED STATES
April 1956

TERESA BREWER
A TEAR FELL
Coral

▲ 9
⑩ 5•
—/250

Although still only in her mid-twenties, the bouncy Miss Brewer was another star who lost ground to rock'n'roll. Her last transatlantic Top 10 entry was a cover of an Ivory Joe Hunter record, which she coupled with another R&B song, Fats Domino's 'Bo Weevil'.

LONNIE DONEGAN
ROCK ISLAND LINE
Imperial

▲ 8
⑩ 1
—/250

See UK entry (January).

MORRIS STOLOFF & HIS ORCHESTRA
MOONGLOW/THEME FROM *PICNIC*
Decca

▲ 2
⑩ 1•
143/250

Rock Around The Clock was not the only film packing in the crowds – there was also the William Holden and Kim Novak movie *Picnic*. A medley of two songs from the latter earned Columbia Pictures' Academy Award-winning musical director Stoloff a gold disc. 'Moonglow' was an old tune that had first been made famous by Benny Goodman and Duke Ellington in the mid-1930s, while the film's theme was a new Steve Allen composition. This recording also shot the Philadelphia born conductor/composer into the UK Top 10.

PLATTERS
(YOU'VE GOT) THE MAGIC TOUCH
Mercury

▲ 5
⑩ 3
—/250

In less than six months the distinctive group fronted by sweet tenor Tony Williams scored their third successive Top 5 entry. Interestingly, the song was originally called 'The Midas Touch' and was penned, as were the act's previous hits, by manager Buck Ram – a man to whom that title surely applied.

UNITED KINGDOM
April 1956

DAVID WHITFIELD
MY SEPTEMBER LOVE
Decca

▲ 3
⑩ 10
129/250

For the second year running composer Tolchard Evans won an Ivor Novello award for a song by David Whitfield. Soon afterwards, a parody by The Famous Eccles (Spike Milligan) also sold well.

RONNIE HILTON
NO OTHER LOVE
HMV

▲ 1
⑩ 3
34/250

Three years after Perry Como had taken it to the top in the US, copyright restrictions on the standout Rodgers & Hammerstein show song were lifted in the UK. Despite tough opposition, Hilton's interpretation easily outsold all other versions including Como's cut, which oddly appeared on HMV's export label and therefore was not properly promoted.

TERESA BREWER
A TEAR FELL
Vogue/Coral

▲ 2
⑩ 2
150/250

See US entry.

UNITED STATES
May 1956

LITTLE RICHARD
LONG TALL SALLY
Specialty

▲ 6
⑩ 1
—/250

If you were asked to list the wildest rock'n'roll records of all time, then this single would surely be high in the Top 10. Its release came at a time when rock was receiving a lot of bad press; the music was tagged as 'immoral' and even banned in certain areas. Little Richard (born Richard Penniman in Georgia) was arguably the music's most frantic performer, and no doubt his wild stage act and uninhibited singing style convinced many concerned parents that rock'n'roll was not suitable for their teenage children.

GEORGE CATES & HIS ORCHESTRA
MOONGLOW/THEME FROM *PICNIC*
Coral

▲ 5
⑩ 1•
—/250

Bing Crosby, Teresa Brewer, Johnny Desmond and the Andrews Sisters were among the singers that New Yorker Cates arranged for. He was musical director at Coral Records and held a similar post with TV's *Lawrence Welk Show* for 25 years. Cates' only major hit in his own right was a version of this medley from the box office smash *Picnic* which, like Morris Stoloff's original recording, managed to sell over a million.

CATHY CARR
IVORY TOWER
Fraternity

▲ 7
⑩ 1•
—/250

After a few years of so-so sellers, the Bronx-born singer/dancer had her only Top 40 entry with a cover of a song written and first recorded by ex-Paul Whiteman Band vocalist Jack Fulton. The petite 19-year-old's treatment was joined in the Top 20 by the R&B hit version from Otis Williams & The Charms. Carr appeared on a handful of labels over the next few years and in 1962 re-recorded 'Ivory Tower' on Laurie, without success.

FOUR LADS
STANDING ON THE CORNER
Columbia

▲ 3
⑩ 4•
234/250

The most popular song from Frank Loesser's Broadway show *The Most Happy Fella* took the foursome into the Top 3 for the third time in five months. Although US radio DJs continued to promote the group's records during the early rock years, their sales slumped and by the time this single became the quartet's only UK Top 40 entry in 1960, they had already bid farewell to the US chart.

GOGI GRANT
THE WAYWARD WIND
Era

▲ 1
⑩ 1•
39/250

Six months after 'Suddenly There's A Valley' introduced the Philadelphia vocalist to the Top 20, she had her biggest seller with a dramatic lost-love ballad that sounded as if it belonged in a western movie. The singer, who previously recorded as Audrey Brown and Audrey Grant, earlier released overlooked versions of such hits as 'Ricochet' and 'Secret Love'. Oddly, Grant's transatlantic Top 10 entry returned to the US chart in 1961, and in 1963 Frank Ifield took it all the way to No 1 in the UK bestsellers.

FATS DOMINO
I'M IN LOVE AGAIN
Imperial

▲ 4
⑩ 1
246/250

Back in 1950 Domino's debut disc, 'The Fat Man', wrote the blueprint for 1950s R&B. The influential singer/songwriter/pianist from New Orleans finally cracked the pop Top 10 with his fifteenth R&B Top 10 entry. A year earlier Pat Boone's cover of 'Ain't That A Shame' had outsold the original version in the pop market. However, this time a rendition by Boone's label-mates, the Fontane Sisters, was left far behind as Domino's disc sold a reported 300,000 in three weeks.

UNITED KINGDOM
May 1956

LOUIS ARMSTRONG
THEME FROM *THE THREEPENNY OPERA*
Philips

▲ 8
⑩ 2
—/250

Three years before Bobby Darin immortalized 'Mack The Knife', this world-renowned jazz ambassador thrust his version into the transatlantic charts. The celebrated New Orleans trumpeter/film star and gravel-voiced vocalist was awarded a posthumous Lifetime Achievement Grammy in 1972 and was elected into the Rock and Roll Hall of Fame (as a forefather of rock) in 1990.

BILLY MAY & HIS ORCHESTRA
MAIN TITLE THEME FROM *THE MAN WITH THE GOLDEN ARM*
Capitol

▲ 9
⑩ 1•
—/250

One of the 1950's most critically acclaimed arrangers had a major UK hit with the Elmer Bernstein-penned title theme from a controversial Frank Sinatra film which dealt with drug abuse. The Pittsburgh-born conductor/arranger/trumpeter, who earlier played in the bands of Glenn Miller,

Charlie Barnet and Les Brown, is best known for his work with Peggy Lee, Nat 'King' Cole and Sinatra himself. Guitarist Jet Harris returned the instrumental to the UK Top 20 in 1962.

LONNIE DONEGAN
LOST JOHN/STEWBALL
Pye Nixa

▲ 2
⑩ 2
133/250

Many music pundits presumed that Donegan and indeed skiffle were one-hit wonders. However, the success of both this double-sider and his first US tour (in which he headlined with top rock acts) proved them wrong. Overnight, Donegan had jumped from jazz band musician to international pop star.

PAT BOONE
I'LL BE HOME
London American

▲ 1
⑩ 2
22/250

See US entry (February).

DON ROBERTSON
THE HAPPY WHISTLER
Capitol

▲ 8
🔟 1•
—/250

See US entry (June).

ELVIS PRESLEY
HEARTBREAK HOTEL
HMV

▲ 2
🔟 1
104/250

See US entry (March).

UNITED STATES
June 1956

DON ROBERTSON
THE HAPPY WHISTLER
Capitol

▲ 9
🔟 1•
—/250

Not only did Peking, China-born Robertson write the early 1950s country No 1s 'I Really Don't Want To Know' (Eddy Arnold) and 'I Don't Hurt Anymore' (Hank Snow), he also master-minded the 'Nashville piano style' that Floyd Cramer subsequently made internationally famous. His only noteworthy hit as an artist was this happy-go-lucky toe-tapper which journeyed into the Top 10 on both sides of the Atlantic. Robertson was later inducted into the Nashville Songwriters Hall of Fame and had his name included in the Country Walkway of Stars.

ELVIS PRESLEY
I WANT YOU, I NEED YOU, I LOVE YOU
RCA

▲ 1
🔟 2
93/250

The artist who had been voted Most Promising Country Singer of 1955 sold 750,000 copies of this single in just three weeks. After he performed it and 'Hound Dog' in a controversial hip-shaking way on the *Milton Berle Show* Presley acquired the nickname 'Elvis the Pelvis'.

PAT BOONE
I ALMOST LOST MY MIND
Dot

▲ 2
🔟 4
179/250

Six years after composer Ivory Joe Hunter took his treatment to the top of the R&B chart, Boone's beat ballad arrangement earned him a gold disc.

Soon afterwards Hunter had a Top 20 pop hit with the similar 'Since I Met You Baby', on which he used a Boone-styled arrangement.

NERVOUS NORVUS
TRANSFUSION
Dot

▲ 8
🔟 1•
—/250

Forty-four-year-old ex-truck driver Jimmy Drake (aka Nervous Norvus) wrote and recorded the most controversial hit of the year. 'Transfusion' was a happy sounding ditty which dealt with the gruesome subject of automobile accidents and blood transfusions. He first cut this slice of macabre fun with his group The Four Jokers, but their version on Diamond died a death. Drake then re-recorded it as a solo and the ghoulish result crashed into the Top 10. Few people in the UK heard it as it was banned by the BBC.

PERRY COMO
MORE
RCA

▲ 4
🔟 17
—/250

Few TV shows were more popular than *Perry Como's Music Hall*, which he hosted throughout the late 1950s; his engaging personality suited the small screen perfectly. Tom Glazer's composition 'More' was one of the show's most requested songs and its bestselling B side, 'Glendora', was probably the only romantic opus about a shop window mannequin.

VIC DAMONE
ON THE STREET WHERE
YOU LIVE
Columbia

▲ 8
⑩ 2•
—/250

A year after beating all-comers in the US with this show-stopping *My Fair Lady* song, the smooth baritone repeated that feat in the UK, where it topped the chart. Damone (yet another Arthur Godfrey discovery) was arguably the last successful romantic balladeer. The Vegas veteran was still entertaining in the 1990s, when he appeared on the bestselling *Sleepless In Seattle* soundtrack.

UNITED KINGDOM
June 1956

BILL HALEY &
HIS COMETS
THE SAINTS ROCK 'N
ROLL

▲ 5
⑩ 5
195/250

Brunswick

This award-winning act's last US Top 20 entry was one of his record-breaking five singles that stood together in the UK Top 20. As it climbed the chart, Haley's film *Rock Around The Clock* had British audiences jiving in the aisles.

PERRY COMO
HOT DIGGITY
HMV

▲ 4
⑩ 4
226/250

See US entry (March).

ELVIS PRESLEY
BLUE SUEDE SHOES
HMV

▲ 9
⑩ 2
—/250

In America, Elvis insisted that his rendition of ex-Sun label-mate Carl Perkins' million seller was only available on an EP (it was the first EP to reach the US Top 20). In the UK, where it was released as a single, it pipped Perkins' original at the post.

CARL PERKINS
BLUE SUEDE SHOES
London American

▲ 10
⑩ 1•
—/250

See US entry (March).

MORRIS STOLOFF &
HIS ORCHESTRA
MOONGLOW/THEME
FROM *PICNIC*
Brunswick

▲ 7
⑩ 1•
—/250

See US entry (April).

NAT 'KING' COLE
TOO YOUNG TO GO
STEADY
Capitol

▲ 8
⑩ 10
—/250

Soon after making an appearance in the first rock film, *Rock'n'Roll Revue*, the easy-on-the-ear entertainer took a second song about being 'Too Young' up the charts. The Jimmy McHugh and Harold Adamson composition came from the musical *Strip For Action*.

JOHNNY DANKWORTH
EXPERIMENTS WITH MICE
Parlophone

▲ 7
⑩ 1
—/250

One of the most unusual UK hits of the year was recorded by a modern jazz pioneer from London and his 20 piece big band. On the George Martin-produced single, Dankworth and his entourage imagined how the big bands of Billy May, Benny Goodman, Glenn Miller and Stan Kenton might have handled the nursery rhyme 'Three Blind Mice'. The witty track also narrowly missed the US Top 40. Dankworth, who subsequently married the band's vocalist Cleo Laine, has never lacked for work since.

UNITED STATES
July 1956

CHORDETTES
BORN TO BE WITH YOU
Cadence

▲ 8
🔟 2
—/250

The versatile vocal quartet, fronted by Lynn Evans, gave songwriter Don Robertson his second simultaneous Top 20 entry. In 1968, a revival by Sonny James headed the country chart, and in 1973 Dave Edmunds returned the song to the UK Top 10.

GENE VINCENT & HIS BLUE CAPS
BE-BOP-A-LULA
Capitol

▲ 7
🔟 1•
—/250

He seldom visited the Top 10, but few rock artists are held in such high esteem as Virginia's Vincent (real name Vincent Eugene Craddock). He is among a handful of rockers whose importance and influence cannot be overstated. The bop-till-you drop performer, whom Capitol launched as their 'Answer to Elvis', is best remembered for this ever popular rock'n'roll anthem. His relocation to the UK in 1960 gave that scene a much needed lift and helped inspire many later British performers.

PLATTERS
MY PRAYER
Mercury

▲ 1
🔟 4
76/250

No black vocal group since The Ink Spots had achieved sales to match The Platters. Their enviable run of hits continued with this distinctive version of a French song ('Avant De Mourir') that The Ink Spots scored with in 1939.

DORIS DAY
WHATEVER WILL BE WILL BE (QUE SERA SERA)
Columbia

▲ 3
🔟 7•
163/250

Soon after signing an unprecedented $1 million deal with Columbia, Day enjoyed her last Top 10 single of the decade with an Academy Award-winning song from her film *The Man Who Knew Too Much*. The photogenic performer continued to be a Top 10 box office star and an extremely popular personality, until she turned her back on show business in the 1970s – 'Que Sera Sera'.

PATTI PAGE
ALLEGHENY MOON
Mercury

▲ 5
🔟 12
—/250

One of the hottest songwriting teams of the decade, Al Hoffman and Dick Manning, composed the melodic tune that gave the top-rated TV host her highest-ranked hit for over two years.

UNITED KINGDOM
July 1956

VARIOUS ARTISTS
ALL STAR HIT PARADE
Decca

▲ 2
⑩ 1
223/250

It may surprise some readers to know that there were bestselling charity records in the 1950s. On this single top names of the day performed others' hits. The tracks were 'Theme From The Threepenny Opera' (Winifred Atwell), 'No Other Love' (Dave King), 'My September Love' (Joan Regan), 'A Tear Fell' (Lita Roza), ' Out of Town' (Dickie Valentine) and 'It's Almost Tomorrow' (David Whitfield). The record raised £10,000 for the National Playing Fields Association.

GOONS
I'M WALKING
BACKWARDS FOR
CHRISTMAS/BLUEBOTTLE
BLUES
Decca

▲ 4
⑩ 1
—/250

Peter Sellers, Spike Milligan and Harry Secombe comprised the zany trio known as the Goons, whose radio show of that name had a huge British following. Who but the Goons could score with a Christmas song in midsummer? Oddly, their single was picked as a hit by reviewers in the US, where it was called 'the craziest record ever'. However, neither the boundary-stretching funny men's version nor Jerry Colona's cover charted there.

TEENAGERS FEATURING FRANKIE LYMON
WHY DO FOOLS FALL
IN LOVE
Columbia

▲ 1
⑩ 1
51/250

See US entry (March).

GOGI GRANT
THE WAYWARD WIND
London American

▲ 9
⑩ 1•
—/250

See US Entry (May).

TONY MARTIN
WALK HAND IN HAND
HMV

▲ 2
⑩ 2•
153/250

Martin was in the UK filming *Let's Be Happy* when his version of this big ballad outsold a handful of local renditions, including one by Ronnie Carroll (which narrowly missed the Top 10). The song was penned by Johnny Cowell and first recorded by fellow Canadian Denny Vaughn. It was the last major hit for the well-seasoned singer who, in the mid-1960s, unexpectedly signed to Motown.

RONNIE HILTON
WHO ARE WE
HMV

▲ 6
⑩ 4
—/250

As Gogi Grant's 'The Wayward Wind' climbed the UK Top 10, it was joined by a cover of her previous single by Ronnie Hilton. The notable Jerry Livingston and Paul Francis Webster composition also charted by Vera Lynn.

DORIS DAY
WHATEVER WILL BE
WILL BE
Philips

▲ 1
⑩ 8
20/250

See US entry.

TEX RITTER
WAYWARD WIND
Capitol

▲ 8
⑩ 1•
—/250

Gene Autry, Roy Rogers and Texas-born Ritter were America's best-loved singing cowboys in the 1930s and 1940s. This rich baritone, whose soundtrack recording of 'High Noon' had sold well on both sides of the Atlantic in 1952, just outpaced Gogi Grant in the UK with his rendition of the western-styled opus. Ritter was the first performer to be elected into both the Country Music Hall of Fame and the Cowboy Hall of Fame.

UNITED STATES
August 1956

ELVIS PRESLEY
HOUND DOG/DON'T
BE CRUEL
RCA

In two weeks this single sold a million; it headed the chart for 11 weeks and ended up selling over five million copies. 'Hound Dog' was a revival of a 1953 R&B No 1 by 'Big Mama' Thornton, and the coupling was a song that R&B group The Bachelors had been offered earlier.

BUCHANAN & GOODMAN
THE FLYING SAUCER
(PARTS 1 & 2)
Luniverse

Music publishers and record companies were up in arms over this 'war of the worlds' inspired release, which sampled a handful of hits without permission or payment. The humorous single featured snippets from acts including The Platters, Teenagers, Little Richard, Fats Domino, Elvis Presley, Carl Perkins and Chuck Berry. Bill Buchanan was a noted publisher and manager. His partner Dickie Goodman coninued to have US-only chart entries with similar 'cut-up' singles until the late 1970s (UK companies never allowed such records to be released).

HUGO WINTERHALTER
(& HIS ORCHESTRA) &
EDDIE HEYWOOD
CANADIAN SUNSET
RCA

Jazz pianist Heywood (who had earlier worked with Billie Holiday) composed and played on Winterhalter's last and biggest hit. As the single reached the Top 3, another Heywood record, 'Soft Summer Breeze', peaked at No 11. Despite his amazing chart start, the public overlooked all future releases by this keyboard playing composer from Atlanta.

UNITED KINGDOM
August 1956

TERESA BREWER
SWEET OLD-FASHIONED
GIRL
Vogue/Coral

▲ 3
⑩ 3•
193/250

Bob Merrill composed the appealing pop/rock'n'roll novelty that lifted the noted performer into the Top 10 for the final time. Brewer's style may have been a little old-fashioned but that did not really harm her future career, as she became a regular attraction in Las Vegas and was still recording in the 1990s.

MEL TORME
MOUNTAIN GREENERY
Vogue/Coral

▲ 4
⑩ 1•
218/250

At a time when critics noted 40 per cent of UK chart entries were 'in the rock'n'roll idiom', the acclaimed cool jazz crooner from Chicago (born Melvin Howard) clocked up a UK-only hit. The smooth singer, whose biggest US hits were 'Again' and 'Careless Hands' in 1949, spent six months on the UK bestsellers with his fast-paced revival of a Rodgers & Hart song from the 1926 musical *Garrick Gaieties*. The track came from the multi-talented

artist's live album entitled *Mel Torme At The Crescendo*.

BILL HALEY & HIS COMETS
ROCKIN' THROUGH
THE RYE
Brunswick

▲ 3
⑩ 6
118/250

In the US, Haley may now have been overshadowed by Presley, but in the UK he could still do no wrong. His rockin' revival of an old Scottish air became his fifth single to reach the Top 10 in eight months.

SLIM WHITMAN
SERENADE
London American

▲ 8
⑩ 3
—/250

Grand Ole Opry performer Whitman notched up another UK hit with an operatic aria from the 1920s. This time it was a Sigmund Romberg composition, which had recently been recorded successfully by Mario Lanza.

UNITED STATES
September 1956

PATIENCE & PRUDENCE
TONIGHT YOU BELONG
TO ME
Liberty

▲ 4
⑩ 1•
244/250

Sisters Patience and Prudence McIntyre, who were aged 11 and 14, found transatlantic success with a

cuter-than-cute rendition of a 30-year-old standard that Gene Austin originally made famous. The Los Angeles duo, who were backed by their father Mark McIntyre's band, also clicked with the follow-up 'Gonna Get Along Without You Now', and were voted Most Promising Group of 1956. The sisters' 1965 re-recording sold few, even though months earlier The Caravelles had had a transatlantic hit with a Patience & Prudence-styled single.

MITCH MILLER & HIS ORCHESTRA
THEME SONG FROM
SONG FOR A SUMMER NIGHT
Columbia

The theme from a *Studio One* TV production transported the decade's top A&R man back into the Top 10 in his own right. In 1958, New Yorker Miller hit upon the idea of a series of 'Sing Along' albums. These proved amazingly successful and led to a popular *Sing Along* TV series in the early 1960s. Miller, who appreciated R&B but was no champion of rock'n'roll, took the art of record production to a new level.

BILL DOGGETT
HONKY TONK
(PARTS 1 & 2)
King

Forty-year-old Doggett and his combo wrote and recorded the biggest-selling R&B instrumental of the decade, which featured guitarist Billy Butler and saxophonist Clifford Scott. The act, who earlier in the year backed other artists on the all-star *Top 10 R&B Show*, were voted Most Promising Instrumental Group of 1956. Veteran organist Doggett, who had previously worked with many of the top names in the R&B and jazz fields, also released a virtually ignored vocal version of 'Honky Tonk' featuring Tommy Brown.

SANFORD CLARK
THE FOOL
DOT

DJ Lee Hazlewood considered Oklahoma native Clark the ideal singer for his wife's composition 'The Fool'. Hazlewood produced this atmospheric, echoey and sparse rock ballad (featuring guitarist Al Casey) which sold a million after Dot picked it up from Hazlewood's MCI label. Later Clark cuts such as 'New Kind Of Fool' and 'A Cheat' did not repeat the feat, and a 1966 re-recording (co-produced by Waylon Jennings) from Clark's *Return Of The Fool* album on Hazlewood's LHI label did little business.

ANDY WILLIAMS
CANADIAN SUNSET
Cadence

When minor celebrities the Williams Brothers disbanded in 1952, the youngest member Andy became a regular on Steve Allen's top-rated *Tonight* show. Before joining Cadence he recorded with little effect for MGM, Decca and RCA. The first of his many bestsellers was a vocal version of a current Hugo Winterhalter and Eddie Heywood hit, utilizing a lyric that leading songsmith Norman Gimble had added to Heywood's haunting music. Its success led to Williams being voted Most Promising Male Vocalist in 1956.

JOHNNIE RAY
JUST WALKING IN THE RAIN
Columbia

After three relatively bleak years, Ray returned to the top end of the US charts with a number written by an inmate of Tennessee State Prison. 'Lifer' Johnny Bragg originally recorded the song at Sun Studios with fellow captives, The Prisonaires. Amazingly, Bragg claims that Elvis helped him with his phrasing on that 1953 session!

UNITED KINGDOM

September 1956

ANNE SHELTON
LAY DOWN YOUR ARMS
Philips

| ▲ 1 |
| ⑩ 1 |
| 52/250 |

This vocalist from London was very popular during the war years, when she recorded the successful English lyric version of the German classic 'Lili Marlene'. Shelton's biggest seller in the 1950s was a march tempo opus about her sweetheart in the forces. The Swedish song's English lyric, which was considered by some to encourage cowardice, was penned by Britain's hit machine, Paddy Roberts. Shelton's single also shot up the charts in America, where a particularly effective cover by The Chordettes stormed into the Top 20.

CHORDETTES
BORN TO BE WITH YOU
London American

| ▲ 8 |
| ⑩ 1 |
| —/250 |

See US entry (July).

PLATTERS
THE GREAT PRETENDER/ONLY YOU
Mercury

| ▲ 5 |
| ⑩ 1 |
| 147/250 |

See US entries (October 1955 and January 1956).

GOONS
BLOODNOK'S ROCK'N' ROLL CALL/YING TONG SONG
Decca

| ▲ 3 |
| ⑩ 2 |
| 244/250 |

Q: What was the first British recorded hit with the words 'Rock'n'Roll' in the title? A: This zany opus by the UK's most innovative funny men of the decade. Unexpectedly, the even odder B side, 'Ying Tong Song', returned to the Top 10 in 1973. Goon Peter Sellers later became an internationally renowned film star, Spike Milligan, composer of these songs, remained a popular oddball entertainer and all-rounder Harry Secombe went on to earn a knighthood.

LONNIE DONEGAN
BRING A LITTLE WATER SYLVIE/DEAD OR ALIVE
Pye Nixa

| ▲ 7 |
| ⑩ 3 |
| —/250 |

'The English Leadbelly' and the 'Irish Hillbilly' were terms Americans used for Britain's 'Sultan of Skiffle'. His third hit single, which coupled a Leadbelly blues with a Woody Guthrie folk song, amassed enviable advance orders of 30,000.

ELVIS PRESLEY
HOUND DOG
HMV

| ▲ 2 |
| ⑩ 3 |
| 91/250 |

See US entry (August).

FRANKIE LAINE
A WOMAN IN LOVE
Philips

| ▲ 1 |
| ⑩ 17 |
| 30/250 |

Nine months after the big ballad from the film musical *Guys And Dolls* returned him to the US Top 20, it took Laine to the top of the UK lists for the last time.

UNITED STATES
October 1956

JIM LOWE
THE GREEN DOOR
Dot

▲ 2
⑩ 1•
112/250

On both sides of the Atlantic record buyers were intrigued by the goings-on behind the green door. In the US, the top pop/rock song became noted New York DJ Lowe's first hit as a vocalist, the man from Missouri having earlier seen Rusty Draper's cover of his composition 'Gambler's Guitar' go gold, and his attempts at rock tunes 'Maybelline' and 'Blue Suede Shoes' make little impression. In the UK, Frankie Vaughan's rendition reached the runner-up spot, and 25 years later a revival by Shakin' Stevens repeated that feat.

ELVIS PRESLEY
LOVE ME TENDER
RCA

▲ 1
⑩ 4
47/250

An unprecedented one million advance orders were amassed by Elvis' fourth No 1 in seven months. Only Presley's previous single, 'Don't Be Cruel', stopped the title song of his first film from entering the Top 50 bestsellers at No 1!

PAT BOONE
FRIENDLY PERSUASION
(THEE I LOVE)/CHAINS
OF LOVE
Dot

▲ 9
⑩ 5
—/250

Before Boone was approached to sing the title song in Gary Cooper's film *Friendly Persuasion*, Perry Como, Nat 'King' Cole, Harry Belafonte and Frankie Laine had apparently turned down the opportunity. The B side, a revival of a 1951 Joe Turner R&B smash, also cracked the Top 20.

FATS DOMINO
BLUEBERRY HILL
Imperial

▲ 3
⑩ 2
164/250

Perhaps surprisingly, in late 1956 more riots were reported at shows starring this relatively relaxed rocker than anyone bar Elvis. This did not stop his revival of 'Blueberry Hill' (which started a stampede of R&B acts cutting standards) becoming Domino's only transatlantic Top 10 entry and his most popular recording.

UNITED KINGDOM
October 1956

FREDDIE BELL & THE BELLBOYS
GIDDY-UP-A-DING-DONG
Mercury

▲ 4
⑩ 1•
—/250

British teenagers loved the film *Rock Around The Clock* and bought records by every rock act in it, including this well-choreographed white R&B sextet, who had been Las Vegas regulars since 1953. The self-penned rocker raced up the UK chart by Bell (born Freddie Bello in Philadelphia) and his group, even though it stalled at the starting gate Stateside. The act, whose bump-and-grind version of 'Hound Dog' inspired Elvis to cut it, toured the UK with Tommy Steele in 1957.

BILL HALEY & HIS COMETS
ROCK AROUND THE CLOCK
Brunswick

▲ 5
🔟 7
—/250

Britain's first million-selling single paid a record-shattering five separate visits to the UK Top 20. The biggest-selling rock single was also sampled on the 1989 million seller, 'Swing That Mood' by Jive Bunny & The Mastermixers.

JOHNNIE RAY
JUST WALKIN' IN THE RAIN
Philips

▲ 1
🔟 8
15/250

See US Entry (September).

UNITED STATES
November 1956

BING CROSBY & GRACE KELLY
TRUE LOVE
Capitol

▲ 5
🔟 7•
239/250

One of the century's most successful and celebrated entertainers scored his last transatlantic Top 10 entry with a timeless love song from the hit movie *High Society*. The Cole Porter composition also showcased the vocal talent of actress Grace Kelly – the future Princess Grace of Monaco. In 1993, Elton John & Kiki Dee's revival reached the UK Top 3.

GUY MITCHELL
SINGING THE BLUES
Columbia

▲ 1
🔟 6
15/250

After almost five years away, the one-time country music performer returned to the US Top 10 with an easily accessible cover of a song that label-mate Marty Robbins took to the top of the country lists. This transatlantic No 1, which featured the orchestra (and indeed whistling) of Ray Conniff, headed the US chart for nine weeks.

EDDIE FISHER
CINDY, OH CINDY
RCA

▲ 10
🔟 19•
—/250

In early 1956, the popular performer signed a $1 million radio and TV contract and his future looked bright. However, rock'n'roll seriously damaged Fisher's fan base and he managed only one more transatlantic hit. The vocalist's version of this catchy calypso out-pointed the original by Vince Martin & The Tarriers (whose label, Glory, sued RCA for copying their arrangement and vocal style). When not beset by personal problems, Fisher was still a good drawing card on the club and cabaret circuit in future years.

UNITED KINGDOM
November 1956

PLATTERS
MY PRAYER
Mercury

▲ 4
🔟 2
240/250

See US entry (July).

JIMMY YOUNG
MORE
Decca

▲ 4
🔟 5•
239/250

Few British vocalists sold more singles in the early 1950s than Young, whose last Top 10 entry was a cover of a Perry Como single. When demand for his records decreased, he moved successfully into radio work. Young, who is still one of the UK's best-loved DJ/presenters, has received both an OBE and CBE from the Queen.

PERRY COMO
MORE
HMV

▲ 10
🔟 5
—/250

See US entry (June).

BILL HALEY & HIS COMETS
RIP IT UP
Brunswick

▲ 4
🔟 8
222/250

At the same time as he was voted World's Outstanding Music Personality in the *NME* poll, Haley had the big UK hit version of the wild rocker that Little Richard took into the US Top 20.

JIM LOWE
THE GREEN DOOR
London American

▲ 8
🔟 1•
—/250

See US entry (October).

FRANKIE VAUGHAN
GREEN DOOR
Philips

▲ 2
🔟 1
122/250

Before his rousing rendition of Jim Lowe's US hit opened the door to the Top 10, this Liverpool-born heart-throb (real name Frank Abelson) had already scored five Top 20 entries. Vaughan was a leading variety entertainer whose earlier bestsellers included covers of such beat songs as 'Tweedle Dee', 'Seventeen' and 'My Boy Flat Top'. The high-kicking showman donated the royalties from 'Green Door' (engineered by talented newcomer Joe Meek), to his favourite charity, the Boys' Club Federation.

MITCHELL TOROK
WHEN MEXICO GAVE UP THE RUMBA
Brunswick

▲ 6
🔟 1•
—/250

Back in 1953, this country singer/songwriter not only wrote Jim Reeves' first chart record, 'Mexican Joe', but also had his biggest US hit with 'Caribbean'. Torok's bestselling UK release was another Mexican opus that musically owed something to 'Caribbean'. The song, which sold few Stateside, was penned by his wife Gale. It was successful enough to earn him a British tour and an appearance at the London Palladium – neither of which were particularly well received by the critics.

ELVIS PRESLEY
BLUE MOON
HMV

▲ 9
🔟 4
—/250

His country-styled arrangement of the well-known Rogers & Hart standard gave Presley a UK-only Top 10 entry. It was taken from his eponymous debut LP, which led the US lists for ten weeks.

MALCOLM VAUGHAN
ST THERESE OF THE
ROSES
HMV

| ▲ 3 |
| ⑩ 2 |
| 123/250 |

Jackie Wilson) lifted the powerful Welsh tenor back
into the charts.

A big ballad that had proved successful Stateside
for Billy Ward & The Dominoes (featuring vocalist

UNITED STATES
December 1956

FRANK SINATRA
HEY! JEALOUS LOVER
Capitol

| ▲ 8 |
| ⑩ 5 |
| —/250 |

In the year that Presley rewrote musical history,
anti-rock spokesman Sinatra only managed one US
Top 20 entry. The song was co-written by his
regular hit supplier Sammy Cahn and Kay Twomey,
who subsequently wrote many tunes that Elvis cut.

GEORGE HAMILTON IV
A ROSE AND A BABY
RUTH
ABC Paramount

| ▲ 7 |
| ⑩ 1• |
| —/250 |

The clean-cut, soft-voiced teenager first heard this
cute love song performed on local TV by fellow
North Carolina native John D. Loudermilk. The
recording by *Arthur Godfrey Show* winner Hamilton
gave him and composer Loudermilk the first of
their many hits. In the UK, where no advertising
was allowed on radio, the title was re-sung by
producer Don Costa (not George) to become 'A
Rose And A Candy Bar'. Hamilton later moved
successfully into country music and become known
worldwide as the 'Ambassador of Country Music'.

ELVIS PRESLEY
LOVE ME
RCA

| ▲ 7 |
| ⑩ 5 |
| —/250 |

R&B duo Willie & Ruth originally released the
dramatic Leiber & Stoller song which joined a
record nine other Elvis recordings in the US Top
100. In 1956 he sold an unprecedented ten million
singles and accounted for 60 per cent of RCA's sales.

TARRIERS
THE BANANA BOAT SONG
Glory

| ▲ 5 |
| ⑩ 1• |
| —/250 |

Noted actor Alan Arkin and Erik Darling (later of
The Rooftop Singers) were members of the folk trio
whose arrangement of this Caribbean classic
joined their recording (with Vince Martin) of
'Cindy, Oh Cindy' in the Top 20. Soon afterwards
Harry Belafonte's treatment joined them and the
Calypso craze was in full swing. The group never
returned to the Top 100, although they released
both 'Tom Dooley' (Kingston Trio) and 'I Know
Where I'm Going' (George Hamilton IV) before the
hit versions.

JERRY LEWIS
ROCK-A-BYE YOUR BABY
WITH A DIXIE MELODY
Decca

| ▲ 10 |
| ⑩ 1• |
| —/250 |

When the extremely popular movie duo, Dean
Martin and Jerry Lewis, acrimoniously split,
who would have thought that the latter would
be the first to have a million-selling single?
Nevertheless, it was the celebrated funny man
from New Jersey (born Joseph Levitch) who struck
gold with a swinging update of an old Al Jolson
jewel. Interestingly, in the next decade Dean and
Jerry's sons fought it out in the charts, with Gary
Lewis proving slightly more successful than Dean
Martin Jr (of Dino, Desi & Billy).

UNITED KINGDOM
December 1956

BING CROSBY & GRACE KELLY
TRUE LOVE
Capitol

▲ 4
⑩ 5
106/250

See US Entry (November).

EDDIE FISHER
CINDY, OH CINDY
HMV

▲ 5
⑩ 8•
246/250

See US entry (November).

WINIFRED ATWELL
MAKE IT A PARTY
Decca

▲ 7
⑩ 9
—/250

Old music hall classics 'Don't Dilly Dally On The Way', 'Down At The Old Bull & Bush' and 'I Belong To Glasgow' were among the songs on the latest of Atwell's annual seasonal singalong singles.

GUY MITCHELL
SINGING THE BLUES
Philips

▲ 1
⑩ 9
29/250

See US entry (November).

DICKIE VALENTINE
CHRISTMAS ISLAND
Decca

▲ 8
⑩ 8•
—/250

Although he retained his crown as Best British Male Vocalist in the *NME* poll, Valentine's update of the seasonal Andrews Sisters' single from 1948 proved to be the entertainer's last Top 10 entry. In 1957 he tried both rock'n'roll and skiffle, but his days as a chart regular were numbered. Always a popular live act, Valentine died in a car crash returning from a show in 1971.

UNITED STATES
January 1957

FRANKIE LAINE
MOONLIGHT GAMBLER
Columbia

After a four-year absence, the man with the most muscular vocal chords of the era reinstalled himself, albeit briefly, in the US Top 10 with this powerful Phil Springer and Bob Hilliard song.

SONNY JAMES
YOUNG LOVE
Capitol

One of country music's most successful singers first recorded for Capitol in 1952. His eighteenth single, a quick cover of singer/songwriter Ric Cartey's teen masterpiece 'Young Love', was his only pop Top 20 entry. It was also the first of a staggering 23 country No 1s (including a record 16 in succession!) for the singer born James Loden in Arkansas. At times James' rendition and Tab Hunter's similarly arranged version stood together in the Top 3. As this single climbed, James was touring with Gene Vincent and Carl Perkins.

PAT BOONE
DON'T FORBID ME
Dot

Although Elvis Presley loved this song, his production team rejected it. Boone then snapped

it up and the track, which took just 15 minutes to record, became the clean-cut teen idol's ninth Top 20 entry in just over 18 months.

TAB HUNTER
YOUNG LOVE
Dot

The photogenic actor (born Arthur Kelm in New York City) joined the long list of Dot recording artists who had major hits with covers in the mid-1950s. Hunter's pop-slanted version of the Sonny James country smash is said to have sold 400,000 in just ten days in the US, while in the UK it headed the charts for an enviable seven weeks.

HARRY BELAFONTE
BANANA BOAT (DAY-O)
RCA

Since early 1956 rock'n'roll had been getting a bad press and many musical prophets tipped Calypso to replace it. Spearheading the new craze was New York-born (of West Indian parents) Belafonte, who first recorded in 1949. Before his cry of 'Day-O' made him internationally famous, he had reached the US Top 20 with 'Mary's Boy Child' and 'Jamaica Farewell' – the latter being the B side of this hit in the UK. The distinctive single, almost inevitably, attracted a wonderful parody by Stan Freberg.

UNITED KINGDOM
January 1957

TOMMY STEELE
SINGING THE BLUES
Decca

▲ 1
⑩ 1
108/250

The UK's first home-grown rock'n'roll star was discovered singing at the 2 I's coffee bar and was managed by Larry Parnes (both the venue and Parnes' names recur throughout the early days of British rock). The 19-year-old Londoner (born Thomas Hicks) was truly an overnight sensation. His first release, the self-penned 'Rock With The Caveman', rocketed into the Top 20, and this distinctive cover of Guy Mitchell's big hit took 'Britain's answer to Elvis' to the top before Presley even managed the feat!

PAT BOONE
FRIENDLY PERSUASION
London American

▲ 3
⑩ 3
161/250

See US entry (October 1956).

FRANKIE VAUGHAN
GARDEN OF EDEN
Philips

▲ 1
⑩ 2
60/250

Vaughan confirmed his status as one of the UK's most popular recording artists when his dramatic rendition of Joe Valino's US Top 20 hit reached No 1 – even though it was banned on several radio and TV shows due to its religious connotations.

FATS DOMINO
BLUEBERRY HILL
London American

▲ 6
⑩ 1•
—/250

See US entry (October 1956).

UNITED STATES
February 1957

ELVIS PRESLEY
TOO MUCH
RCA

▲ 1
⑩ 6
97/250

The controversial singer, who topped the US chart for an unprecedented 24 weeks in 1956, started off the new year with another No 1. He introduced the repetitive rocker (which Bernard Hardison had recorded first) during his last *Ed Sullivan Show* appearance.

FATS DOMINO
BLUE MONDAY
Imperial

▲ 9
⑩ 3
—/250

No R&B performer could match Domino's run of hits in the 1950s. He was at his peak of popularity in early 1957, when this single replaced 'Blueberry Hill' at No 1 on the R&B charts and gave him 15 consecutive weeks at the top. The rotund performer sang this self-penned piano-pounder in the film *The Girl Can't Help It*.

JOHNNIE RAY
YOU DON'T OWE ME A
THING
Columbia

▲ 10
⑩ 7•
—/250

After Guy Mitchell successfully covered two of label-mate Marty Robbins' records, Columbia's A&R head Mitch Miller let Ray rework the hooky Robbins' composition. The result of this typically melodramatic and mannered vocal workout was another transatlantic Top 20 entry for one of the era's most distinctive song stylists.

**TERRY GILKYSON &
THE EASY RIDERS**
MARIANNE
Columbia

▲ 6
⑩ 1•
—/250

Lead singer Gilkyson was one of the 1950s most successful songwriters and, with the other members of the trio, had written and sung on Dean Martin's 1956 transatlantic No 1, 'Memories Are Made of This'. The group composed this captivating Caribbean-flavoured ditty, which also reached the Top 20 by The Hilltoppers. Pennsylvanian Gilkyson's other compositions include the following 1950s Top 10 entries: 'The Cry Of The Wild Goose', 'Tell Me A Story' and 'Where The Wind Blows', and 'Christopher Columbus'.

UNITED KINGDOM
February 1957

LONNIE DONEGAN
DON'T YOU ROCK ME
DADDY-O
Pye Nixa

▲ 4
⑩ 4
172/250

Soon after he became the first British artist to reach the singles chart with both an EP ('Skiffle Session') and an album (*Lonnie Donegan Showcase*), the Glasgow-born entertainer outsold rivals The Vipers with his treament of this standout skiffle stomper.

**VIPERS SKIFFLE
GROUP**
DON'T YOU ROCK ME
DADDY-O
Parlophone

▲ 10
⑩ 1
—/250

As Britain's first pop TV shows, *Cool For Cats* and *6.5 Special*, were launched, skiffle was spreading like wild fire, and the London-based Vipers were helping Lonnie Donegan fan the flames. George Martin produced the act's second single, which the group's Walley Whyton based on a 1920s folk/country song, 'Darneo' (aka 'Sail Away Ladies'). Not only did Donegan cover the track in the UK, but in the US it was also released by Bob Cort's Skiffle Group and Billy Sherrill, who subsequently became a leading country music writer/producer.

TAB HUNTER
YOUNG LOVE
London American

▲ 1
⑩ 1
18/250

See US entry (January).

PAT BOONE
DON'T FORBID ME
London American

▲ 2
⑩ 4
120/250

See US entry (January).

BILL HALEY & HIS COMETS
DON'T KNOCK THE ROCK
Brunswick

▲ 7
⑩ 9•
—/250

Haley's first tour was the most anticipated musical event of the decade in the UK. Perhaps inevitably it could not live up to people's expectations and sales slumped overnight, the last hit being the title song from his movie, *Don't Knock The Rock*. Haley's music may have owed something to Louis Jordan, Joe Turner and other R&B acts, but there is no denying that it was his group that introduced rock'n'roll to the world. In later years the band were given their due respect and packed houses right around the globe.

GUY MITCHELL
KNEE DEEP IN THE BLUES
Philips

▲ 3
⑩ 10
203/250

For the second time in a row the popular entertainer covered a Marty Robbins record that had been written by 22-year-old polio victim Melvin Endsley. Also for the second successive time, his version soared higher than British idol Tommy Steele's treatments.

UNITED STATES
March 1957

TOMMY SANDS
TEEN-AGE CRUSH
Capitol

▲ 2
⑩ 1•
249/250

Before he discovered Presley, Colonel Tom Parker managed this youthful recording veteran from Chicago. After refusing the lead in the TV production The *Singing Idol* (based roughly on Presley's life) for Elvis, Parker recommended Sands for the part. The role made Sands, who had been recording and touring to little effect since 1949, an overnight sensation, and the single amassed advance orders of over 500,000. Although hotly tipped to eclipse Elvis at the time, the photogenic performer's later releases and films failed to make him a top star.

CHARLIE GRACIE
BUTTERFLY
Cameo

▲ 3
⑩ 1•
—/250

White rock'n'rollers were now no longer a rarity, and one of the year's most successful was this singer/songwriter and guitarist born Charles Gracie in Philadelphia, whose previous recordings included 'Rockin' 'n' Rollin'' in 1951 (when he was just 15). The song was penned by Bernie Lowe and Kal Mann and was the first of scores of hits on the prolific pair's Cameo label. Not only did it fly up the charts for Gracie, but it was also a transatlantic smash by Andy Williams.

ANDY WILLIAMS
BUTTERFLY
Cadence

▲ 4
⑩ 2
—/250

This critically acclaimed balladeer from Iowa briefly boarded the rock'n'roll bandwagon with a credible cover of Charlie Gracie's high-flying hit. In the UK, his recording outsold Gracie's and topped the bestsellers chart.

PERRY COMO
ROUND AND ROUND
RCA

▲ 1
⑩ 18
107/250

Perhaps the song and singer were a little square for 1957, but that did not stop the record from returning the easy-on-the-ear Emmy winner to the top again. Incidentally, Como should be given credit for promoting many rock'n'roll performers on his TV show.

BUDDY KNOX
PARTY DOLL
Roulette

▲ 1
⑩ 1•
128/250

Rockabilly-pioneering Knox apparently composed this country rocker while at school in the late 1940s. Both the A side and its coupling, Jimmy Bowen's 'I'm Sticking With You', were cut at Norman Petty's studio and released on the singers' Triple D label. Roulette picked up both tracks and released them separately as their first two singles – and amazingly both reached the Top 20. As the record hit, Knox was drafted for six months. Despite a handful of mid-table chart entries, this early Tex-Mex rocker never received his due acclaim.

FATS DOMINO
I'M WALKIN'
Imperial

▲ 5
⑩ 4
—/250

Rock'n'roll's most successful songwriting partnership before Lennon & McCartney were Domino and his producer/bandleader Dave Bartholomew. Among their many million-selling compositions was this peerless rocker that soon afterwards also earned Ricky Nelson a gold disc. Curiously, Fats' recording reappeared in the German Top 20 in 1992.

DIAMONDS
LITTLE DARLIN'
Mercury

▲ 2
⑩ 1
172/250

A year after introducing Canadian vocal quartet The Crew-Cuts to Mercury, Cleveland DJ Bill Randle took this Canadian foursome to the label. Both groups specialized in covers of R&B songs, although The Diamonds' interpretations often sold well in the R&B market too. Before their tongue-in-cheek rendition of The Gladiolas' calypso rocker 'Little Darlin'' made them international hit makers, they had Top 40 US entries with covers of singles by The Teenagers, Willows, Clovers and G-Clefs. This single held the runner-up spot for a record eight weeks.

PAT BOONE
WHY BABY WHY
Dot

▲ 5
⑩ 7
—/250

Weeks after signing a lucrative $1 million TV deal, the teen-targeted crooner clicked with a Luther Dixon composition. Boone coupled it with a revival of Lucky Millinder's 1951 R&B hit 'I'm Waiting Just For You' which also added to his most impressive Top 40 tally.

UNITED KINGDOM
March 1957

DAVID WHITFIELD
ADORATION WALTZ
Decca

▲ 9
⑩ 11•
—/250

Al Lewis and Larry Stock, composers of 'Blueberry Hill', reportedly wrote the dated ballad especially for Whitfield. It was the last Top 10 entry for the internationally renowned tenor whose home town, Hull, named a street after him. Whitfield, whose voice was unsuited to rock'n'roll, spent much of his later life touring the world and died in 1980, while working in Australia.

LITTLE RICHARD
LONG TALL SALLY
London American

▲ 3
⑩ 1
181/250

See US entry (May 1956).

HARRY BELAFONTE
BANANA BOAT SONG
HMV

▲ 2
⑩ 1
132/250

See US entry (January).

SHIRLEY BASSEY
BANANA BOAT SONG
Philips

▲ 8
⑩ 1
—/250

Britain's best-known female cabaret artist debuted on the UK chart with a song that also sailed into the Top 20 by American recording artists Harry Belafonte and The Tarriers. At the time, 20-year-old Bassey, who hailed from Tiger Bay, Cardiff, was performing to appreciative audiences in both Las Vegas and Hollywood.

UNITED STATES
April 1957

DELL-VIKINGS
COME GO WITH ME
Dot

▲ 4
⑩ 1
—/250

The first successful inter-racial rock'n'roll group was formed in the US Air Force. Bass singer Clarence E. Quick composed the doo-wop quintet's breakthrough hit, which they initially recorded a cappella for Buchanan & Goodman's Luniverse label. However, it was a later version cut in a Pittsburgh DJ's small basement studio, and originally released on Fee Bee, that spent six months on the chart. Later in the year the group's similarly styled invitation, 'Come Along With Me' enticed few buyers.

FERLIN HUSKY
GONE
Capitol

▲ 5
⑩ 1•
—/250

During his long career this country singer from Missouri performed under a variety of names. He first recorded the memorable rock-a-ballad in 1952 as Terry Preston, although few people noticed. Husky, or Huskey as he was then known, first hit the headlines in 1953 thanks to his duet with Jean Shepard, 'A Dear John Letter'. After a few minor country charters as a solo singer, Husky re-recorded 'Gone', and the resulting single led the country bestsellers for 10 weeks and gave him his biggest-selling pop release.

ELVIS PRESLEY
ALL SHOOK UP
RCA

▲ 1
⑩ 7
43/250

Presley, who always admitted his debt to R&B music, was delighted when 'All Shook Up' (a song earlier cut by David Hill) became the first record by a white act to head the R&B sales, jukebox and radio play charts. It was also the first of the King's many UK No 1s.

CHUCK BERRY
SCHOOL DAY
Chess

▲ 3
⑩ 2
—/250

Between his first two Top 10s, the original guitar-playing rock singer/songwriter had released such classics as 'Thirty Days', 'Roll Over Beethoven' and 'Brown-Eyed Handsome Man'. Teen-angst tune 'School Day' was one of the all-time great rock'n'roll records. When he rewrote it in 1964 as 'No Particular Place To Go' it was a smash all over again.

UNITED KINGDOM
April 1957

LONNIE DONEGAN
CUMBERLAND GAP
Pye Nixa

For the second successive time, skiffle's foremost performer won a chart battle with rivals The Vipers. This frenzied folk stomper hit the top as he headed the bill (with The Platters) at the London Palladium.

LITTLE RICHARD
THE GIRL CAN'T HELP IT
London American

Due to label problems, Richard's first two US hits, 'Tutti Frutti' and 'Long Tall Sally', were coupled in the UK and released a year after their American success. That double-sider was joined in the Top 20 by 'The Girl Can't Help It' and its flip, 'She's Got It', both of which he sang in Jayne Mansfield's movie *The Girl Can't Help It.*

JOHNNIE RAY
LOOK HOMEWARD ANGEL
Philips

The Four Esquires originally recorded this dramatic Wally Gold-composed ballad. In the US, it was the other side, 'You Don't Owe Me A Thing', that reached the Top 10.

VIPERS SKIFFLE GROUP
CUMBERLAND GAP
Parlophone

On Lonnie Donegan's chart-topping treatment of this song he was '15 miles from the Cumberland Gap', whereas these skiffle pioneers still had 19 miles to go. Nevertheless, it was to be the group's last journey into the Top 20 as their popularity faded with that of skiffle music. Leader Wally Whyton became a top children's TV presenter and a well-respected country music DJ for the BBC.

FRANKIE LYMON & THE TEENAGERS
BABY BABY
Columbia

In the UK, 'Baby Baby' and the coupling, 'I'm Not A Juvenile Delinquent', were Top 20 entries as the youthful showmen became the youngest act ever to top the bill at the London Palladium. However, in the US, these songs from their film *Rock, Rock, Rock* went nowhere. Soon after the UK tour, the widely imitated group split up and, to quote their last hit title, were 'Out In The Cold Again'. Sadly, Lymon died from drug abuse in 1968, aged 25. In 1993 they were inducted into the Rock and Roll Hall of Fame.

TAB HUNTER
NINETY-NINE WAYS
London American

A song that composer Charlie Gracie put on the B side of his high-flying 'Butterfly' quickly returned this teen pin-up to the transatlantic Top 20. Soon afterwards, Hunter's film company, Warner Brothers, signed him to their newly launched record label, where he had minor hits with revivals of 'Don't Get Around Much Anymore', 'Jealous Heart' and 'In Apple Blossom Time'.

NAT 'KING' COLE
WHEN I FALL IN LOVE
Capitol

This is one of very few records to reach the UK Top 5 on two separate occasions, and even more remarkable is the fact that there was a 30 year gap between entries! In the US, it was only available on his No 1 album *Love Is The Thing*. Cole's original recording joined Rick Astley's revival in the UK Top 5 in 1988 – the year that Cole's daughter, Natalie, had a minor US hit with the song.

UNITED STATES
May 1957

JIMMY DORSEY & HIS ORCHESTRA
SO RARE
Fraternity

▲ 3
⑩ 1•
161/250

Legendary bandleader Dorsey's highest-placed hit since the war was a contemporary cut featuring a 'doo-wahing' female vocal chorus. The saxophonist and clarinettist who, along with his equally famous brother Tommy, had been playing since the 1920s, formed his own band in 1935. Among his wartime bestsellers were 'The Breeze And I', 'Amapola', 'Green Eyes' and 'Maria Elena' (all featuring vocalist Bob Eberly). Sadly, as this single entered the Top 5, Dorsey himself succumbed to cancer.

GUY MITCHELL
ROCK-A-BILLY
Columbia

▲ 10
⑩ 7
—/250

This one-time country performer (as Al Cernick and Al Grant) boarded the fast-moving rockabilly bandwagon with an up-tempo tune that gave him his fourth and last UK No 1. The memorable, if repetitive, song was co-written by Woody Harris, who later penned hits for Bobby Darin.

RICKY NELSON
A TEENAGER'S ROMANCE/I'M WALKING
Verve

▲ 2
⑩ 1
216/250

As the transatlantic music media prophesied the death of rock'n'roll, one of the genre's top acts debuted on the chart. America had watched New Jersey-born Nelson grow since 1949 via regular appearances on his parents' radio and TV show, *The*

Adventures of Ozzie & Harriet. When an Elvis skit received a good reaction, Ricky decided to try for a recording career. Although 20 labels rejected it, his version of Fats Domino's 'I'm Walking' and its archetypal teen coupling joined Domino's rendition in the Top 20.

MARTY ROBBINS
A WHITE SPORT COAT (AND A PINK CARNATION)
Columbia

▲ 2
⑩ 1
212/250

After seeing his country bestsellers 'Singing The Blues', 'You Don't Owe Me A Thing' and 'Knee Deep In The Blues' go up the charts by other Columbia artists, Robbins insisted that he was produced by the label's whiz kid, Ray Conniff. This teaming gave the country singer/songwriter (born Martin Robinson) from Arizona his first major pop hit. In the UK, however, he still suffered from covers, and versions by The King Brothers and Terry Dene easily outsold Robbins' recording.

PAT BOONE
LOVE LETTERS IN THE SAND
Dot

▲ 1
⑩ 8
38/250

Boone's revival of a Ted Black hit from 1931 topped the US best sellers for five weeks and stood at No 2 in the UK for almost two months. As his best-known single exited the chart, Boone was voted the World's Outstanding Male Singer (above Elvis) in the *NME* poll.

UNITED KINGDOM
May 1957

GUY MITCHELL
ROCK-A-BILLY
Philips

| ▲ 1 |
| ⑩ 11 |
| 103/250 |

See US entry.

ANDY WILLIAMS
BUTTERFLY
London American

| ▲ 1 |
| ⑩ 1 |
| 88/250 |

See US entry (March).

CHAS McDEVITT
SKIFFLE GROUP
FREIGHT TRAIN
Oriole

| ▲ 5 |
| ⑩ 1• |
| —/250 |

Folk singer Nancy Whiskey was recruited by fellow Glaswegian McDevitt to share vocal chores in his skiffle group, and their reworking of the folk blues favourite 'Freight Train' (which they featured in the film *The Tommy Steele Story*) steamed up the UK chart. Despite an appearance on Ed Sullivan's US TV show, a cover version by Rusty Draper sold more Stateside. The speedy demise of skiffle's popularity harmed the progress of the group's strong follow-up, 'Greenback Dollar'/'I'm Satisfied'.

JOHNNIE RAY
YES TONIGHT JOSEPHINE
Philips

| ▲ 1 |
| ⑩ 10• |
| 65/250 |

One of the greats of the decade ended his Top 10 career with this fast-paced UK No 1, penned by R&B songsmith Winfield Scott. When he arrived on the scene, the 'Cry Guy' had caused a sensation, and when Elvis appeared many dismissed him as a

pale impersonation of Ray. Inevitably though, rock stars eventually replaced him in the charts, but he spent many of his remaining years on the lucrative nightclub circuit.

ELVIS PRESLEY
TOO MUCH
HMV

| ▲ 6 |
| ⑩ 5 |
| —/250 |

See US entry (February).

SLIM WHITMAN
I'LL TAKE YOU HOME
AGAIN KATHLEEN
London American

| ▲ 7 |
| ⑩ 4• |
| —/250 |

Even though the British press said he had 'no personality and lacked showmanship', Whitman achieved a remarkably long and successful UK career. Although presumed to be about Ireland, his last hit of the decade was written in the nineteenth century by an American homesick for Germany. Whitman remained popular in the UK, and in the late 1970s the fifty-something singer scored two No 1 LPs in a row.

PEGGY LEE
MR WONDERFUL
Brunswick

| ▲ 5 |
| ⑩ 1 |
| —/250 |

The title song from the Broadway musical *Mr Wonderful* (which starred Sammy Davis Jr) gave the popular husky-voiced singer/actress a major UK hit a year after it had reached the US Top 40.

UNITED STATES
June 1957

GALE STORM
DARK MOON
Dot

▲ 6
⑩ 2•
—/250

Her cover of a country song by label-mate Bonnie Guitar took the star of TV's *The Gale Storm Show* into the charts for the last time. The singer, whose Top 20 entries included her versions of 'Why Do Fools Fall In Love', 'Teen Age Prayer' and 'Ivory Tower', was backed on this track by the Billy Vaughn Orchestra.

SAL MINEO
START MOVIN' (IN MY DIRECTION)
Epic

▲ 9
⑩ 1•
—/250

Eighteen-year-old New York actor Mineo, who received an Oscar nomination for his role in James Dean's *Rebel Without A Cause*, was already a target of teen adulation before he recorded. David Hill penned his debut disc, which sold a reported 484,000 in 11 days. In the UK, both Sal's single and fellow newcomer Terry Dene's treatment moved into the Top 20. Mineo, whose singing was unlikely to win him many awards, returned to the movies full time in the early 1960s, and was murdered in 1976.

BONNIE GUITAR
DARK MOON
Dot

▲ 10
⑩ 1•
—/250

When Dot signed a deal with country label Fabor, their first releases were Ned Miller's 'From A Jack To A King' (which finally hit in 1963) and this memorable Miller-composed ballad. To begin with, Fabor had only wanted Guitar (who changed her name from Buckingham due to her prowess on that instrument) to play on the session, but she

convinced them that she was the ideal vocalist. Later in the decade, Guitar launched her own Dolphin/Dolton labels and struck gold with The Fleetwoods and The Ventures.

EVERLY BROTHERS
BYE BYE LOVE
Cadence

▲ 2
⑩ 1
147/250

In 1957, country was as influential on the pop chart as R&B, and one of the most successful country acts was Nashville-based Don and Phil Everly. The brothers, who previously recorded for Columbia, had their debut hit with a song written for another country duo, Johnny & Jack (which had supposedly been rejected by over two dozen artists, including Elvis). The addition of a Bo Diddley-style guitar intro (taken from the duo's own composition 'Give Me A Future') helped give the track its distinctive and commercial sound.

COASTERS
SEARCHIN'/YOUNG BLOOD
Atco

▲ 3
⑩ 1
174/250

The Coasters were a spin-off act from noted R&B group The Robins, and they were produced by Leiber & Stoller, who also wrote most of the quartet's successes. The Coasters' third R&B charter, a novelty number that name-dropped many fictional detectives, gave the unmistakable combo their first pop hit and earned Atlantic Records its first gold disc. Incidentally, Leiber & Stoller penned the humorous and somewhat lecherous girl-watching flip side (which was part of The Beatles' early repertoire) some years before, but held it for the right time.

UNITED KINGDOM
June 1957

RONNIE HILTON
AROUND THE WORLD
HMV

▲ 4
⑩ 5•
205/250

Five versions of this film theme reached the UK Top 30 with Hilton's heading the crowded field, and it was one of 11 Top 20 entries he amassed in the decade. After his hits halted, Hilton still remained a top drawing card on the UK club circuit, and in the 1990s he hosted the BBC radio series *Sounds Of The Fifties*, which looked back nostalgically at the music of the era.

GRACIE FIELDS
AROUND THE WORLD
Columbia

▲ 8
⑩ 1•
—/250

'Our Gracie', as she was affectionately known, was one of the great British entertainers of the twentieth century. The Lancashire lass (born Grace Stansfield) helped to lift the spirits of the British during the depression and war years with her films, records and live appearances. The singer/comedienne/actress, who is best known for such songs as 'Sally' and 'The Biggest Aspidistra In The World', had a Top 10 hit at age 59 with this popular film theme.

BING CROSBY
AROUND THE WORLD
Brunswick

▲ 5
⑩ 6
—/250

One of the legends of twentieth-century music had his last major hit with the much-recorded theme song. The man with the made-for-radio voice and film-friendly persona was awarded a Lifetime Achievement Grammy in 1962. Crosby's perennially popular 'White Christmas' returned to the UK Top 10 weeks after he died in 1977, and one of Bing's last recordings, 'Peace On Earth – Little Drummer Boy' with David Bowie, followed suit five years later. In 1993, the US Post Office issued a stamp to commemorate his life.

LONNIE DONEGAN
GAMBLIN' MAN/PUTTING
ON THE STYLE
Pye Nixa

▲ 1
⑩ 6
66/250

Only Dickie Valentine received more votes in the *NME* poll for the UK's Musical Personality of 1956 than the singer, who clocked up his second No 1 in two months. 'Gamblin' Man', which had recently been popularized as 'The Rovin' Gambler', was coupled with another traditional folk/country song that Valentine covered unsuccessfully.

DIAMONDS
LITTLE DARLIN'
Mercury

▲ 3
⑩ 1•
159/250

See US entry (March).

KING BROTHERS
A WHITE SPORT COAT
Parlophone

▲ 6
⑩ 1
—/250

Before being tagged 'Britain's rock'n'roll kids', this talented Essex trio frequently appeared on children's TV and had even played at the London Palladium. The fact that they were not rock'n'rollers, but essentially all-round entertainers, did not harm their career. The clean-cut combo's bouncy cover of Marty Robbins' high school prom song outsold all other versions in the UK. The trio were voted Britain's Top Group up until the arrival of label-mates The Beatles. Youngest brother Denis became one of the most prolific TV theme writers in the UK.

ELVIS PRESLEY
ALL SHOOK UP
HMV

▲ 1
⑩ 6
13/250

See US entry (April).

RUSS HAMILTON
WE WILL MAKE LOVE
Oriole

▲ 2
🔟 1•
140/250

Seven years before Merseybeat swept the world, the Merseyside singer (born Ronald Hulme) sold a million of his composition 'Rainbow' in the US. Amazingly, in the UK, it was the other side, 'We Will Make Love', that took the honours – giving Hamilton a double-sided transatlantic hit with his debut disc! Despite this staggering start, there was no more gold at the end of the rainbow for the performer voted second Most Promising Male Singer of 1957 in the US (pushing Paul Anka into third position).

UNITED STATES
July 1957

ELVIS PRESLEY
TEDDY BEAR
RCA

▲ 1
🔟 8
36/250

Many fans feel that *Loving You* was Elvis' best movie and that his performance in it of 'Teddy Bear' was one of the highlights of his Hollywood years. The renowned rocker sold 1.6 million in just two weeks, and the soundtrack LP remained at No 1 until Elvis' *Christmas Album* replaced it.

FATS DOMINO
VALLEY OF TEARS/IT'S
YOU I LOVE
Imperial

▲ 6
🔟 5
—/250

Some R&B purists disliked the use of female backing singers on this memorable beat ballad which, like its equally popular coupling, was composed by the prolific pairing of Domino and Dave Bartholomew.

JOHNNY MATHIS
IT'S NOT FOR ME TO SAY
Columbia

▲ 6
🔟 1
—/250

Despite current trends, Mitch Miller was convinced that Mathis, who owed more to Nat 'King' Cole than rock'n'roll, was a potential superstar. After six months' promotion the San Francisco-born singer's debut single, 'Wonderful Wonderful', cracked the US Top 20. This Al Stillman-composed follow-up, which was heard in the Eleanor Parker film *Lizzie*, fared even better. Both singles were included on his 1958 album *Johnny's Greatest Hits*, which astoundingly spent nearly ten years in the US LP chart!

BILLY WILLIAMS
I'M GONNA SIT RIGHT
DOWN AND WRITE
MYSELF A LETTER
Coral

▲ 7
🔟 1•
—/250

In the 1940s this Texan's group, The Charioteers, sang with Bing Crosby and Frank Sinatra and had hits of their own. He formed The Billy Williams Quartet in 1950 and they became regulars on Sid Caesar's *Your Show Of Shows*. After stints with MGM and Mercury, the act released several cover versions on Coral including 'Sh-Boom', 'Love Me' and 'Butterfly'. The quartet's biggest seller was a foot-tapping revival of a Fats Waller standard, which they performed on Alan Freed's new TV show and on the first nationally seen edition of *Bandstand*.

ANDY WILLIAMS
I LIKE YOUR KIND OF
LOVE
Cadence

▲ 10
🔟 3
—/250

Melvin 'Singing The Blues' Endsley penned both sides of Williams' second successive transatlantic Top 20 entry. He was assisted on this pop/rocker by the seductive-sounding Peggy Powers.

JOHNNIE & JOE
OVER THE MOUNTAIN;
ACROSS THE SEA
Chess

Zell Sanders, the owner of J&S Records, liked Joe Rivers' voice and teamed him with her daughter, Johnnie. Their third release, 'I'll Be Spinning', attracted some sales, but it was Johnnie & Joe's next single, a slow R&B doo-wop track, that made them short-lived stars. The single, which allegedly needed 25 takes to get right, was penned by Joe's long-time friend Rex Garvin (who also played piano on it). The track, which is rightfully regarded as gem of the genre, returned to the US chart once again in 1960.

LITTLE RICHARD
JENNY JENNY/MISS ANN
Specialty

The piano-pounding headliner of Alan Freed's all-star *Holiday Rock'n'Roll Show* had another transatlantic Top 20 entry with one of the wildest waxings ever recorded. 'Jenny Jenny', which owes a nod to Johnny Moore & The Three Blazers' 1952 single 'Johnny Johnny', was coupled with an outstanding slow blues shouter.

NAT 'KING' COLE
SEND FOR ME/MY
PERSONAL POSSESSION
Capitol

Ollie Jones from The Cues composed the contemporary track which returned Cole to the Top 10 after a two-year absence. The coupling (which featured The Four Knights) was penned by Rose Marie McCoy, writer of his earlier success 'If I May'.

LARRY WILLIAMS
SHORT FAT FANNIE
Specialty

Specialty, the label that released Little Richard's records, added to their gold discs with a self-penned rocker by another piano-pounding singer/songwriter. The one-time valet and chauffeur for ex-Specialty star Lloyd Price followed a closely cloned cover of Price's 'Just Because' with a track packed with titles of current rock hits. The follow-up, 'Boney Maronie', was the underrated New Orleans rocker's only transatlantic Top 20 entry. Williams' singles were consistently good, and his songs were subsequently recorded by such acts as The Beatles and Rolling Stones.

PATTI PAGE
OLD CAPE COD
Mercury

Almost ten years after she introduced record buyers to multi-track vocalizing, the host of pop TV show *The Big Record* dueted with herself again on this paean to one of America's most beautiful holiday resorts. Page, who outsold every other female singer in the decade, has reputedly sold over 60 million records in her long career (she was still appearing on TV in the mid-1990s).

DELL-VIKINGS
WHISPERING BELLS
Dot

Soon after recording their follow-up to 'Come Go With Me', four of the vocal quintet signed to Mercury. The only member not leaving was Corinthian 'Kripp' Johnson, who sang lead on 'Whispering Bells' (which bass singer Clarence E. Quick had written as a ballad). This meant there were two groups called the Dell-Vikings, neither of whom returned to the Top 20.

DEBBIE REYNOLDS
TAMMY
DOT

Eddie Fisher's equally famous wife, who was born in the West Texas town of El Paso, had her bestselling single with a beautiful Jay Livingston and Ray Evans ballad from her film *Tammy And The Bachelor*. Interestingly, R&B producer/songwriter Berry Gordy was so impressed with 'Tammy' that he wanted to name his record label after it – but he was legally forced to amend it to Tamla.

UNITED KINGDOM
July 1957

TOMMY STEELE
BUTTERFINGERS
Decca

▲ 8
⑩ 2
—/250

Less than a year after he first burst on to the scene, this chirpy cockney rocker was starring in *The Tommy Steele Story*. In the film, the UK's first working-class hero sang this worthy beat ballad, which Steele had composed with Lionel Bart.

PAT BOONE
LOVE LETTERS IN THE SAND
London American

▲ 2
⑩ 5
98/250

See US entry (May).

ELVIS PRESLEY
TEDDY BEAR
HMV

▲ 3
⑩ 7
154/250

See US entry.

UNITED STATES
August 1957

PAUL ANKA
DIANA
ABC Paramount

▲ 1
⑩ 1
99/250

Teenage singer/songwriters were thin on the ground in the 1950s and the most successful was Canadian Anka. A cha-lypso tune that the 16-year-old had written about his one-time babysitter (Diana Ayoub) rocketed to No 1 on both sides of the Atlantic. In the UK, where it topped the chart for nine weeks, it was only the third single to sell a million copies. With total sales of over ten million, it is one of the all-time Top 10 best-selling singles.

RUSS HAMILTON
RAINBOW
Kapp

▲ 7
⑩ 1•
—/250

See UK entry (June).

DON RONDO
WHITE SILVER SANDS
Jubilee

▲ 9
⑩ 1•
—/250

This powerful baritone, who narrowly missed the Top 20 in 1956 with the ballad 'Two Different Worlds', had his biggest seller with a version of an up-tempo track previously recorded by Dave Gardner (who scored with several humorous hit albums in the early 1960s as Brother Dave Gardner). The New York-based singer never returned to the Top 40, but in 1960 Bill Black's

Combo reinstated the song in the Top 10, and in 1972 a revival recorded by Sonny James was a country smash.

CRICKETS
THAT'LL BE THE DAY
Brunswick

▲ 1
⑩ 1•
138/250

A year after rockabilly performer Buddy Holly's solo version went nowhere, his re-recording of this

self-penned stomper (released under his group's name) rocketed to No 1 on both sides of the Atlantic. The track, which had been rejected by a handful of top labels, was the first record to be played on Dick Clark's *Bandstand* TV show when it went national. It was also the first song to be demoed by The Quarry Men (Beatles), whose bass player, Paul McCartney, later bought the rights to Holly's compositions.

UNITED KINGDOM
August 1957

HARRY BELAFONTE
ISLAND IN THE SUN
RCA

▲ 3
⑩ 2
112/250

The self-composed title song from his third movie was a bigger hit in the UK than the US. However, the album it was extracted from, *Belafonte Sings Of The Caribbean*, was the 'King of Calypso's' fifth US Top 3 album in less than two years.

LITTLE RICHARD
LUCILLE
London American

▲ 10
⑩ 3
—/250

When Specialty bought Little Richard's contract for $600 they signed one of the era's most successful singers and writers. 'Lucille' is just one of his songs that has been recorded numerous times. Interestingly, a version of this R&B/rocker by Waylon Jennings reached the top of the country chart in 1983.

EVERLY BROTHERS
BYE BYE LOVE
London American

▲ 6
⑩ 1
—/250

See US entry (June).

JOHNNY DUNCAN & THE BLUE GRASS BOYS
LAST TRAIN TO SAN FERNANDO
Columbia

▲ 2
⑩ 1•
128/250

Initially this Tennessee-born performer (who had reportedly played in Bill Monroe's celebrated Bluegrass Band) was billed in Britain as 'The original rockabilly kid'. The singer/guitarist stayed in the UK after being drafted there by the US Army, and he replaced Lonnie Donegan in Chris Barber's Band before forming his own bluegrass/skiffle group. Duncan's only big hit, produced by Denis Preston and engineered by Joe Meek, was a lively cover of a single by Bobby Short (cousin of R&B chart maker Rudy Render).

PAUL ANKA
DIANA
Columbia

▲ 1
⑩ 1
8/250

See US entry.

PETULA CLARK
WITH ALL MY HEART
Pye Nixa

| ▲ 4 |
| ⑩ 3 |
| 207/250 |

After a two-year chart absence, the popular singer/actress from Surrey returned with a beat ballad that had given Jodie Sands her only US hit. The song was composed by Sands' producer Bob Marcucci and her musical arranger Peter De Angelis.

CHARLIE GRACIE
FABULOUS
Parlophone

| ▲ 8 |
| ⑩ 1 |
| —/250 |

Even though both sides of his previous single, 'Butterfly' and '99 Ways', had sold better in Britain by Andy Williams and Tab Hunter respectively, Gracie's Elvis-like rockin' follow-up reached the UK Top 10.

UNITED STATES
September 1957

JERRY LEE LEWIS
WHOLE LOT OF SHAKIN' GOING ON
Sun

| ▲ 3 |
| ⑩ 1 |
| —/250 |

Not since the arrival of Elvis had any performer caused such a stir as the piano pounder from Louisiana. His debut hit was a rip-up-the-seats rocker that had previously been recorded by R&B vocalist Big Maybelle and rockabilly artist Roy Hall (whom Lewis worked with earlier). This single, which is rightfully regarded as one of rock'n'roll's finest, topped both the country and R&B charts.

JIMMIE RODGERS
HONEYCOMB
Roulette

| ▲ 1 |
| ⑩ 1 |
| 92/250 |

The vocalist from Washington had included this Bob Merrill composition (which was the B side of Georgie Shaw's 1954 hit, 'Till We Two Are One') in his folk club act since 1955. Rodgers left a tape of it with Roulette, who took six months to trace him as he forgot to include an address! The single also topped the R&B chart, at a time when the first four places were astonishingly taken by white artists! In the UK the uplifting song was banned by the BBC on religious grounds.

BOBBETTES
MR LEE
Atlantic

| ▲ 7 |
| ⑩ 1• |
| —/250 |

Not only was this quintet the youngest group to grace the Top 10 (with an average age of 12), but they were also the first female R&B vocal team to reach that chart. The youngsters composed their million seller about a fifth grade teacher who, in reality, the girls did not like. Despite many other noteworthy releases, the teenagers, voted Most Promising R&B Vocal Group of 1957, never returned to the Top 40, although a sequel, 'I Shot Mr Lee', only narrowly missed.

TONY BENNETT
IN THE MIDDLE OF AN ISLAND
Columbia

| ▲ 9 |
| ⑩ 5• |
| —/250 |

'Rock-A-Hula' is how Columbia tagged the last Top 10 entry by this singer's singer. Of the early 1950s crooners, only Bennett and his No 1 fan, Frank Sinatra, remained headliners throughout the 1960s, 1970s and 1980s. In the 1990s, Bennett was 'discovered' by the MTV generation and also earned several more trophies, including a couple of Grammy awards.

PAT BOONE
REMEMBER YOU'RE
MINE/THERE'S A
GOLD MINE IN THE SKY
DOT

▲ 10
⑩ 9
—/250

Guitar legend Link Wray's brother Ray Vernon first recorded this Kal Mann and Bernie Lowe composition, which had a similar title to Boone's unsuccessful second release, 'Remember To Be Mine'. The B side, a 1938 composition by the writers of 'Love Letters in The Sand', also entered the Top 20.

JOHNNY MATHIS
CHANCES ARE/
THE TWELFTH OF NEVER
Columbia

▲ 4
⑩ 2
211/250

One of the year's classiest double-sided smashes came from a youthful song stylist who had intended to be a jazz vocalist. Like his previous hit,

'Chances Are' was composed by Al Stillman and Robert Allen. Both Cliff Richard and Donny Osmond later successfully revived 'The Twelfth Of Never'.

TUNE WEAVERS
HAPPY, HAPPY BIRTHDAY
BABY
Checker

▲ 8
⑩ 1•
—/250

Margo Sylvia fronted this family foursome whose sole hit was a teen-oriented ballad, which she had written with her brother Gilbert in 1952. Checker Records picked up the rights from the small Casa Grande label, and the fact that follow-ups by the act appeared on both labels may have harmed their future career. Later, similar-sounding singles such as 'Congratulations On Your Wedding' and 'Merry, Merry Christmas Baby' also failed to give the group any happy returns to the chart. The tune topped the country lists in 1986 by Ronnie Milsap.

UNITED KINGDOM
September 1957

TOMMY STEELE
WATER WATER/HANDFUL
OF SONGS
Decca

▲ 5
⑩ 3
—/250

These standout songs from *The Tommy Steele Story* were joined in the Top 20 by Steele's recording of the self-penned title tune from the film *Shiralee*. 'Handful Of Songs', co-written by Mike Pratt (Randall from the cult TV series *Randall & Hopkirk*), won the Ivor Novello Award for Song of the Year.

CHARLIE GRACIE
WANDERIN' EYES
London American

▲ 6
⑩ 2•
—/250

Thanks partly to a well-received British tour, both 'Wanderin' Eyes' and the B side, a revival of the country song 'I Love You So Much It Hurts Me',

joined Gracie's previous single, 'Fabulous', in the UK Top 20. The pioneering singer/guitarist who, unlike most of his contemporaries, was actually a virtuoso on his instrument, was still drawing crowds on UK tours in the 1990s.

ELVIS PRESLEY
PARALYSED
HMV

▲ 8
⑩ 8
—/250

Otis Blackwell composed this underrated rocker, which joined four other Presley platters in the UK Top 20. Elvis says he patterned his vocal after Jackie Wilson's treatment of an earlier Blackwell song, 'Don't Be Cruel', which the King considered 'better than mine'.

DEBBIE REYNOLDS
TAMMY
Vogue Coral

▲ 2
⑩ 2•
131/250

See US entry (July).

UNITED STATES
October 1957

EVERLY BROTHERS
WAKE UP LITTLE SUSIE
Cadence

▲ 1
⑩ 2
109/250

Noted Nashville tunesmiths Boudleaux and Felice Bryant composed the majority of the brothers' early hits, including this slightly suggestive song which was banned by some radio stations. The single topped the US pop, country and R&B charts and reached the runner-up spot in the UK.

ELVIS PRESLEY
JAILHOUSE ROCK
RCA

▲ 1
⑩ 9
31/250

In the UK, this red hot Leiber & Stoller-penned rocker amassed record advance orders of 250,000 and became the first single to enter the chart at No 1. In the US, the title song from his third film took Presley's tally of No 1 hits to nine in less than two years.

LITTLE RICHARD
KEEP A KNOCKIN'
Specialty

▲ 9
⑩ 3•
—/250

As his frantic reworking of this old blues song sped up the bestsellers, Little Richard announced that he was retiring. After a verse about drinking gin was deleted, the finished track was less than a minute long and only by some nifty editing was it stretched to over two minutes.

RICKY NELSON
BE-BOP BABY/HAVE I TOLD YOU LATELY THAT I LOVE YOU
Imperial

▲ 3
⑩ 2
238/250

When the actor-turned-teen idol signed a $250,000 deal with Imperial, his previous label, Verve, sued for $1 million. Nonetheless, Nelson's first Imperial release amassed a reported 750,000 advance orders. Incidentally, a version of the B side was featured on Elvis' 'Just For You' EP, which was charting simultaneously.

RAYS
SILHOUETTES
Cameo

▲ 4
⑩ 1•
241/250

After the New York vocal quartet left Chess Records, producer/songwriters Bob Crewe and Frank Slay signed them to their XYZ label. 'Silhouettes', the group's second single on that label, was leased to Cameo for $1,500 (after top DJ Hy Lit tipped them off about it). Despite appearances on Ed Sullivan's TV show, The Rays failed to follow up this hit. 'Silhouettes' was subsequently revived successfully by Herman's Hermits (1965) and Cliff Richard (1990), while its popular flip side, 'Daddy Cool', was a UK Top 10 entry by The Darts in 1977.

SAM COOKE
YOU SEND ME
Keen

▲ 1
🔟 1
85/250

Six years after he first recorded with top gospel group The Soul Stirrers, the soulful singer/ songwriter from Mississippi released his first secular single on Specialty. When his gospel fans objected,

the label let him go to Keen, whose third release (cut initially for Specialty) rocketed off like the recently launched Sputnik, leaving a handful of covers on the launching pad. Cooke, who heaped up a pile of transatlantic hits before his untimely death in 1964, is rightfully regarded as one of the most influential singers of the rock era.

UNITED KINGDOM
October 1957

CRICKETS
THAT'LL BE THE DAY
Vogue Coral

▲ 1
🔟 1
79/250

See US entry (August).

ELVIS PRESLEY
PARTY
RCA

▲ 2
🔟 9
148/250

This UK-only single was one of a record-breaking 13 tracks that Presley put into the UK chart in 1957. Not only did the Jessie Mae Robinson-written rock gem race up, but its frantic flip, 'Got A Lot O' Livin' To Do', also reached the Top 20.

PAT BOONE
REMEMBER YOU'RE
MINE/THERE'S A
GOLD MINE IN THE SKY
London American

▲ 5
🔟 6
—/250

See US entry (September).

JERRY LEE LEWIS
WHOLE LOTTA SHAKIN'
GOIN' ON
London American

▲ 8
🔟 1
—/250

See US entry (September).

UNITED STATES
November 1957

THURSTON HARRIS
LITTLE BITTY PRETTY
ONE
Aladdin

▲ 6
🔟 1•
—/250

Bobby Day wrote and originally recorded the song that put the ex-lead singer of The Lamplighters in the record books. Indianapolis-born Harris was

backed here by The Sharps, who subsequently added 'rebel yells' to Duane Eddy tracks and released some outstanding soul sides as The Rivingtons. Future singles by Harris & The Sharps (including a cover of Day's 'Over And Over') fell flat. This infectious number later charted for Frankie Lymon, Clyde McPhatter and The Jackson Five.

BOBBY HELMS
MY SPECIAL ANGEL
Decca

▲ 7
⑩ 1
—/250

Indiana-born Helms was the most popular new country artist of 1957. His first hit, 'Fraulein' (which numerous artists had earlier rejected), was a country No 1 and remarkably stayed on that chart for a year. This follow-up was even more successful and earned him a gold disc. The outstanding ballad was penned by Jimmy Duncan about his young daughter (and not a wife/girlfriend as might be imagined). In the UK, Malcolm Vaughan's cover outsold Helms' version, and in 1968 The Vogues brought the song back to the US Top 10.

PAT BOONE
APRIL LOVE/WHEN THE
SWALLOWS COME BACK
TO CAPISTRANO
DOT

▲ 1
⑩ 10
84/250

The title tune from the vocal superstar's second film was his tenth Top 10 single. It was coupled with an R&B song that was first recorded in the early 1940s by Celle Burke, and Boone's revival was in direct competition with Bobby Day's version.

BILL JUSTIS
RAUNCHY
Phillips

▲ 2
⑩ 1•
219/250

When Sun Records' head Sam Phillips told Justis that his band needed to get 'that raunchy sound', it inspired the jazz-based saxophonist to change the name of a rocking instrumental he had written, with the band's guitarist Sid Manker, from 'Backwoods' to 'Raunchy'. It became one of the best-known rock instrumentals of all time and also charted for Ernie Freeman and Billy Vaughn (and Ken Mackintosh in the UK). Success, however, was short lived for Justis, although his band can be heard backing many Sun artists of the era.

UNITED KINGDOM
November 1957

FRANKIE VAUGHAN
MAN ON FIRE/WANDERIN'
EYES
Philips

▲ 6
⑩ 3
—/250

Even though his two follow-ups to the No 1 'Garden Of Eden' failed to chart, the larger-than-life headliner returned to the heights with this double-sided smash. It coupled the title song from Bing Crosby's latest film with a distinctive cabaret-styled cover of Charlie Gracie's hit.

JIM DALE
BE MY GIRL
Parlophone

▲ 2
⑩ 1•
176/250

As *Billboard* noted that 'UK artists are getting more interested in recording US flops', Dale had his biggest hit with a George Martin-produced cover of an American flop by Johnny Madara. The one-time comedian and impressionist, who was born James Smith in Northamptonshire, aimed to be an all-round entertainer. His aim was true and the performer whose first film, *6.5 Special*, was released soon after this record, went on to appear in several successful British and American movies in the 1960s.

FRANKIE VAUGHAN & THE KAYE SISTERS
GOTTA HAVE SOMETHING IN THE BANK FRANK
Philips

▲ 8
⑩ 4
—/250

Teaming the popular British heart-throb with this attractive female vocal trio proved financially rewarding. Their first hit together was a lively reading of a Bob Hilliard-composed novelty that both Bob Jaxon and Steve Allen had failed to chart with Stateside.

LONNIE DONEGAN
MY DIXIE DARLING
Pye Nixa

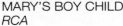

▲ 10
⑩ 7
—/250

The skiffle craze was all but over and only Donegan continued to register hits. His fourth Top 10 of the year was a fast-paced treatment of a song recorded in 1936 by country pioneers The Carter Family (although its roots go back even further).

HARRY BELAFONTE
MARY'S BOY CHILD
RCA

▲ 1
⑩ 3
5/250

In a record six weeks, this Christmas classic sold a million in the UK by the singer/actor who first found fame in the 1954 movie *Carmen Jones*. 'Mary's Boy Child', which had reached the US chart a year earlier, returned to the UK Top 10 12 months later. The performer, whose album *Calypso* (which RCA at first were not keen to record) was top for six months, was a major equal rights campaigner and has since worked steadfastly for UNICEF and the USA for Africa charity.

PAUL ANKA
I LOVE YOU BABY
Columbia

▲ 3
⑩ 2
184/250

Surprisingly, in the US Anka's bouncy self-penned follow-up to the chart-topping 'Diana' sold few copies. However, in the UK, where he was successfully touring, it was another big hit. Freddie & The Dreamers' 1964 revival also cracked the UK Top 20.

EVERLY BROTHERS
WAKE UP LITTLE SUSIE
London American

▲ 2
⑩ 2
165/250

See US entry (October).

JOHNNY OTIS SHOW
MA HE'S MAKING EYES AT ME
Capitol

▲ 2
⑩ 1•
126/250

One of America's bestselling R&B acts of the early 1950s made their UK chart debut with a supposedly live recording, which had failed to dent the US Top 100. The old vaudeville standard was belted out by the show's girl group, The Three Tons Of Joy, fronted by big-voiced Marie Adams. Soon afterwards, Otis (born John Veliotes) and his show revived another similarly themed standard, 'What Do You Want To Make Those Eyes At Me For', but it was a cover by Emile Ford that topped the UK hit parade.

UNITED STATES
December 1957

BUDDY HOLLY
PEGGY SUE
Coral

▲ 3
⑩ 1•
230/250

Unbelievably, this was the only Top 10 entry Holly had in the US under his own name. The legendary rock'n'roll song started out as 'Cindy Lou' (after two close relatives) and ended up being named after Cricket Jerry Allison's girlfriend and later wife. It was Allison's distinctive drumming, combined with Holly's unique hiccuping vocal style, that helped the track to stand out from the pack.

CHUCK BERRY
ROCK & ROLL MUSIC
Chess

▲ 9
⑩ 3
—/250

Records like this were the foundation stones that much of the 1960's music was built on. Sixties stalwarts The Beatles, Beach Boys, Dave Clark Five, Gerry & The Pacemakers and Status Quo were among the acts who recorded this gem from the pen of the duck-walking musical wizard.

DANNY & THE JUNIORS
AT THE HOP
ABC Paramount

▲ 1
⑩ 1•
56/250

One of the late 1950's best-loved dance tracks was first called 'Do The Bop'. However, when Dick Clark suggested that the title was dated, the youthful Philadelphia foursome rewrote it and released it initially on Singular. When Little Anthony & The Imperials cancelled an appearance on *Bandstand*, Clark substituted them with Danny & The Juniors, and the rest is history. Their similar follow-up, 'Rock And Roll Is Here To Stay', also reached the Top 20, although subsequent singles including 'Back To The Hop' were less rewarding.

JERRY LEE LEWIS
GREAT BALLS OF FIRE
Sun

▲ 2
⑩ 2
214/250

Apparently, label-mate Carl Perkins was first offered the song which gave this rock'n'roll legend his highest-placed hit. The frantic masterpiece was performed by 'The Killer' in the movie *Disc Jockey Jamboree* (aka *Jamboree*) and *Great Balls of Fire* was also the title of Jerry Lee's 1989 biopic.

JIMMIE RODGERS
KISSES SWEETER
THAN WINE
Roulette

▲ 8
⑩ 2
—/250

At a time when rock ruled on both sides of the Atlantic, the pop/folk performer had his first transatlantic hit with a sped-up revival of an old Leadbelly/Weavers song, to which he added hand claps and some exciting key changes.

UNITED KINGDOM
December 1957

MALCOLM VAUGHAN
MY SPECIAL ANGEL
HMV

▲ 3
⑩ 3
187/250

The actor/singer, who had initially felt his future lay in the zany comedy duo Earle & Vaughan, scored a fifth Top 20 single with his treatment of Bobby Helms' US crossover country hit.

ELVIS PRESLEY
SANTA BRING MY BABY
BACK TO ME
RCA

▲ 7
⑩ 10
—/250

Elvis' *Christmas Album*, which racked up record advance orders of over 200,000, was considered sacrilegious by many critics. Nevertheless, that did not stop it topping the US charts, or this stomping seasonal single taken from it from giving Presley his fifteenth UK Top 20 entry in 18 months.

PETULA CLARK
ALONE
Pye Nixa

▲ 8
⑩ 4
—/250

This 1940s child star scored her fifth Top 20 entry of the decade with a UK-aimed cover of an American hit by the Shepherd Sisters. Unlike most of her peers, the best was yet to come for Petula, who in 1966 was voted the US' Most Popular Female Singer. The perennial bill-topper has spent over 50 years in show business and sold more than 30 million records.

JACKIE WILSON
REET PETITE
Coral

▲ 6
⑩ 1
—/250

Not only did this uninhibited slab of rockin' R&B introduce Wilson to the hit parade, but it was also the first hit for composer Berry Gordy Jr, who later founded the Motown empire. Oddly, the single fared far better in the UK than in the Detroit native's homeland. Equally curious was the fact that 'Reet Petite' was his last UK Top 20 single until 1969 – by which time he had stored up 14 US Top 20 entries. Stranger still, the single returned to top the UK chart in 1986.

FRANK SINATRA
ALL THE WAY
Capitol

▲ 3
⑩ 5
152/250

Soon after his *Songs For Swingin' Lovers* became the first album to sell enough copies to enter the UK Top 20 singles chart, the decade's most popular LP artist clicked with this Oscar-winning Sammy Cahn composition. Both 'All The Way' and its equally in-demand B side, 'Chicago', came from Sinatra's film *The Joker Is Wild*.

WINIFRED ATWELL
LET'S HAVE A BALL
Decca

▲ 4
⑩ 10
—/250

The arrival of rock'n'roll and skiffle did not harm the sales of Atwell's latest Christmas singalong. Among the songs featured were recent hits 'Last Train To San Fernando', 'Bring A Little Water Sylvie' and 'Puttin' On The Style'.

JERRY LEE LEWIS
GREAT BALLS OF FIRE
London American

▲ 1
⑩ 2
92/250

See US entry.

UNITED STATES
January 1958

RICKY NELSON
STOOD UP/WAITIN' IN SCHOOL
Imperial

▲ 2
⑩ 3
233/250

Both sides of the photogenic singer's fourth Top 20 entry in 1957 were rockers. 'Stood Up' was composed by country performer Dub Dickinson, while later hit makers Johnny and Dorsey Burnette penned the equally in-demand flip.

BOBBY HELMS
JINGLE BELL ROCK
Decca

▲ 7
⑩ 2•
—/250

Helms ended his hottest year with one of the biggest-selling Christmas records of all time. In fact, the single sells well every December and is truly an essential part of Christmas in America. It was the last major hit for the country singer, who in 1957 had made a major mark on the US pop scene. In the UK, the song reached the Top 10 in 1959 by Max Bygraves.

SILHOUETTES
GET A JOB
Ember

▲ 2
⑩ 1•
235/250

In just three weeks this almost unintelligible doo-wop diamond sold a million copies. The Philadelphia foursome's (named after The Rays' recent hit) self-penned song was originally released as a B side on DJ Kae Williams' Junior label. Among many answer records was 'Got A Job' by The Miracles, who were headliners long after The Silhouettes had gotten other jobs. The first major rock revival act, Sha Na Na, named themselves after the vocal refrain on 'Get A Job'.

BILLY VAUGHN & HIS ORCHESTRA
SAIL ALONG SILVERY MOON/RAUNCHY
Dot

▲ 5
⑩ 3•
—/250

Arguably, Vaughan fronted the most successful orchestra of the early rock years. Their sweet sax-led update of Bing Crosby's 1937 bestseller sold over a million in both the US and Germany, and the B side, 'Raunchy', also reached the Top 40. Vaughan's album of the same name was one of 16 Top 20 entries for the orchestra between 1958 and 1965.

DIAMONDS
THE STROLL
Mercury

▲ 7
⑩ 2•
—/250

When *Bandstand* dancers started doing the stroll, the quartet, who were known for their cover versions, released an original stroll song penned by Clyde Otis and 14-year old Nancy Lee. Although not a cover, The Diamonds' interpretation was similar to Brook Benton's demo of 'The Stroll'. The group, whose follow-up was Buddy Holly's 'Words Of Love', returned unsuccessfully to the dance in 1959 with 'Walking The Stroll'.

McGUIRE SISTERS
SUGARTIME
Coral

▲ 7
⑩ 4•
—/250

At the time, no record received more radio play than this singalong single, which was heard 'in the morning, in the evening and at supper time' and had originally been recorded by composer Charlie Phillips with producer Norman Petty and session guitarist Buddy Holly. The trio split in 1968 after vanishing under a pile of sixties girl groups. The sisters, who have sung for five presidents, successfully reunited for live work in the mid-1980s.

BILLY & LILLIE
LA DEE DAH
Swan

▲ 10
⑩ 1•
—/250

Mentioning titles of hit singles in your song proved a good commercial move in the late 1950s. Frank Slay and Bob Crewe composed this cha-cha rocker that gave veteran R&B performer Billy Ford and teenager Lillie Bryant their biggest seller. It was helped on its way by the act's appearance on *Bandstand*, which was now watched by an average audience of 8.5 million every day. The duo (backed by Ford's entertaining band, The Thunderbirds) took another title-dropping tune, 'Lucky Ladybug', into the Top 20 in 1959.

UNITED KINGDOM
January 1958

JIMMIE RODGERS
KISSES SWEETER THAN WINE
Columbia

▲ 7
⑩ 1
—/250

See US entry (December 1957).

BUDDY HOLLY
PEGGY SUE
Coral

▲ 6
⑩ 1
—/250

See US entry (December 1957).

FRANKIE VAUGHAN
KISSES SWEETER THAN WINE
Philips

▲ 8
⑩ 5
—/250

It may have surprised some people when this Victor Mature lookalike was voted Top Screen Singing Star in the UK above both Elvis and Pat. However, it was no major shock when his recording of the folk favourite joined Jimmie Rodgers' US hit revival in the Top 10.

CRICKETS
OH, BOY!
Coral

▲ 3
⑩ 2
196/250

Norman Petty not only co-wrote this renowned rocker with singer Sonny West (who originally recorded it as 'Alla My Love'), but also produced the Crickets' record, which quickly reinstated the group from Texas in the transatlantic Top 20. Mud's 1975 re-recording headed the UK chart.

ELVIS PRESLEY
JAILHOUSE ROCK
RCA

▲ 1
⑩ 11
75/250

See US entry (October 1957).

MICHAEL HOLLIDAY
THE STORY OF MY LIFE
Columbia

▲ 1
⑩ 1
77/250

Michael Milne was the real name of the Bing Crosby soundalike from Liverpool, who gave celebrated composer Burt Bacharach his first UK No 1. The singer, whose stage debut had been at New York's prestigious Radio City Music Hall, was signed to Columbia by Norrie Paramor in 1955. After several minor hits, he reached the top with a tune that Marty Robbins took to No 1 in the US country chart. Amazingly, it was replaced at the top in the UK by another Bacharach song, 'Magic Moments' (Perry Como).

PAT BOONE
APRIL LOVE
London American

▲ 7
⑩ 7
—/250

See US entry (November 1957).

UNITED STATES
February 1958

ELVIS PRESLEY
DON'T/I BEG OF YOU
RCA

▲ 1
🔟 10
74/250

After a run of standout rock'n'roll songs, Presley recorded an emotion-wrenching, dirge-like, Leiber & Stoller-penned ballad, which more than a million fans ordered before hearing. If they were hoping for another rocker, then the Rose Marie McCoy-composed coupling fitted that bill.

ROYAL TEENS
SHORT SHORTS
ABC Paramount

▲ 4
🔟 1•
—/250

Among the many acts that enjoyed five minutes of fame in 1958 was a self-contained teenage quartet from New Jersey, who clicked with a simple but simply irresistible rocker about a new female fashion craze. The track was released on Power, and ABC paid a staggering $14000 for the rights. The group performed this mainly instrumental novelty in the film *Keep It Cool*. 'Short Shorts' inspired several similar singles, including their own 'Leotards' and 'Short Shorts Twist'. Member Bob Gaudio later joined The Four Seasons and penned many of that top quartet's hit songs.

PERRY COMO
CATCH A FALLING
STAR/MAGIC MOMENTS
RCA

▲ 3
🔟 19
225/250

This Grammy-winning single was the US's first authenticated Gold Record. In the UK, which had recently started airing Como's weekly TV show, both sides of the single made the Top 10 in their own right. In fact, the Burt Bacharach-penned 'Magic Moments' hit the top.

FRANKIE AVALON
DEDE DINAH
Chancellor

▲ 9
🔟 1
—/250

In 1954, 14-year-old Avalon (born Avallone) released two unsuccessful trumpet solos on RCA. Four year later, his third release on manager Bob Marcucci's fledgling label, Chancellor, gave him the first of 25 US chart entries. According to the legend, Avalon held his nose (as a joke) while singing the teen-targeted track. The resulting record started an avalanche of hits for the photogenic Philadelphian. Marcucci and partner Peter De Angelis penned the song about youthful Dinah ('She's a minor') which, despite its pop leanings, featured a standout rocking sax break.

PAUL ANKA
YOU ARE MY DESTINY
ABC Paramount

▲ 9
🔟 2
—/250

The youngest transatlantic chart regular of the decade notched up his first ballad hit with another of his top-class compositions. As the record climbed the transatlantic bestsellers, Anka was touring Australia alongside Buddy Holly and Jerry Lee Lewis.

CRESCENDOS
OH JULIE
Nasco

▲ 6
🔟 1•
—/250

As the boundaries between pop, R&B and country became more blurred, this white vocal group from Nashville also took 'Oh Julie' into the R&B Top 10, despite a cover by hit makers Otis Williams & The Charms. The recording, which boasted little in the way of backing instrumentation, featured lead singer George Lanius and session singer Janice Green. The group split after the hit and future Crescendos' singles were cut by completely different people.

UNITED KINGDOM
February 1958

DANNY & THE JUNIORS
AT THE HOP
HMV

▲ 3
⑩ 1•
192/250

See US entry (December 1957).

MARION RYAN
LOVE ME FOREVER
Pye Nixa

▲ 5
⑩ 1•
—/250

Few British female singers appeared as often on TV in the late 1950s as this vivacious vocalist from Middlesbrough, who was married to top impresario Harold Davison. The performer, who previously sang with the bands of Edmundo Ros and Ray Ellington, had her only chart entry with a contemporary pop ballad which reached the US

bestsellers by both Eydie Gorme and The Four Esquires. She retired shortly before her sons Paul & Barry Ryan started on a string of UK hits in the mid-1960s.

PERRY COMO
MAGIC MOMENTS
RCA

▲ 1
⑩ 6
14/250

See US entry.

PAUL ANKA
YOU ARE MY DESTINY
Columbia

▲ 6
⑩ 3
—/250

See US entry.

UNITED STATES
March 1958

FOUR PREPS
26 MILES (SANTA
CATALINA)
Capitol

▲ 5
⑩ 1
—/250

Four flops preceded the first of The Four Preps' six US Top 40 singles. The quartet, who were a teen-oriented version of The Four Freshman or Four Lads, scored with a song that members Glenn Larson and Bruce Belland had started writing in 1953. The ex-Hollywood High School students' biggest hit put the island of Santa Catalina (26 miles off the California coast) on the musical map.

CHUCK BERRY
SWEET LITTLE SIXTEEN
Chess

▲ 2
⑩ 4
242/250

The headliner of Alan Freed's *Big Beat Show* earned a gold disc for his tale about a typical teenage rock'n'roll fan. Several later hits owed something to this bona fide classic, including the Beach Boys' Top 10 debut, 'Surfin' USA'. Coincidentally, in the UK it was Berry's only Top 20 entry of the 1950s and it peaked at 16.

PAT BOONE
A WONDERFUL TIME UP
THERE/IT'S TOO SOON
TO KNOW
Dot

Boone's tenth successive double-sided hit coupled two songs first recorded ten years earlier. The A side was an uplifting Sister Rosetta Tharpe gospel gem which was coupled with a love ballad originally released by The Orioles.

CONNIE FRANCIS
WHO'S SORRY NOW
MGM

When her ninth single in a row failed, MGM decided to release only one more record by the New Jersey vocalist (born Concetta Francionero). Her father had long pestered Connie to cut this big 1923 hit, but she considered it 'too square'. The story goes that she cut it in the last four minutes of her (supposed) last MGM session. Be that as it may, it lay dormant for three months before Dick Clark kick-started it and launched the career of the first female superstar of the rock age.

CHAMPS
TEQUILA
Challenge

A group of session musicians fronted by Dave Burgess and Chuck Rio recorded 'Tequila' in ten minutes (at the end of a Jerry Wallace session), as the B side of 'Train To Nowhere'. Despite numerous covers, The Champs' version was a transatlantic hit and even earned them the Grammy for Best R&B Recording of 1958. The group, who named

themselves after label owner Gene Autry's wonder horse Champion, could not sustain their popularity, and several similarly themed tracks including 'Cantina', 'Sombrero' and 'Too Much Tequila' sold far fewer copies.

CHORDETTES
LOLLIPOP
Cadence

The first group ever to appear on *Bandstand* chalked up eight Top 20 singles before their beat-barbershop sound became too dated for the charts. The act, who started recording on Columbia in 1950, had their last transatlantic Top 10 hit with a cover of a bubblegum rocker that Ronald & Ruby (aka the song's composer Beverly Ross) released first.

JOHN ZACHERLE
DINNER WITH DRAC
(PART 1)
Cameo

Forty-year-old Zacherle played Roland, host of spook movie show *Shock Theater*, on Philadelphia's WCAU-TV. In that role, he often recited self-composed ghoulish limericks similar to those found on this most unusual million seller. The spine-chilling single, originally released as 'Igor', was banned by numerous radio stations and received no play in the UK. Under the gruesome lyric was an outstanding rock instrumental played by The Cool Ghouls (Cameo house band Dave Appell & The Applejacks featuring saxophonist Buddy Savett). Zacherle's follow-ups in a similar vein all died a death.

UNITED KINGDOM
March 1958

ELVIS PRESLEY
DON'T
RCA

▲ 2
⑩ 12
197/250

See US entry (February).

TOMMY STEELE
NAIROBI
Decca

▲ 3
⑩ 4
231/250

Only Elvis received more votes as World's Most Popular Music Personality in the *NME* poll than the singer who scored his seventh Top 20 entry in 18 months with a novelty item composed by Bob Merrill. Coincidentally, in 1992 Steele starred in Merrill's stage musical *Some Like It Hot*.

LITTLE RICHARD
GOOD GOLLY MISS MOLLY
London American

▲ 8
⑩ 4
—/250

Although it was recorded first, Richard's rendering of the uninhibited rock gem was released after The Valiants' version. Interestingly, the piano intro on the rock giant's last transatlantic Top 20 entry is almost identical to that on Jackie Brenston's 1951 R&B chart topper 'Rocket 88'.

PERRY COMO
CATCH A FALLING STAR
RCA

▲ 9
⑩ 7
—/250

See US entry (February).

MARVIN RAINWATER
WHOLE LOTTA WOMAN
MGM

▲ 1
⑩ 1•
74/250

A year after his only US pop Top 20 entry, 'Gonna Find Me A Bluebird', this country singer/ songwriter from Kansas (born Marvin Percy) took the relatively minor American rockabilly hit to the top of the UK charts. The performer, known as 'The Singing Cherokee', was yet another act who had appeared successfully on Arthur Godfrey's *Talent Scouts* show. Rainwater's only other UK bestseller, the follow-up 'I Dig You Baby', was recorded at Abbey Road studios during a British tour.

JACKIE DENNIS
LA DEE DAH
Decca

▲ 4
⑩ 1•
—/250

6.5 Special launched the short but spectacular career of this 15-year-old singer from Edinburgh. Two weeks after Jackie's TV debut, his cover of Billy & Lillie's US hit was in the Top 20 and he was being filmed for the *6.5 Special* movie. Just weeks later the wee lad was whisked off to America for the *Perry Como Show* (Como called him 'Britain's Ricky Nelson') and plans for his biopic were announced! However, the kilt-clad lad's next singles stiffed and his fall was as meteoric as his rise.

CRICKETS
MAYBE BABY
Coral

▲ 4
⑩ 3
—/250

Lead singer Buddy Holly composed this outstanding rocker, which joined three others by the act in the UK Top 20 as The Crickets toured the country. Their tour was one of the highlights of the late 1950s, and inspired many would-be British rock stars to form groups.

UNITED STATES
April 1958

LAURIE LONDON
HE'S GOT THE WHOLE
WORLD (IN HIS HANDS)
Capitol

▲ 2
⑩ 1•
204/250

London was discovered at the 1957 Radio Show exhibition, when he volunteered to sing on the BBC stand. His debut single, which narrowly missed the UK Top 10, earned the 13-year-old Londoner a US gold disc. According to Capitol, London's revival of this famous spiritual was their fastest seller since Tennessee Ernie Ford's 'Sixteen Tons'. It looked as if the youngster had the world in his hands, but future releases fell by the wayside, a planned US tour was cancelled and soon afterwards the talented teenager returned to school.

JERRY LEE LEWIS
BREATHLESS
Sun

▲ 9
⑩ 3•
—/250

Otis Blackwell, composer of the standout showman's previous smash, 'Great Balls Of Fire', also penned the rock'n'roll jewel that gave the controversial entertainer his third transatlantic Top 10 entry in six months. Soon afterwards, Lewis' career was badly harmed when it was revealed that he had married a 13-year-old second cousin. This unique performer, who later moved successfully into the country field, still packs houses around the world.

RICKY NELSON
BELIEVE WHAT YOU
SAY/MY BUCKET'S GOT
A HOLE IN IT
Imperial

▲ 4
⑩ 4
—/250

With his regular team of leading rock musicians, including guitarist James Burton, behind him, the TV star-cum-teen idol clicked with another double-sided rocker. The Burnette brothers (who

composed 'Waitin' In School') penned the top deck, while the flip covered Sonny Burgess' revival of an old Hank Williams classic.

PLATTERS
TWILIGHT TIME
Mercury

▲ 1
⑩ 5
120/250

As they were working in Europe when their vocal version of the old Three Suns instrumental was released, the internationally famous quintet were filmed singing it in Rome. This early 'video' helped it go all the way to No 1. Incidentally, leader Tony Williams sang the wrong melody, but producer/composer/manager Buck Ram liked it and left it.

MONOTONES
BOOK OF LOVE
Argo

▲ 6
⑩ 1•
—/250

The famous Pepsodent toothpaste commercial, 'You'll wonder where the yellow went...', supposedly inspired the teenage New Jersey sextet to write 'The Book Of Love'. Also, the story goes that the sound of kids playing basketball against their rehearsal studio wall gave them the idea of including that distinctive bass drum thud on the track. When the single attracted attention, Chess/Argo picked up the rights from Mascot Records. Subsequent singles, including 'Reading The Book Of Love' and 'Book Of Dance', failed to make the grade.

DAVID SEVILLE
WITCH DOCTOR
Liberty

▲ 1
⑩ 1•
90/250

Veteran songwriter/actor/singer and musician Seville earlier tasted success as a composer under his real name, Ross Bagdasarian, and previously reached the transatlantic charts as Alfi and Harry ('The Trouble With Harry'). However, Seville's major contribution to music was the introduction of sped-up vocals. The humorous novelty 'Witch Doctor' shot to the top of the US bestsellers in just three weeks and started a rush of similar sped-up singles. Although he never achieved similar sales under his own name, Seville sold millions of singles and albums as The Chipmunks.

ELVIS PRESLEY
WEAR MY RING AROUND YOUR NECK
RCA

▲ 2
⑩ 11
223/250

Recorded on his last session before joining the army, this all-out rocker and its equally outstanding B side, 'Doncha' Think It's Time',

notched up a million advance orders as Presley did his basic training at Fort Hood, Texas.

EVERLY BROTHERS
ALL I HAVE TO DO IS DREAM
Cadence

▲ 1
⑩ 3
71/250

This timeless recording headed the US pop, country and R&B charts and took Don and Phil to the top in the UK for the first time. The ballad, which supposedly was written in 15 minutes, was later a hit for several other acts including Phil Everly and Cliff Richard, whose duet reached the UK Top 20 in 1994.

UNITED KINGDOM
April 1958

EDDIE CALVERT
MANDY
Columbia

▲ 9
⑩ 4•
—/250

'La Panse' was the original Italian title of the infectious instrumental that brought the UK's best-known trumpeter back after a two-year chart absence. Nevertheless, Calvert's dated style of music could not survive the rise of rock, as was made clear when the trumpeter toured the UK tour with up-and-coming rock'n'roller Cliff Richard. Calvert relocated to South Africa in 1968, where he died ten years later.

TED HEATH & HIS MUSIC
SWINGIN' SHEPHERD BLUES
Decca

▲ 3
⑩ 4•
228/250

When the 20 year touring ban between the US and UK was lifted, Ted Heath & His Music were the first artists the Americans wanted. Their US shows sold out and *Billboard* said 'They have no rivals in the commercial dance band field'. Nevertheless, the

band's treatment of Canadian Moe Koffman's contagious sax instrumental was their last UK Top 10 entry – Heath's classy big band swing sound was no longer in demand by singles buyers.

CHAMPS
TEQUILA
London American

▲ 5
⑩ 1•
—/250

See US entry (March).

CONNIE FRANCIS
WHO'S SORRY NOW
MGM

▲ 1
⑩ 1
16/250

See US entry (March).

PAT BOONE
A WONDERFUL TIME UP THERE
London American

▲ 2
⑩ 9
146/250

See US entry (March).

PAT BOONE
IT'S TOO SOON TO KNOW
London American

▲ 7
⑩ 8
—/250

See US Entry (March).

JERRY LEE LEWIS
BREATHLESS
London American

▲ 8
⑩ 3
—/250

See US entry.

UNITED STATES
May 1958

DON GIBSON
OH LONESOME ME/
I CAN'T STOP LOVIN' YOU
RCA

▲ 7
⑩ 1•
—/250

These songs earned singer/songwriter Gibson a small fortune. The much recorded A side, which was written as 'Ole Lonesome Me' (a typing error changed it!), led the country lists for two months. The flip, which subsequently topped the transatlantic bestsellers by Ray Charles, has been recorded by over 700 artists! It was the first of numerous country hits for the North Carolina native, who had been recording since 1949. Many people consider it to be the single that introduced the new 'Nashville Sound' to the pop chart.

DEAN MARTIN
RETURN TO ME
Capitol

▲ 4
⑩ 3
—/250

After a couple of relatively quiet sales years, Dino returned to the transatlantic Top 10 with a multi-lingual song co-written by veteran Carmen Lombardo, who had sung with his brother Guy's band since the 1920s.

NAT 'KING' COLE
LOOKING BACK/DO I
LIKE IT
Capitol

▲ 5
⑩ 9
—/250

One of the century's finest vocalists last charted in the decade with a Brook Benton-penned ballad. Cole, who sold as many albums as singles, broke down numerous barriers for black performers during a long career. His records continued to sell after his death in 1965, and he was awarded a posthumous Lifetime Achievement Grammy in 1990. Cole reached the US Top 20 singles in 1991, and the legendary entertainer's albums were still charting in the mid-1990s – 50 years after his first No 1 LP!

CHUCK BERRY
JOHNNY B. GOODE
Chess

▲ 9
⑩ 5
—/250

Berry aimed 'to write lyrics as good as Louis Jordan' – he achieved this and much more. Acts from almost every musical genre have recorded his songs. For example, this gem was later cut by such diverse artists as Elvis, The Sex Pistols, Grateful Dead, Beatles, Tom Jones, Shadows, Jimi Hendrix, Buck Owens, Meat Loaf and Jive Bunny! Berry, who was the biggest influence on the 1960s Beat Boom, was rightly among the first acts inducted into the Rock and Roll Hall of Fame.

PAT BOONE
SUGAR MOON/CHERIE
I LOVE YOU
Dot

▲10
⑩12
—/250

Only Elvis could better Boone's late-1950's track record. He strung together a staggering run of hit singles, LPs and EPs, hosted a TV series, wrote a top-selling book (*Twixt Twelve and Twenty*) and was idolized by millions. Boone, whose last 1950's Top 10 entry revived a bestseller from 1910, retained his popularity in the early 1960s when he moved into country and then Christian music. Incidentally, in 1977 Pat's daughter Debbie followed in her father's and grandfather's (Red Foley) footsteps by having a No 1 single.

UNITED KINGDOM
May 1958

CHORDETTES
LOLLIPOP
London American

▲ 6
⑩ 2•
—/250

See US entry (March).

ELVIS PRESLEY
WEAR MY RING AROUND
YOUR NECK
RCA

▲ 3
⑩ 13
—/250

See US entry (April).

ELIAS & HIS ZIGZAG JIVE FLUTES
TOM HARK
Columbia

▲ 2
⑩ 1•
157/250

The UK's most unlikely hit makers of the decade were a ten piece South African kwela outfit, led by Elias Lerole, which included seven flute players. The track, which was recorded (supposedly 'live') after a game of dice on the streets of Johannesburg) in October 1956, found fame after being used as the theme for the TV series *The Killing Stones*. 'Tom Hark' was slang for the roving police van that picked up dice players and their musical style, 'kwela', was the word used by police to hurry along the people they bundled into them!

LONNIE DONEGAN
GRAND COOLIE DAM
Pye Nixa

▲ 6
⑩ 8
—/250

Long before Bob Dylan praised Woody Guthrie's work, Donegan frequently turned the folk legend's songs into hits. The latest given his no-holds-barred skiffle treatment honoured one of the great American hydroelectric achievements. The traditional tune was also used for the country classic 'Wabash Cannonball'.

MUDLARKS
LOLLIPOP
Columbia

▲ 2
⑩ 1
208/250

Mary, Fred and Jeff Mudd were a clean-cut family act from Bedford, whom *NME* readers voted the UK's Top Vocal Group in both 1958 and 1959. The trio, who were discovered by leading DJ David Jacobs, were regulars on TV's *6.5 Special*. They first tasted success with their second single, which in the UK licked the US hit version recorded by The Chordettes.

VIC DAMONE
ON THE STREET WHERE YOU LIVE
Philips

▲ 1
⑩ 1•
82/250

See US entry (June 1956).

PERRY COMO
KEWPIE DOLL
RCA

▲ 9
⑩ 8
—/250

Despite opposition from UK heart-throb Frankie Vaughan, the 46-year-old ex-big-band vocalist had the bestselling version of Tepper & Bennett's tale of teen romance at the fair.

MAX BYGRAVES
YOU NEED HANDS/
TULIPS FROM
AMSTERDAM
Decca

▲ 3
⑩ 5
110/250

Coupling a self-composed 'show biz' opus with a German ditty about Holland gave Bygraves one of his hits. In the US, Eydie Gorme covered both 'Hands' and the follow-up, 'Gotta Have Rain'. Pat Boone's TV producer wrongly prophesied 'Max could be bigger in the US than any other British star'. Nevertheless, he had a string of successful *Singalong* albums in the 1970s, received the OBE in 1982 and was still charting in the 1990s.

UNITED STATES
June 1958

FOUR PREPS
BIG MAN
Capitol

Arranger Lincoln Mayorga's distinctive piano playing helped propel this self-composed pop pearl into the transatlantic Top 10. In the 1960s, the quartet introduced a pop parody style that British group The Barron Knights later borrowed successfully. Members Glenn Larson and Bruce Belland subsequently became top TV executives, while Ed Cobb wrote and produced many hits. Incidentally, two of Belland's daughters front the 1990s band Voice Of The Beehive.

SHEB WOOLEY
THE PURPLE PEOPLE EATER
MGM

Hot on the heels of 'Witch Doctor' came another novelty featuring a sped-up vocal, and yet again the performer was a relative veteran with previous success as a composer and actor. Earlier in the decade Oklahoma-born Wooley, the first singer to record in Nashville (1945), had appeared in the hit films *High Noon* and *Giant* and played Pete Nolan in the popular TV western series *Rawhide*. This single rocketed to the top in two weeks and inspired many answer records, including 'The Witch Doctor Meets The Purple People Eater'.

JIMMIE RODGERS
SECRETLY
Roulette

The one-time Arthur Godfrey *Talent Scouts* winner continued his run of US hits with this bouncy teen-targeted ballad, which was coupled with another popular track, 'Make Me A Miracle'. In 1978, Rodgers' re-recording of 'Secretly' reached the country chart.

BOBBY FREEMAN
DO YOU WANT TO DANCE
Josie

As the music press screamed that 'rock'n'roll is going out of fashion' and Alan Freed, after a much publicized riot in Boston, announced that his shows would no longer feature just rock'n'roll artists, this San Francisco teenager clicked with a self-penned R&B/rock classic. The ex-doo-wop singer sang and played keyboard on the track (the only other musician being a drummer), which after a slow start sold over a million. Freeman released several other standout singles before 'C'Mon And Swim' briefly returned him to the heights in 1964.

COASTERS
YAKETY YAK
Atco

For the second year running, The Coasters picked up the *Cash Box* award for Top R&B Vocal Group and this humorous parent-put-down was voted Top R&B Single, as was their 'Searchin'' in 1957. The record included two new members, Cornel Gunter (an original Platter) and Will 'Dub' Jones from The Cadets.

JAN & ARNIE
JENNIE LEE
Arwin

Californians Jan Berry and Arnie Ginsburg were inspired to write this lyrically unfathomable rocker after watching a stripper called Jennie 'The Bazoom Girl' Lee. They recorded it with some friends, including Dean Torrence, in Jan's garage (with Arnie playing a cardboard-box drum!) and it was released on Doris Day's Arwin label. Later Torrence teamed with Berry to form Jan & Dean, who became one of the most successful duos of all time.

JODY REYNOLDS
ENDLESS SLEEP
Demon

▲ 5
⑩ 1•
—/250

Stopping your lover from committing suicide may not be the most romantic story for a song, but it helped this rockabilly singer/songwriter from Arizona achieve his only hit. Distinctive session guitarist Al Casey can be clearly heard on the track, which took just 20 minutes to record. The single, which has been called the first 'swamp rock' hit, heralded a string of successful death ditties. Reynold's subsequent releases, including remakes of his million seller, failed to breathe life back into the recording career of the one-time mortician's assistant.

UNITED KINGDOM
June 1958

MICHAEL HOLLIDAY
STAIRWAY OF LOVE
Columbia

▲ 3
⑩ 2
236/250

With the aim of repeating the success of his earlier No 1, 'The Story Of My Life', the easy-on-the-ear vocalist covered a Marty Robbins record again. This time it was a bouncy little number written by regular hit makers Tepper & Bennett. Holliday, who went on to become the first Liverpool act to top the UK chart in the 1960s, sadly committed suicide in 1963.

DON LANG &
HIS FRANTIC FIVE
WITCH DOCTOR
HMV

▲ 5
⑩ 1•
—/250

6.5 Special's most frequently seen act were fronted by a Yorkshireman born Gordon Langhorn, who had played in various bands including those of Vic Lewis and Ken Mackintosh (he co-wrote the latter's Top 10 entry, 'The Creep'). Although basically a jazz trombonist and scat vocalist, Lang covered many US rock hits, and his lively interpretation of David Seville's US chart topper, complete with sped-up vocals, outsold the original in the UK. Interestingly, The Beatles later enlisted him to play on their *White Album*.

FRANKIE VAUGHAN
KEWPIE DOLL
Philips

▲ 10
⑩ 6
—/250

Such was Vaughan's popularity that his treatment of this cute up-tempo Tepper & Bennett tune sold as well as the original by TV's most successful show host, Perry Como.

EVERLY BROTHERS
ALL I HAVE TO DO IS
DREAM/CLAUDETTE
London American

▲ 1
⑩ 3
12/250

See US entry (April).

TV CAST
ARMY GAME
HMV

▲ 5
⑩ 1•
—/250

The cast of the popular TV comedy show *The Army Game* reached the Top 10 with the only single they released. The track, which was a humorous vocal version of their show's signature tune, featured actors Alfie Bass, Michael Medwin, Leslie Fyson and Bernard Bresslaw. The latter also had a hit in his own right a couple of months later with 'Mad Passionate Love'.

MUDLARKS
BOOK OF LOVE
Columbia

▲ 8
⑩ 2•
—/250

Seven years after these siblings first performed as The Mudd Trio, they chalked up two successive UK Top 10 entries with Norrie Paramor-produced covers of US hits. Fronted by hiccuping vocalist Mary Mudd, the lively vocal group left The Monotones' original recording of 'Book Of Love' at the starting post in the UK. It was, however, the last bestseller for the chirpy performers.

FOUR PREPS
BIG MAN
Capitol

▲ 2
⑩ 1•
162/250

See US entry.

UNITED STATES
July 1958

ELVIS PRESLEY
HARD HEADED WOMAN
RCA

▲ 1
⑩ 12
137/250

Private Presley clocked up another million seller with a hard-hitting rocker taken from his fourth film, *King Creole*. For the second time in the decade, RCA kept their No 1 act (previously Eddie Fisher) red hot even though he was in the services.

PEREZ PRADO & HIS ORCHESTRA
PATRICIA
RCA

▲ 2
⑩ 2•
188/250

Three years after his 'Cherry Pink' had helped make the mambo internationally famous, Prado's self-penned 'Patricia' spread the popularity of the cha cha. A vocal treatment by label-mate Ray Peterson created little interest, but Prado's 1962 twist re-recording dented the US chart. Interestingly, the follow-up, 'Guaglione', which was only a mid-table success in 1958, sold half a million copies in the UK in 1995!

BOBBY DARIN
SPLISH SPLASH
Atco

▲ 3
⑩ 1
—/250

After leaving Decca, this New York singer/songwriter (born Robert Walden Cassotto) signed a three-single deal with Atco. When the first two releases went nowhere, he released 'Early In The Morning' as The Ding Dongs on Brunswick. His luck then changed. The title-dropping novelty rocker 'Splish Splash' became a smash and 'Early In The Morning' (now released under the name of The Rinky Dinks on Atco) joined it in the Top 40. Interestingly, Darin penned 'Splish Splash' (one of the first stereo singles) with DJ Murray The K's mother.

RICKY NELSON
POOR LITTLE FOOL
Imperial

▲ 1
⑩ 5
110/250

Until this single it looked as if Nelson was a US-only phenomenon. His first transatlantic Top 10 entry was penned by Sharon Sheeley (later Eddie Cochran's fiancée). He headed the hit parade 23 years after father Ozzie had achieved a US No 1 and 22 years before his sons Gunnar and Matthew topped the chart!

DUANE EDDY
REBEL-'ROUSER
Jamie

▲ 6
⑩ 1
—/250

Thanks to his revolutionary 'twangy' guitar sound (achieved by playing the bass strings of his Gretsch through an echo chamber), New York-born and Arizona-based Eddy had a long string of transatlantic hits. Like the majority of his singles, he composed this track with producer Lee Hazlewood. The instrumental, which owed something to 'When The Saints Go Marching In', also featured noted sax player Gil Bernal and Thurston Harris' backing vocalists The Sharps (later Rivingtons), who provided the hand claps and rebel yells.

KALIN TWINS
WHEN
Decca

| ▲ 5 |
| ⑩ 1• |
| —/250 |

Composer Paul Evans initially intended to launch his own recording career with 'When'. However, he wasn't too disappointed when New Yorkers Herb and Hal Kalin's version (which started out as the B side) bolted up the bestsellers. In the UK, the single reached No 1 and a tour (with support acts Cliff Richard and Eddie Calvert) was hurriedly

arranged. Nevertheless, British record buyers soon forgot the twins, whose follow-up, 'Forget Me Not', was their only other US Top 20 entry. 'When' was also a big UK hit in 1977 by Showaddywaddy.

JACK SCOTT
MY TRUE LOVE/LEROY
Carlton

| ▲ 3 |
| ⑩ 1 |
| —/250 |

When Joe Carlton left ABC-Paramount to form Carlton Records, he brought Canadian rockabilly singer/songwriter Scott (born Jack Scafone), and his distinctive backing vocal group The Chantones, with him. At first the A side was 'Leroy', a stomper written about a friend, Bill 'Leroy' Johnson (which Scott first recorded as 'Greaseball'). However, the romantic ballad on the flip soon took over and pushed the single over the million sales mark. In the UK, after sleeping for five months, 'My True Love' also cracked the Top 10.

UNITED KINGDOM
July 1958

PLATTERS
TWILIGHT TIME
Mercury

| ▲ 3 |
| ⑩ 3 |
| 217/250 |

See US entry (April).

PAT BOONE
SUGAR MOON
London American

| ▲ 6 |
| ⑩ 10 |
| —/250 |

See US entry (May).

BUDDY HOLLY
RAVE ON
Coral

| ▲ 5 |
| ⑩ 2 |
| —/250 |

After composer Sonny West's original recording ran aground, his producer and co-writer, Norman Petty, cut this epic rock song with his top act and the result kept Holly red hot in the UK.

ELVIS PRESLEY
HARD HEADED WOMAN
RCA

| ▲ 2 |
| ⑩ 14 |
| 212/250 |

See US entry.

MARTY WILDE
ENDLESS SLEEP
Philips

| ▲ 4 |
| ⑩ 1 |
| 225/250 |

Although he had built up a strong following through live shows and appearances on such TV shows as *6.5 Special*, the UK's most popular teen idol since Tommy Steele did not crack the chart with his first three singles. Londoner Wilde (born Reginald Smith), who, like Steele, was managed by Larry Parnes, finally broke through with a moody interpretation of Jody Reynolds' suicide saga.

UNITED STATES
August 1958

JOHNNY OTIS SHOW
WILLIE AND THE
HAND JIVE
Capitol

▲ 9
⑩ 1•
—/250

Six months after their huge UK-only smash, 'Ma, He's Making Eyes At Me', this celebrated Californian R&B band had its only major US pop hit with a self-penned single inspired by a digital dance craze that started in UK coffee bars. Among the act's subsequently overlooked singles were the similar 'Willie Did The Cha Cha' and 'Hand Jive One More Time'.

PEGGY LEE
FEVER
Capitol

▲ 8
⑩ 2•
—/250

Her finger-snapping treatment (arranged by ex-husband Dave Barbour) of Little Willie John's 1956 R&B No 1 took the acclaimed vocalist into the transatlantic Top 10. The song returned to the charts in 1993 by Madonna – who coincidentally was born as Lee's recording climbed the US Top 20. Lee, fondly remembered for her work in Disney's *The Lady And The Tramp*, was dogged by bad health in later years.

DOMENICO MODUGNO
NEL BLU DIPINTO DI BLU
(VOLARE)
Decca

▲ 1
⑩ 1•
64/250

A song about a man painting himself blue and soaring through the air hardly sounds like the formula for a hit, but that's what Modugno's multi-million seller was about. Despite over a dozen covers, his original Italian-language recording jetted to the top in the US. The song, which had won the prestigious San Remo Festival in Italy, grabbed three trophies at the first Grammy awards, including Record of the Year and Song of the Year. None of Modugno's subsequent US

singles (including three more San Remo winners) flew chartwards.

JIMMY CLANTON
JUST A DREAM
Ace

▲ 4
⑩ 1
—/250

For a change, America's latest teen pin-up was not a photogenic Philadelphian but a good-looking lad from Louisiana. Clanton originally cut this self-penned teen ballad with his band, The Rockets, but Ace re-recorded it using top New Orleans R&B session men. Initially it sold few copies; however, an appearance on *Bandstand* kick-started it and the single rocketed up the pop and R&B charts. It was the first of three Top 10 entries for the singer, who starred in many late 1950s package shows.

ELEGANTS
LITTLE STAR
Apt

▲ 1
⑩ 1•
116/250

Five of the acts that headed the US chart in 1958 never managed to acheive another Top 40 entry. This white doo-wop quintet from New York, fronted by Vito Picone, were among that number. The Elegants' self-composed debut single, which was based on 'Twinkle Twinkle Little Star', sold over two million copies. Although The Elegants never became big stars, their sole smash influenced many later vocal groups.

EVERLY BROTHERS
BIRD DOG
Cadence

▲ 2
⑩ 4
186/250

No group in the 1950s stockpiled as many transatlantic Top 10 hits as the distinctive duo, who earned their fourth gold disc in just over a year with this unusual Boudleaux Bryant rocker. The flip, 'Devoted To You', also graced the Top 20.

PONI-TAILS
BORN TOO LATE
ABC Paramount

▲ 7
⑩ 1•
—/250

Eighteen months after Joy Layne successfully covered their debut disc, 'Your Wild Heart', this fresh-faced Ohio trio tasted fleeting transatlantic fame with a teen-angst ballad, which followed the group's similarly themed flop, 'It's Just My Luck To Be Fifteen'. Amazingly, when they arrived in the UK for appearances on BBC TV's *Drumbeat*, Toni, Laverne and Patti were met at the airport by the entire cast performing 'Born Too Late'! On the subject of birth, Michael Jackson was born as this girl group gem climbed the chart.

UNITED KINGDOM
August 1958

KALIN TWINS
WHEN
Brunswick

▲ 1
⑩ 1•
36/250

See US entry (July).

DEAN MARTIN
RETURN TO ME
Capitol

▲ 2
⑩ 8
124/250

See US entry (May).

PEREZ PRADO & HIS ORCHESTRA
PATRICIA
RCA

▲ 8
⑩ 2
—/250

See US entry (July).

CHARLIE DRAKE
SPLISH SPLASH
Parlophone

▲ 7
⑩ 1•
—/250

Popular slapstick comedian Drake surprised many people when he proved that he could rock'n'roll as well, if not better, than the majority of British performers. The London entertainer's rousing rendition of 'Splish Splash' outsold composer Bobby Darin's original version, and his later George Martin-produced covers of 'Sea Cruise' and 'Itchy Twitchy Feeling' also merited attention. In 1962 Drake's self-penned novelty song 'My Boomerang Won't Come Back' gave him his only transatlantic Top 40 hit.

CONNIE FRANCIS
CAROLINA MOON/
STUPID CUPID
MGM

▲ 1
⑩ 2
25/250

For the second time in five months, Francis headed the UK charts with a song written before she was born. In her homeland, it was the Neil Sedaka-penned B side (written for the Shepherd Sisters) that reached the Top 20.

PEGGY LEE
FEVER
Capitol

▲ 5
⑩ 2•
—/250

See US entry.

UNITED STATES
September 1958

FRANKIE AVALON
GINGER BREAD
Chancellor

▲ 9
⑩ 2
—/250

Philadelphia's leading teen idol of the late 1950s clicked with a cute teen beat novelty about a girl who was 'Kinda naughty, but naughty and nice'. It was composed by later chart regulars Clint Ballard and Hank Hunter.

JIMMIE RODGERS
ARE YOU REALLY MINE
Roulette

▲ 10
⑩ 4•
—/250

Cash Box magazine's Most Promising Male Singer of 1958 clocked up his fourth Top 10 entry in a year with a song penned by producers Hugo (Peretti) and Luigi (Creatore), and top composer Al Hoffman. As the record climbed, Rodgers was the subject of TV's *This is Your Life*, and soon afterwards hosted his own NBC TV series.

BOBBY DAY
ROCK-IN' ROBIN/OVER AND OVER
Class

▲ 2
⑩ 1•
200/250

In 1957, this singer/songwriter from Texas (born Robert Byrd) wrote the Top 20 hits 'Little Bitty Pretty One' (Thurston Harris & The Sharps) and 'Buzz Buzz Buzz' (by his group The Hollywood Flames). Producer Leon Rene penned the A side of Day's biggest solo success and top saxophonist Plas Johnson played the distinctive piccolo solo. 'Rock-In' Robin' reached No 2 again in 1972 by Michael Jackson, and the flip (which Thurston Harris also covered) was taken to No 1 in 1965 by The Dave Clarke Five.

OLYMPICS
WESTERN MOVIES
Demon

▲ 8
⑩ 1•
—/250

Western movies were the most popular shows on US TV in 1958, and The Olympics name dropped many of them (although some were hard to decipher) on this superior single penned by their prolific producers Fred Smith and Cliff Goldsmith. The Coasters-influenced cut, which came complete with gunshot sounds, was recorded in Ted Brinson's garage studio, where The Penguins had earlier cut 'Earth Angel'. 'Western Movies' also shot up the UK charts and earned The Olympics a gold disc. They subsequently released many other outstanding, if less successful, singles.

TOMMY EDWARDS
IT'S ALL IN THE GAME
MGM

▲ 1
⑩ 1•
51/250

Future vice-president Charles Gates Dawes composed this much recorded song (as 'Melody In A Major') in 1912, and Carl Sigman added the lyric. In 1951 Edwards' original version reached the Top 20, and seven years later his re-recording, which utilized a beat-ballad backing, topped the transatlantic charts. Among the Virginia-born vocalist's subsequent hits were updates of his earlier tracks 'Please Mr Sun' and 'Morning Side Of The Mountain'. Interestingly, the B side 'Please Love Me Forever' took Cathy Jean & The Roommates into the Top 20 in 1961.

LITTLE ANTHONY & THE IMPERIALS
TEARS ON MY PILLOW
End

▲ 4
⑩ 1
—/250

Richard Barrett, producer of Frankie Lymon & The Teenagers' smashes, was also behind this similar-sounding vocal team. The New York quintet, who first recorded as The Chesters, were fronted by high tenor Anthony Gourdine (tagged Little Anthony by Alan Freed). The lost-love ballad, the backing vocals of which were based on The Penguins' 'Earth Angel', started out as the B side. The talented vocal group strung together an impressive run of hits in the mid-1960s, although a 1966 re-remake of 'Tears' sold few. In UK, the song finally charted in 1990 by Kylie Minogue.

ROBIN LUKE
SUSIE DARLIN'
DOT

▲ 5
⑩ 1•
—/250

Billboard called 1958 'the year that one-hit acts dominated the disc landscape'. One of those artists was Hawaii-based Luke, whose sole hit topped the Hawaiian chart (then not a US state) before Dot picked it up from Bertram International. They re-cut the track but decided to release Luke's original home-recorded rendition. The Los Angles-born 16-year-old had written this haunting opus for his eight-year-old sister Susie, and in 1962 a revival by Tommy Rose returned it to the transatlantic Top 40.

EDDIE COCHRAN
SUMMERTIME BLUES
Liberty

▲ 8
⑩ 1•
—/250

Despite radio's backlash against basic rock'n'roll, there was still room on the transatlantic Top 20 for the track which has gone down in history as one the genre's greatest recordings. Minnesota-born singer/songwriter and guitarist Cochran was another performer whose few chart entries belie his influence and importance. He was especially popular in the UK, where this ground-breaking release returned to the Top 40 in 1968 – the year that hard rock band Blue Cheer took Cochran's composition back into the US Top 20.

ROGER WILLIAMS
NEAR YOU
Kapp

▲ 10
⑩ 2
—/250

Three years after his last bestseller, 'Autumn Leaves', the popular pianist returned with an update of a song that composer Francis Craig had topped the chart with in 1947 for 12 weeks. It was also the title track of Williams' eighth Top 20 LP. In total, the award-winning musician charted an enviable 38 albums – none of which, curiously, graced the UK bestsellers.

UNITED KINGDOM
September 1958

DEAN MARTIN
VOLARE
Capitol

▲ 2
⑩ 9
158/250

One of the year's top songs also reached the transatlantic charts by the amiable Italian American, who always sounded as if he had stopped off at a bar *en route* to the studio or show. Unlike many of his contemporaries, Martin's magic continued to work throughout the 1960s, when the Vegas veteran appeared in several movies, hosted a TV series and added many more hits to his enviable collection.

RICKY NELSON
POOR LITTLE FOOL
London American

▲ 4
⑩ 1
238/250

See US entry (July).

DOMENICO MODUGNO
VOLARE
Oriole

▲ 10
⑩ 1•
—/250

See US entry (August).

BERNARD BRESSLAW
MAD PASSIONATE LOVE
HMV

Soon after the theme from TV's *The Army Game* exited the UK chart, Bresslaw, who played the gormless 'Popeye' in the show, marched in with a hit of his own. The tall Londoner performed this Dick Sherman-penned novelty and its noted B side, 'You Need Feet', in character. It was the first hit for one of the most successful composers of the 1960s and the last for the popular comedy actor.

EVERLY BROTHERS
BIRD DOG
London American

See US Entry (August).

UNITED STATES
October 1958

TOMMY DORSEY ORCHESTRA
TEA FOR TWO CHA CHA
Decca

In their earlier days, the band recorded such influential tracks as 'Boogie Woogie' (1938) and 'Yes Indeed' (1941), and topped the first official US chart in 1940 with 'I'll Never Smile Again' (featuring their vocalist Frank Sinatra). Two years after Dorsey's death, his band, under the leadership of fellow trombonist Warren Covington, had a million seller with a cha-cha revival of this well-known song from the 1925 musical *No, No, Nanette*. Almost instantly, scores of other acts climbed on to the cha-cha bandwagon, bringing it to a premature halt.

EARL GRANT
THE END
Decca

This distinctive vocalist/organist from Oklahoma started his singles chart career with 'The End' – a noteworthy love ballad composed by Sid Jacobson, whose later hits included the oddball 1960 million seller 'Yogi' by the Ivy Three. The Nat 'King' Cole-styled entertainer, who released over four dozen easy-listening albums in the 1960s, unfortunately met his end in an automobile accident in 1970.

COZY COLE
TOPSY II
Love

One of the most respected jazz drummers (who played with Louis Armstrong, Cab Calloway, Dizzy Gillespie, Jelly Roll Morton and Charlie Parker) had this million seller shortly before his fiftieth birthday. Cole stretched his revival of 'Topsy' over two sides and both independently reached the Top 40. Numerous labels cashed in on the single's success by re-releasing old Cole cuts, which probably harmed his official follow-up, 'Turvy I & II'. The drummer soon returned to jazz circles and even the later 'Topsy 3 & 4' was a flopsy.

CONWAY TWITTY
IT'S ONLY MAKE BELIEVE
MGM

After recording unsuccessfully for Sun, Harold Lloyd (named after the silent movie comic) Jenkins renamed himself after two towns: Conway, Arkansas and Twitty, Texas. In mid-1957, advertisements urged 'Remember the name, Conway Twitty' but few did until this dramatic rock-a-ballad shot him to the top of the transatlantic charts. Twitty and his drummer Jack Nance composed the song (which structurally resembled 'I Believe') in just ten minutes in a motel room in Ontario, and it was initially intended as the B side to the equally Elvis-esque track 'I'll Try'.

KINGSTON TRIO
TOM DOOLEY
Capitol

▲ 1
⑩ 1
96/250

Their eponymous debut album was the first LP by a group to head the US chart, and the act's revival of the nineteenth-century song 'Tom Dula' (taken from it by public demand) hurled the San Francisco folk trio to No 1. The hit inspired many answer and sequel singles, and oddly grabbed the Grammy for Best Country Record. The act most responsible for the 1960s folk revival also took five of their next six LPs to the top. Interestingly, folk team The Tarriers' earlier revival of this death ditty had gone almost unnoticed.

BIG BOPPER
CHANTILLY LACE
Mercury

▲ 6
⑩ 1•
—/250

For his rock show on KTRM in Beaumont, Texas, DJ Jape Richardson called himself the Big Bopper and used catchphrases such as 'Hello baby' and 'You know what I like'. After a couple of country singles as Jape Richardson, Mercury flipped his third single, 'The Purple People Eater Meets The Witch Doctor' and released 'Chantilly Lace' (which included his catchphrases) as by the Big Bopper. The self-penned pearl was in the UK Top 20 on the week he died in a plane crash alongside Buddy Holly and Ritchie Valens.

UNITED KINGDOM
October 1958

ELVIS PRESLEY
KING CREOLE
RCA

▲ 2
⑩15
209/250

This UK-only single took Elvis to the runner-up spot in the UK for the third time in the year. As his Leiber & Stoller film-title song charted, the King visited Europe for the only time when he started an army tour of duty in Germany.

CLIFF RICHARD
MOVE IT
Columbia

▲ 2
⑩ 1
189/250

Britain's most successful solo singer made his chart debut with a song penned *en route* to the studio by Ian Samwell, who was then a member of Cliff's backing band, The Drifters. Producer Norrie Paramor intended it to be the B side (to a cover of Bobby Helms' single 'School Boy Crush') but influential TV producer Jack Good thought otherwise. The Indian-born entertainer, whose real name was Harry Webb, sang this top-drawer rocker on the first *Oh Boy!* TV show and it was an instant hit.

PONI-TAILS
BORN TOO LATE
HMV

▲ 5
⑩ 1•
—/250

See US entry (August).

JOHNNY MATHIS
A CERTAIN SMILE
Fontana

▲ 4
⑩ 1
215/250

Although he had no US Top 20 singles in 1958, Mathis was never off the album chart, and at times four of his LPs were riding high. His first big UK hit was the Webster & Fain-composed title song from a film starring Christine Carere and Rossano Brazzi.

MARINO MARINI & HIS QUARTET
COME PRIMA
Durium

▲ 2
⑩ 1•
170/250

Astonishingly, both sides of Naples-born Marini's debut UK hit entered the Top 20 independently in the same week. His interpretation of 'Volare' gave countryman Domenico Modugno a good run, and his rendition of this much recorded Italian composition outsold the English-language version ('More Than Ever') by Malcolm Vaughan. Marini and his quartet, who appeared at the London Palladium for two weeks in 1957, had a further Top 40 entry with a cover of another Modugno song, 'Ciao Ciao Bambino'.

TOMMY EDWARDS
IT'S ALL IN THE GAME
MGM

▲ 1
⑩ 1•
63/250

See US entry (September).

MALCOLM VAUGHAN
MORE THAN EVER
(COME PRIMA)
HMV

▲ 5
⑩ 4•
—/250

With eight Top 20 singles in the late 1950s, Vaughan was arguably the last 'old school' British vocalist to be replaced by rock. The performer, who early in his career acted alongside Sir Lawrence Olivier, last visited the heights with the English-lyric version of the Italian hit 'Come Prima', supported by the Mike Sammes Singers.

LORD ROCKINGHAM'S XI
HOOTS MON
Decca

▲ 1
⑩ 1•
46/250

TV producer Jack Good and noted musical arranger Harry Robinson were the masterminds behind the 13 piece house band on TV's *Oh Boy!* The pair wanted to create a unique, amusing and unorthodox sound – 'Hoots Mon' was proof that they succeeded. This Celtic cousin of 'Tequila', which included humorous broad Scottish one-liners from composer Robinson, was the first rock'n'roll instrumental to top the UK hit parade. Their similar follow-up, 'Wee Tom', also reached the Top 20, and 35 years later in 1993 'Hoots Mon' returned briefly to the chart.

UNITED STATES
November 1958

TEDDY BEARS
TO KNOW HIM, IS TO LOVE HIM
Dore

▲ 1
⑩ 1•
78/250

Only three members of this teenage quartet sang on the track which they recorded hurriedly as a B side. Member Phil Spector was inspired to write the haunting ballad by the words on his father's gravestone, 'To Know Him Was To Love Him'. When it took off, the quartet, who named themselves after a recent Elvis hit, became a trio. Although The Teddy Bears soon disbanded, both Spector and distinctive lead vocalist Annette Kleinbard (aka Carol Connors) subsequently had long and successful careers in music.

RICKY NELSON
I GOT A FEELING
Imperial

▲ 10
⑩ 6
—/250

Sun Records' head Sam Phillips admiringly said 'Nelson could take a rocker and make it sound like a ballad' – which he did again on this track. Both 'I Got A Feeling' and its equally successful flip, 'Lonesome Town', were composed by singer/songwriter Baker Knight.

PLAYMATES
BEEP BEEP
Roulette

▲ 4
⑩ 1•
—/250

Connecticut trio The Playmates were no new-comers – they had been performing a mix of music and comedy (originally as The Nitwits) since the early 1950s. Ten months after 'Jo-Ann' introduced them to the Top 20, the group scored the biggest of their five Top 40 hits with a David and Goliath novelty about a race between a Nash Rambler and a Cadillac. In the UK, where 'Beep Beep' stalled outside the chart, the names of the participants were changed to a bubble car and a limousine in order to get radio play.

RICKY NELSON
LONESOME TOWN
Imperial

▲ 7
⑩ 7
—/250

Not only had Nelson accumulated an enviable run of double-sided hits, he also notched up three Top 20 albums in just 15 months. The latest, *Ricky Sings Again*, included this teen-targeted ballad (the demo for which was recorded by Eddie Cochran), which Baker Knight penned with the Everly Brothers in mind.

BOBBY DARIN
QUEEN OF THE HOP
Atco

▲ 9
⑩ 2
—/250

Darin earned his second successive gold single

with a rock track about a girl who 'tuned into *Bandstand* every day', which was recorded at the same session as the talented singer's previous title-dropping smash, 'Splish Splash'.

ELVIS PRESLEY
ONE NIGHT
RCA

▲ 4
⑩ 14
—/250

Many critics considered his revival of Smiley Lewis' 1956 R&B to be 'too suggestive', even though the original lyric had been toned down somewhat. Coincidentally, the song was melodically likened to 'O Sole Mio', which Presley later recorded as 'It's Now Or Never'.

ELVIS PRESLEY
I GOT STUNG
RCA

▲ 8
⑩ 13
—/250

Both sides of every Elvis single reached the US charts and this was one of his biggest double-sided hits. David Hill, who originally recorded 'All Shook Up', co-wrote the rugged rocker, which racked up over 250,000 advance orders in the UK.

JACK SCOTT
MY TRUE LOVE
London American

▲ 9
⑩ 1•
—/250

See US entry (July).

CONWAY TWITTY
IT'S ONLY MAKE BELIEVE
MGM

▲ 1
⑩ 1
42/250

See US entry (October).

TOMMY DORSEY ORCHESTRA
TEA FOR TWO CHA CHA
Brunswick

▲ 3
⑩ 1•
160/250

See US entry (October).

LONNIE DONEGAN
TOM DOOLEY
Pye Nixa

▲ 3
⑩ 9
191/250

As Donegan was on tour, he recorded this fast-paced rendition of the Kingston Trio's US No 1 at a converted Glasgow TV studio. Unlike most of his British contemporaries, he very rarely covered American singles and never aped anyone else's arrangements.

PERRY COMO
LOVE MAKES THE WORLD
GO ROUND
RCA

▲ 6
🔟 9
—/250

Tennessee Ernie Ford first recorded the bouncy pop item, which fared better in the UK than in the TV star's homeland. It was written by Ollie Jones from noted R&B session singers The Cues.

UNITED STATES
December 1958

EVERLY BROTHERS
PROBLEMS
Cadence

▲ 2
🔟 5
250/250

Shortly after being voted World's Top Group in the *NME*, these youthful music business veterans headlined Alan Freed's *Christmas Rock'n'Roll Spectacular* show. It appeared that the brothers had few of the problems they sang about on this archetypal 'teenage troubles' tune.

PLATTERS
SMOKE GETS IN YOUR
EYES
Mercury

▲ 1
🔟 6
83/250

Their French-recorded revival of this pre-war standard was the award-winning act's only transatlantic No 1. The mixed group, who were seen in numerous films, probably played in more countries than any other 1950s rock act. The quintet also racked up five Top 20 LPs before lead vocalist Tony Williams left in 1961. The Platters have remained a popular draw on the club circuit and were one of the first groups elected to the Rock and Roll Hall of Fame.

CHIPMUNKS
THE CHIPMUNK SONG
Liberty

▲ 1
🔟 1
106/250

Soon after he headed the charts with the gimmicky 'Witch Doctor', David Seville decided to use three sped-up voices instead of one. He called this 'group' The Chipmunks and individually named them after top executives at Liberty, Alvin (Bennett), Simon (Waronker) and Theodore

(Keep). Their first release was the fastest-selling single to date, with sales of almost four million in six weeks. The Grammy-winning record has since been a frequent visitor to the Christmas bestsellers and is said now to have sold over seven million.

CLYDE McPHATTER
A LOVER'S QUESTION
Atlantic

▲ 6
🔟 1
—/250

One of the decade's most distinctive and influential vocalists had his biggest solo success with this bouncy Brook Benton composition. It charted as McPhatter's earlier recordings with Billy Ward & The Dominoes and The Drifters (a group he formed in 1953) were being played on the first 'oldies but goodies' styled radio shows. The R&B superstar, who died in 1972, was inducted into the Rock and Roll Hall of Fame in 1987, and in 1993 his likeness was seen on a commemorative US stamp.

FATS DOMINO
WHOLE LOTTA LOVING
Imperial

▲ 6
🔟 6
—/250

As the unmistakable vocalist's label, Imperial, claimed that Domino had sold over 40 million singles (plus three million LPs and four million EPs) in the decade, he returned to the Top 10 with a catchy, if somewhat repetitive, self-penned easy rock number.

UNITED KINGDOM
December 1958

KINGSTON TRIO
TOM DOOLEY
Capitol

▲ 5
🔟 1•
—/250

See US entry (October).

CLIFF RICHARD
HIGH CLASS BABY
Columbia

▲ 7
🔟 2
—/250

Britain's biggest rock phenomenon since Tommy Steele followed 'Move It' with another Ian Samwell-penned stomper. The song, which Cliff personally disliked (and later refused to sing on stage), was coupled with his former hit in the US, where it received rave reviews but mediocre sales.

RICKY NELSON
SOMEDAY
London American

▲ 9
🔟 2
—/250

Although only available on an album, DJ Pete Murray pushed this revival of the old Mills Brothers' hit. The public responded by buying the only available single version by Jodie Sands. When London released Nelson's rendition it overtook Sands' single in the Top 20.

HARRY BELAFONTE
MARY'S BOY CHILD
RCA

▲ 10
🔟 4•
—/250

See previous UK entry (November 1957).

JANE MORGAN
THE DAY THE RAINS CAME
London American

▲ 1
🔟 1•
97/250

Before finding fame in the US and UK, this Boston-born vocalist (real name Jane Currier) had been a bill-topper in France. Her big US break came in 1957, when she took the old French song 'Fascination' into the Top 20. In the UK, her treatment of another French composition, Gilbert Becaud's 'Le Jour Ou La Pluie Viendra', with English words by Carl Sigman, briefly lifted Miss Morgan into the limelight. It was coupled with the original French-language version.

TOMMY STEELE
COME ON LET'S GO
Decca

▲ 10
🔟 5
—/250

On 3 February 1959, when youthful rocker Ritchie Valens died in a plane crash (alongside Buddy Holly), Steele's Joe Meek-produced cover of his first US hit was in the UK Top 20.

UNITED STATES
January 1959

CONNIE FRANCIS
MY HAPPINESS
MGM

▲ 2
⑩ 2
232/250

Soon after being voted World's Top Female Singer in the UK (a title she held for the rest of the decade) the vocalist, once tagged 'Johnnie Ray's protégé', notched up another transatlantic smash with her revival of Jon & Sondra Steele's 1948 million seller.

BILLY GRAMMER
GOTTA TRAVEL ON
Monument

▲ 4
⑩ 1•
—/250

This coal miner's son from Illinois, who first recorded in 1949, joined the daily *Jimmy Dean Show* in 1955. The singer/guitarist's hit was a revival of a nineteenth-century British song which had been arranged and earlier recorded by The Weavers. Perhaps surprisingly, it travelled up the pop chart before climbing the country lists. Both sides of Grammer's follow-up, 'Bonaparte's Retreat' and 'The Kissing Tree', charted, but his only other successes came in the country field. Grammer, a much in-demand session musician, later had a flat-top guitar named after him.

RITCHIE VALENS
DONNA
Del-Fi

▲ 2
⑩ 1•
192/250

The first Chicano rock star was born Richard Valenzuela in California. Both sides of the 17-year-old singer/songwriter/guitarist's second single were zooming up the US Top 40 when he joined the Winter Dance Party – the tour which ended with the deaths of Valens, Buddy Holly and the Big Bopper. Valens had penned this teen ballad about his girlfriend Donna Ludwig, and it was coupled with a rocking rendition of the old Mexican standard 'La Bamba'. In the UK, Valens remained virtually unknown until the release of the film *La Bamba* in 1987.

CRESTS
16 CANDLES
Coed

▲ 2
⑩ 1•
221/250

Johnny Maestro (born Mastrangelo) fronted the multi-racial vocal quartet from Brooklyn, who chalked up five Top 40 entries. A year after the group's debut disc 'Sweetest One' charted, they scored their biggest hit with a Luther Dixon (writer and producer of many Shirelles' successes) teen ballad, which started out as '21 Candles'. Interestingly, the song had been intended as the B side of 'Beside You'. Among The Crests' subsequent singles were the sequels 'A Year Ago Tonight' and 'You Blew Out The Candles'. Maestro later charted as a soloist and leader of Brooklyn Bridge.

LLOYD PRICE
STAGGER LEE
ABC Paramount

▲ 1
⑩ 1
80/250

Few records in the 1950s were as hard hitting as this Louisiana born singer/songwriter's update of the old blues number 'The Ballad Of Stack O Lee'. Price, one of 1959's bestselling acts, was no newcomer, having headed the R&B chart in 1952 with his ground-breaking composition 'Lawdy Miss Clawdy'. After a slow start, the big-band R&B rocker was a top transatlantic hit, even though America's League of Decency forced Price to revocal the track and lose the references to gambling and murder on the LP version.

JACKIE WILSON
LONELY TEARDROPS
Brunswick

▲ 7
⑩ 1
—/250

One of the 1960's bestselling R&B vocalists debuted in the US Top 20 with a song penned by Berry Gordy Jr. Wilson was a standout showman and singer who influenced countless singers including Elvis Presley, James Brown and Michael Jackson. The one-time lead vocalist of Billy Ward

& The Dominoes collapsed on stage in 1975 while singing 'Lonely Teardrops' and was semi-comatose until his death in 1984.

JACK SCOTT
GOODBYE BABY
Carlton

▲ 8
⑩ 2
—/250

Among the many fine sides released by the rich-voiced baritone and his equally distinctive backing group, The Chantones, was this self-penned mid-tempo rocker, which climbed the chart as Scott entered the services (he was discharged five months later with an ulcer). Before the end of the decade he joined Top Rank in a $50,000 deal, and in the early 1960s added to his hit tally.

UNITED KINGDOM
January 1959

RUSS CONWAY
MORE PARTY POPS
Columbia

▲ 10
⑩ 1
—/250

Every Christmas since 1953, pianist Winifred Atwell had taken a medley of popular songs into the Top 10 – this year it was Bristol-born keyboard player Conway's (born Trevor Stanford) turn. Interestingly, among the tunes on the single were 'Honeysuckle And The Bee', 'Hello Hello Who's Your Lady Friend', ' Yes Sir That's My Baby' and 'Music Music Music', all of which were included on Atwell's earlier seasonal smashes.

LITTLE RICHARD
BABY FACE
London American

▲ 2
⑩ 5•
199/250

A track recorded before his UK chart debut in 1956 gave the larger-than-life performer his biggest UK hit a year after he (first) retired. Interestingly, the song's composer Benny Davis had sung on Jan Garber's original recording in 1926. Richard's music and showmanship influenced many later acts including The Beatles, James Brown and Elton John. He has made many comebacks, and is now as much a professional 'celebrity' as he is a rock star.

TEDDY BEARS
TO KNOW HIM, IS TO LOVE HIM
London American

▲ 2
⑩ 1•
179/250

See US entry (November 1958).

SHIRLEY BASSEY
KISS ME HONEY HONEY KISS ME
Philips

▲ 3
⑩ 2
185/250

In 1956, an astute reviewer described Bassey as 'a raw talent who will be a star of tomorrow – with proper supervision'. As 1959 started, she had two singles in the UK Top 3 – the first was a personality-packed version of a Latin American opus first recorded by Gogi Grant.

ELVIS PRESLEY
ONE NIGHT/I GOT STUNG
RCA

▲ 1
⑩ 16
86/250

See US entry (November).

SHIRLEY BASSEY
AS I LOVE YOU
Philips

▲ 1
⑩ 3
43/250

Livingston & Evans composed the beautiful ballad that became the distinctive Welsh singer's highest-ranked hit of the 1950s. For the record, earlier executions of the song by top vocalists Jo Stafford (1955) and Carmen McCrae (featured in the 1957 film *The Big Beat*) were non-starters. The unmistakable vocalist, who ranks among the world's most popular cabaret entertainers, has had more album chart entries than any other British female artist.

EVERLY BROTHERS
PROBLEMS
London American

| ▲ 6 |
| ⑩ 5 |
| —/250 |

See US Entry (December 1958).

PLATTERS
SMOKE GETS IN YOUR EYES
Mercury

| ▲ 1 |
| ⑩ 4• |
| 72/250 |

See US entry (December 1958).

UNITED STATES
February 1959

BILL PARSONS
ALL AMERICAN BOY
Fraternity

| ▲ 2 |
| ⑩ 1• |
| —/250 |

Soon after Parsons left the services and before fellow Ohio native Bobby Bare (who had recorded for Capitol) was drafted, they co-wrote this humorous talkin' blues about a rock'n'roller going into the army. Bare handled the recitation and rush recorded it as a possible B side. Fraternity accidentally credited Parsons as the performer on the song that many assumed to be about Elvis, and since Bare was in the army, Parsons promoted the single alone. Bare (later a top country star) subsequently released an overlooked sequel 'I'm Hanging Up My Rifle'.

REG OWEN & HIS ORCHESTRA
MANHATTAN SPIRITUAL
Palette

| ▲ 10 |
| ⑩ 1• |
| —/250 |

For the first time since the US charts started in 1940, three British acts were simultaneously in the Top 20. Leading the way was London bandleader Owen, who had been voted Arranger of the Year in the 1954 *NME* poll. The sax-playing one-time member of both Harry Roy and Ted Heath's Bands

scored with a bouncy instrumental written by Billy Maxted, composer of the standard 'Satin Doll'. After its US success, the record (which was released on the Belgian-owned Palette label) reached the UK Top 20.

COASTERS
CHARLIE BROWN
Atco

| ▲ 2 |
| ⑩ 3 |
| 231/250 |

Back in 1956 The Cues first asked 'Why's everybody always picking on me', but it took this West Coast supergroup to turn the amusing Peanuts-inspired slice of rock'n'roll into a transatlantic hit. Several sequels were released, including 'Charlie Brown Got Expelled' by future soul star Joe Tex.

LAVERN BAKER
I CRIED A TEAR
Atlantic

| ▲ 6 |
| ⑩ 1• |
| —/250 |

Eighteen years after she first recorded (aged 11), the Chicago-born R&B headliner notched up her biggest pop single with a track reminiscent of earlier hits by label-mate Chuck Willis. Baker, who was one of the most covered acts of the mid-1950s (see 'Tweedle Dee' by Georgia Gibbs – US/February 1955), had been voted Top Female R&B Artist several years in succession. The star of numerous R&B and rock'n'roll package shows was inducted into the Rock and Roll Hall of Fame in 1990.

ANNETTE
TALL PAUL
Disneyland

Richard and Robert Sherman, who later wrote many memorable Disney songs, first charted with the teen tune that gave ex-Disney Mouseketeer Annette Funicello the first of four Top 20 entries. Annette, a regular performer on *Bandstand* and *the Dick Clark Show*, was backed on her third single by The Afterbeats. Interestingly, fellow Mouseketeer Judy Harriet had released an overlooked version of the tune a few months earlier. Singer/actress Annette possibly dedicated it to boyfriend Paul Anka, who returned the favour by recording 'Who's Our Pet, Annette'.

CHRIS BARBER JAZZ BAND
PETITE FLEUR (LITTLE FLOWER)
Laurie

(See UK entry).

RAY ANTHONY & HIS ORCHESTRA
PETER GUNN
Capitol

Henry Mancini composed the big band's highest-ranking hit since 1953, when another TV series theme, 'Dragnet', had been good for them. Incidentally, in the UK, where the series was not seen, Duane Eddy had the bestselling version. Although pushed to the rock audience through appearances in films like *The Girl Can't Help It*, Anthony's brassy band style seemed out of place in the late 1950s.

UNITED KINGDOM
February 1959

LONNIE DONEGAN
DOES YOUR CHEWING GUM LOSE ITS FLAVOUR
Pye Nixa

His revival of a 35-year-old novelty number gave Britain's most consistent hit maker his thirteenth UK Top 20 entry in three years. Almost three years later this tasty tune also reached the US Top 10 – making him the first post-war British male to have made that journey twice.

PAUL ANKA
(ALL OF A SUDDEN) MY HEART SINGS
Columbia

A ballad Kathryn Grayson introduced in the 1945 film *Anchor's Aweigh*, took Anka way up the

transatlantic charts. The noteworthy Harold Rome song was given a similar treatment to Conway Twitty's recent transatlantic No 1.

SLIM DUSTY
A PUB WITH NO BEER
Columbia

Australia's most famous country singer was born Gordon Kirkpatrick in New South Wales and signed to EMI in 1946. He initially recorded his only major UK hit in 1957 as the B side of 'Saddle Boy'. The novelty song, which was based on the World War II poem 'A Pub Without Beer', earned him Australia's only gold 78rpm single! The singer, who received an MBE from the Queen for services to music, finally toured the UK in 1996, 37 years after his sole success.

CHRIS BARBER JAZZ BAND
PETITE FLEUR
Pye Nixa

▲ 3
⑩ 1•
115/250

Hertfordshire-born Barber fronted the UK's most popular traditional jazz band of the 1950s. Not only were the band at the forefront of the burgeoning trad jazz craze, but they had earlier introduced the British public to skiffle (via their banjo player Lonnie Donegan) and American R&B (Barber brought over acts like Muddy Waters and Louis Jordan). Their sole transatlantic hit was recorded in 1956 and reached the chart in the last few weeks of composer Sidney Bechet's life. Oddly, trombonist Barber did not play on 'Petite Fleur', which featured the band's clarinettist Monty Sunshine.

BEVERLEY SISTERS
THE LITTLE DRUMMER BOY
Decca

▲ 6
⑩ 2•
—/250

Amazingly, this Christmas song peaked in the UK chart in the spring, and its composer Harry Simone took his version into the US Top 40 every year between 1958 and 1962. The UK's best-known girl group had their last topselling single later that year with another Christmas classic, 'Little Donkey'. They officially retired in 1967 but have made several comebacks since.

UNITED STATES
March 1959

FRANKIE AVALON
VENUS
Chancellor

▲ 1
⑩ 3
72/250

Soon after briefly replacing the late Buddy Holly on the ill-fated Winter Dance Party tour, this somewhat vocally challenged teen idol had his biggest seller with an ode to the goddess of love. In the UK, the string-filled ballad was a mid-table hit alongside a cover by Dickie Valentine.

CHIPMUNKS
ALVIN'S HARMONICA
Liberty

▲ 3
⑩ 2•
—/250

Surely no other gimmick-based recoding act can equal the 20 million albums sold by The Chipmunks, who have remained popular for almost 40 years. This humorous novelty picked up three more Grammy awards for their creator David Seville. After his death in 1972, Seville's son Ross Jr took over the group and they continued to sustain their popularity through both cartoons and records.

BELL NOTES
I'VE HAD IT
Time

▲ 6
⑩ 1•
—/250

Lead singers Ray Caroni and Carl Bonura penned the simple but hypnotic number that gave this short-lived Long Island quintet their only bestseller. Noted New York DJ Alan Fredericks produced the record, which the group performed on Dick Clark's top-rated TV show and on an all-star package tour headed by Frankie Avalon and Duane Eddy. The combo released several more singles, including the nattily named 'White Buckskin Sneakers And Checkerboard Socks', but chart-wise the Bell Notes had had it.

BROOK BENTON
IT'S JUST A MATTER OF TIME
Mercury

▲ 3
⑩ 1
—/250

Not long after his compositions 'Looking Back' and 'A Lover's Question' had earned gold discs for Nat 'King' Cole and Clyde McPhatter respectively, this singer/songwriter from South Carolina (born Benjamin Peay) clocked up the first of two dozen US Top 40 hits of his own. Benton's timeless ballad also headed the country chart in 1970 by Sonny James and again in 1989 by Randy Travis.

THOMAS WAYNE
TRAGEDY
Fernwood

▲ 5
🔟 1•
—/250

Both Elvis and Thomas Wayne (Perkins) attended Humes High School in Memphis, and Presley's guitarist Scotty Moore produced the latter's hit. After 'This Time' (later a smash for Troy Shondell) failed, Wayne covered this heartfelt rock-a-ballad, which composer Gerald Nelson had earlier recorded. The track, which also featured female trio The DeLons, was on release over six months before a Dick Clark TV show appearance helped kick-start it. A revival by The Fleetwoods in 1961 returned the song to the Top 10. Tragically, Wayne died in an automobile accident in 1971.

RICKY NELSON
NEVER BE ANYONE ELSE
BUT YOU
Imperial

▲ 6
🔟 8
—/250

In the US, Ricky, Elvis and Pat Boone were the most popular teen idols of the late 1950s. Both this romantic Baker Knight-penned ballad and its B side 'It's Late' reached the Top 10 as Nelson's big-screen debut *Rio Bravo* reached the cinema.

FLEETWOODS
COME SOFTLY TO ME
Dolphin

▲ 1
🔟 1
87/250

'Come Softly To Me' was born when a 'dom-doobie-do' hook Gary Troxel dreamed up was put together in counterpoint with a song Barbara Ellis and Gretchen Christopher had written independently. The trio recorded it almost a cappella – the only instruments being label owner Bonnie Guitar's acoustic guitar and a set of keys being jangled. After a name change from the rather obvious Two Girls And A Guy, the record was released and in a matter of weeks this soothing teen-targeted single topped the chart.

DODIE STEVENS
PINK SHOE LACES
Crystalette

▲ 3
🔟 1•
—/250

Although it sold few copies, Stevens (born Geraldine Pasquale) released her first single as Geri Pace in 1954, when aged only eight. The young performer was frequently seen on Frankie Laine's nationwide TV show in the mid-1950s and recorded her sole million seller when she was 12. Stevens considered the cute song about the sharp-dressing Dooley to be 'dumb', and was not too happy when re-christened Dodie by her label. After a few minor hits and a film role with Fabian, she quit at 16 to get married.

RICKY NELSON
IT'S LATE
Imperial

▲ 9
🔟 9
—/250

Although his TV series, *The Adventures of Ozzie & Harriet*, was not shown in the UK, Nelson racked up seven UK Top 20 entries in the 1950s. The most successful was this Dorsey Burnette-written rocker, which Shakin' Stevens returned to the UK Top 20 in 1983.

UNITED KINGDOM
March 1959

RUSS CONWAY
SIDE SADDLE
Columbia

▲ 1
⑩ 2
21/250

'Come And Dance' was the original title of the instrumental, which Conway started writing in 1956 for the musical *Beauty & The Beast*. His rendition was only released when he could not get Joe 'Mr Piano' Henderson to record it, and this single galloped to No 1, staying in the Top 20 for 25 weeks. In the US, a handful of acts, including Ferrante & Teicher, covered 'Side Saddle', but none of the versions rode up the chart.

CONNIE FRANCIS
MY HAPPINESS
MGM

▲ 4
⑩ 3
235/250

See US entry (January).

LLOYD PRICE
STAGGER LEE
HMV

▲ 7
⑩ 1
—/250

See US entry (January).

BILLY ECKSTINE
GIGI
Mercury

▲ 8
⑩ 2•
—/250

A year after his treatment of this Academy Award winner flopped Stateside, the unique vocalist took the title song from the Lerner & Loewe-penned screen musical into the UK winner's circle. It was a welcome, if brief, return to the heights for the singer who, like many, tried unsuccessfully to make some recordings in a rock'n'roll-influenced vein. Interestingly, in the 1960s he had small sellers on both major soul labels, Motown and Stax.

BUDDY HOLLY
IT DOESN'T MATTER
ANYMORE
Coral

▲ 1
⑩ 3
38/250

Undoubtedly Holly was one of the most innovative, imaginative and imitated rock artists, and the tracks cut during his 18 months at the top have influenced countless acts ever since. His first posthumous release, which headed the UK chart and returned him to the US Top 20, was penned by Paul Anka (who donated his royalties to Holly's widow). Holly's music is still amazingly popular and *Buddy*, the musical based on his life, has broken longevity and box office records.

UNITED STATES
April 1959

VIRTUES
GUITAR BOOGIE SHUFFLE
Hunt

▲ 5
⑩ 1•
—/250

Guitarist Frank Virtue (born Virtuoso) from Philadelphia recorded for a handful of labels before briefly tasting fame as leader of The Virtues. The act's sole hit was a shuffle rock rendition of an instrumental originally released in the mid-1940s by one of Virtue's old Navy buddies, Arthur Smith. Smith's composition was based on the earlier tunes 'Boogie Woogie' and 'Pinetop's Boogie Woogie'. Subsequent singles included the similar 'Virtues Boogie Woogie', 'Guitar Boogie Shuffle Twist' and 'Guitar Boogie Shuffle '65'.

ELVIS PRESLEY
A FOOL SUCH AS I
RCA

▲ 2
⑩ 16
—/250

Elvis returned to his country roots with a revival of a Hank Snow hit that he had often heard when supporting Snow on tour in 1955. Coincidentally, the King's cut was released the same week as an overlooked version by the old King, Bill Haley.

ELVIS PRESLEY
I NEED YOUR LOVE TONIGHT
RCA

▲ 4
⑩ 15
—/250

Even though he had been in the army a year, a million advance orders were still placed for this double-sided smash. Interestingly, Bix Reichner, who co-wrote the rocker, is the person credited for renaming Bill Haley's backing band The Comets.

DAVE 'BABY' CORTEZ
THE HAPPY ORGAN
Clock

▲ 1
⑩ 1
150/250

It's no surprise that organist Cortez (born David Clowney in Detroit) was the only doo-wop singer to top the chart with an instrumental. The ex-member of The Pearls and Valentines clocked up a million seller with a self-written stomper which bore a marked resemblance to 'Shortnin' Bread'. Like many other late 1950s hits, it had started as a B side to the soulful ballad 'Love Me As I Love You'. Cortez returned to the Top 20 in 1962 with 'Rinky Dink' and later released a handful of worthy soul sides.

TRAVIS & BOB
TELL HIM NO
Sandy

▲ 8
⑩ 1•
—/250

Among the 22 acts whose only Top 10 entry came in 1959 were Alabama-based Travis Pritchett and Bob Weaver. Like many duos of the era, Travis & Bob's style owed much to Don & Phil (Everly Brothers). Travis composed the catchy song with its easy-to-grasp chorus and Dot Records paid $12,000 to distribute it, beating hot competition from Cameo and Liberty. For the record, Dean & Marc, whose timely cover of 'Tell Him No' also charted, were members of the successful 1960s hit-making trio The Newbeats.

IMPALAS
SORRY (I RAN ALL THE WAY HOME)
Cub

▲ 2
⑩ 1•
248/250

Like many 1950's groups, Brooklyn quartet The Impalas named themselves after an automobile. However, unlike most they had a black lead singer (15-year-old Joe 'Speedo' Frazier) and three white backing vocalists. When recording the intro, Frazier uttered 'uh oh' after making a mistake, it sounded cute and was left in. Incidentally, the single took off only after the quartet joined Alan Freed's Easter Show at the Brooklyn Fox. Despite reported advance orders of 100,000 copies the follow-up, 'Oh, What A Fool', did not run all the way up the chart.

FABIAN
TURN ME LOOSE
Chancellor

▲ 9
⑩ 1
—/250

Few singers have received as many brickbats about their vocal ability as Philadelphia-born Fabian (Fabiano Forte), who Chancellor admittedly signed for his looks rather than his musical talent. Despite a big 'Who is Fabian' campaign, answered by ads that proclaimed 'This is the Fabulous Fabian – destined to be America's latest record sensation', the photogenic teenager's first two singles fell flat, even though he promoted them on *Bandstand*. His first major hit came with a superior Pomus & Shuman rocker, which he performed with some aplomb.

UNITED KINGDOM
April 1959

PERRY COMO
TOMBOY
RCA

▲ 10
⑩ 10
—/250

This playful pop song ended Como's staggering string of hits in the 1950s. Musical trends came and went in the decade but his popularity never waned. The laid-back entertainer with the warm and friendly vocal style has sold an estimated 60 million records overall. He had a successful recording comeback in the early 1970s (including a UK No 1 LP) and was still playing to packed houses in the 1990s.

MARTY WILDE
DONNA
Philips

▲ 3
⑩ 2
206/250

One of the most popular performers on the UK's top pop TV show *Oh Boy!* returned to the Top 10 with his treatment of the late Ritchie Valens' biggest US hit.

EDDIE COCHRAN
C'MON EVERYBODY
London American

▲ 6
⑩ 1
—/250

The legendary rocker fared better in the UK with this standout stomper (which he had originally recorded as 'Let's Get Together') than in his homeland. Cochran, who died in an automobile accident in Britain in early 1960, was rightfully elected to the Rock and Roll Hall of Fame in 1987; a year before, this timeless single re-entered the UK Top 20.

COASTERS
CHARLIE BROWN
London American

▲ 6
⑩ 1•
—/250

See US entry (February).

ELVIS PRESLEY
A FOOL SUCH AS I/I NEED
YOUR LOVE TONIGHT
RCA

▲ 1
⑩ 17
35/250

See US entry.

UNITED STATES
May 1959

EDWARD BYRNES & CONNIE STEVENS
KOOKIE, KOOKIE (LEND ME YOUR COMB)
Warner

▲ 4
🔟 1•
—/250

Gerald Lloyd 'Kookie' Kookson III, was the name of the hip-talking character that New Yorker Byrnes (born Edward Breitenberger) played in the top TV series *77 Sunset Strip* from 1958 to 1963. Since Kookie was the utmost and cool chicks flipped their wigs over him, it was therefore no surprise when this novelty, based on that character, took him into hitsville. Joining Byrnes on the track was the future Mrs Eddie Fisher, actress Connie Stevens, who later had chart entries of her own.

WILBERT HARRISON
KANSAS CITY
Fury

▲ 1
🔟 1•
122/250

In 1953, Harrison, a one-man-band from North Carolina, released his debut single and Little Willie Littlejohn had a minor R&B hit with the Leiber & Stoller song 'K.C. Loving'. When Harrison's label, Savoy, rejected his idea to revive Littlejohn's single, he cut it for Fury as 'Kansas City'. Despite covers by acts like Hank Ballard and Little Richard, and legal problems with Savoy and Leiber & Stoller, the record reached the top. Later tracks by this distinctive performer, which included 'Kansas City Twist' and 'Goodbye Kansas City', sold far fewer copies.

DION & THE BELMONTS
A TEENAGER IN LOVE
Laurie

▲ 5
🔟 1
—/250

Before teaming together, Dion DiMucci (backed by The Timberlanes) and The Belmonts both recorded separately on New York's Mohawk label. When their forces were combined they became top teen idols and achieved an impressive seven Top 40 hits before 1960, when Dion went solo. The fourth of these was this Pomus & Shuman-penned teen classic, which reportedly started out with the title 'Great To Be Young And In Love'. The noted New York quintet were added to the Rock and Roll Hall of Fame in 1989.

BOBBY DARIN
DREAM LOVER
Atco

▲ 2
🔟 3
207/250

Atlantic Records' first successful white artist penned this catchy cha-lypso which took him to the top of the UK chart. Joining him on the track were pianist Neil Sedaka and noted R&B session vocalists The Cues.

JOHNNY HORTON
THE BATTLE OF NEW ORLEANS
Columbia

▲ 1
🔟 1
82/250

As a follow-up to his first country No. 1, 'When It's Springtime in Alaska', Texas-based Horton recorded a folk/country saga penned by singer/songwriter Jimmy Driftwood. The song's melody was taken from a fiddling tune, 'The Eighth Of January', which had been written to celebrate that 1814 battle. In the US, it scooped the Grammy Awards for Best Song of the Year and Best Country Performance. In the UK, Lonnie Donegan's cover (which amended the 'bloody British' reference to 'blooming British') defeated Horton's interpretation.

THE EXOTIC SOUNDS OF MARTIN DENNY
QUIET VILLAGE
Liberty

▲ 4
🔟 1•
—/250

One of 1959's biggest left-field hits came from the No 1 album *Exotica* (which had been recorded in less than four hours!) by this Hawaii-based New Yorker and his quartet. The tropical instrumental had been written and originally cut in 1950 by Les Baxter, and this vibe-driven version featured frog noises courtesy of Denny and bird calls by bongo player August Colon. Later Denny discs, including 'Quiet Village Bossa Nova', 'Latin Village' and 'Hawaiian Village', made less noise.

LLOYD PRICE
PERSONALITY
ABC Paramount

▲ 2
⑩ 2
208/250

The unmistakable Lloyd Price and his power-packed big band clocked up another transatlantic Top 10 entry with an extremely infectious self-penned pop/R&B opus, which was reminiscent of the gospel tune 'Wade in The Water'.

FRANK POURCEL'S FRENCH FIDDLES
ONLY YOU
Capitol

▲ 9
⑩ 1•
—/250

Four years after Buck Ram's noteworthy song introduced The Platters to the bestsellers, it gave this French string orchestra their only US hit. Marseilles-born bandleader and violinist Pourcel arranged the lush treatment of the rock ballad which earned the venerable French maestro his biggest international record – with sales reported to be over ten million. Pourcel, who over the years has released scores of albums, later co-wrote the 1963 chart topper 'I Will Follow Him' (Little Peggy March).

UNITED KINGDOM
May 1959

RICKY NELSON
IT'S LATE
London American

▲ 3
⑩ 3
149/250

See US entry (March).

FLEETWOODS
COME SOFTLY TO ME
London American

▲ 6
⑩ 1•
—/250

See US Entry (March).

ANTHONY NEWLEY
I'VE WAITED SO LONG
Decca

▲ 3
⑩ 1
174/250

Since 1949, when he appeared as the Artful Dodger in David Lean's film *Oliver Twist*, Londoner Newley had appeared in numerous films without becoming a household name. All that changed when he played conscripted rock'n'roll singer Jeep Jackson in the rock'n'roll satire *Idle On Parade*. Not only did

this rock-a-ballad chart, but an EP from the film (including the track) joined it in the Top 20. Before Newley knew it, the record 'made for a giggle' made him a teen idol.

FRANKIE VAUGHAN & THE KAYE SISTERS
COME SOFTLY TO ME
Philips

▲ 9
⑩ 7
—/250

After a quiet sales period, the celebrated British entertainer clicked with his version of The Fleetwoods' hypnotic US hit. The performer, whom Ed Sullivan described as 'sensational', was backed by Carol, Sheila and Shan, the (unrelated) Kaye Sisters.

CLIFF RICHARD
MEAN STREAK
Columbia

▲ 10
⑩ 3
—/250

Soon after *NME* described a TV appearance by Cliff as 'The most crude exhibition ever seen on TV', he clocked up his third Top 10 entry in seven months with another Ian Samwell song. The flip, Samwell's rocker 'Never Mind', also charted.

RUSS CONWAY
ROULETTE
Columbia

▲ 1
⑩ 3
64/250

The UK's first silver disc (awarded for 250,000 sales) went to Conway's second successive self-penned No 1. As the record hit the top, he appeared in the Royal Variety Show with label-mate Cliff Richard and fellow pianist Liberace.

NEIL SEDAKA
I GO APE
RCA

▲ 9
⑩ 1
—/250

Even though several earlier singles on other labels failed, RCA had a lot of faith in this singer/songwriter from New York. Sedaka followed his first US Top 20 entry, 'The Diary', with a piano-pounding rocker inspired by a current kid slang phrase (incidentally, it was not the first tune titled 'I Go Ape'), which fared better in the UK than in America. Prior to this hit, he composed successful songs for such acts as Connie Francis, Lavern Baker and Clyde McPhatter.

UNITED STATES
June 1959

FREDDY CANNON
TALLAHASSEE LASSIE
Swan

▲ 6
⑩ 1
—/250

A tape of Freddy Karmon (born Frederick Picariello) singing his mother's composition 'Rock'n'Roll Baby' was sent to hot producer/songwriters Frank Slay and Bob Crewe. They rewrote it as 'Tallahassee Lassie' and changed the singer's stage name to Cannon. The single not only put Tallahassee on the musical map, but also started a string of successful singles for the Massachusetts-born performer. Cannon, the most frequent visitor to *Bandstand*, was nicknamed 'Boom Boom' because of the hard-hitting bass drum sounds on his records.

PAUL ANKA
LONELY BOY
ABC Paramount

▲ 1
⑩ 3
77/250

Anka's biggest US hit of the 1950s came from his debut film *Girl's Town*. It charted as the 18-year-old headlined in Las Vegas for the first time. Donny Osmond's 1972 revival was also a US Top 20 entry.

COASTERS
ALONG CAME JONES
Atco

▲ 9
⑩ 4
—/250

The West Coast quartet's fifth Top 10 entry was a tongue-in-cheek spoof about TV western heroes who always appear just in the nick of time. As usual, it was written and produced by Leiber & Stoller and featured a sax break from the unmistakable 'fifth Coaster', King Curtis.

CONNIE FRANCIS
LIPSTICK ON YOUR COLLAR
MGM

▲ 5
⑩ 3
—/250

This one-time winner on Arthur Godfrey's *Talent Scouts* show, who specialized in updating standards, collected her third gold disc with an unforgettable new pop/rock song.

UNITED KINGDOM
June 1959

BERT WEEDON
GUITAR BOOGIE SHUFFLE
Top Rank

▲ 10
⑩ 1•
—/250

The UK's best-known guitarist of the decade had previously played in various bands including those of Ambrose, Ted Heath and Cyril Stapleton. Londoner Weedon played on more records than any other guitarist of his era, and can be heard on hits by such diverse acts as Eddie Calvert, Cliff Richard, David Whitfield, Tommy Steele, Laurie London, Marty Wilde and Russ Conway. His only bestseller as an artist was a cover of an Arthur 'Guitar Boogie' Smith instrumental that The Virtues took into the US Top 10.

BOBBY DARIN
DREAM LOVER
London American

▲ 1
⑩ 1
40/250

See US entry (May).

MARTY WILDE
A TEENAGER IN LOVE
Philips

▲ 2
⑩ 3
137/250

Both sides of Wilde's third Top 5 single had previously been recorded by Dion & The Belmonts. The Pomus & Shuman-penned teen classic was coupled with 'Danny', a song written for Elvis and turned into a hit by Conway Twitty (as 'Lonely Blue Boy') in 1960.

JOAN REGAN
MAY YOU ALWAYS
HMV

▲ 9
⑩ 5•
—/250

One of the UK's most popular British female vocalists of the mid-1950s last visited the Top 10 with her treatment of a standout song that also gave fellow 1950s stars the McGuire Sisters their last Top 20 entry. Regan, who hosted the top-rated TV show *Be My Guest*, moved to the US in the late 1960s. Her one-time accompanist, Russ Conway, convinced her to return to the UK for several successful shows in the 1990s.

LONNIE DONEGAN
BATTLE OF NEW
ORLEANS
Pye

▲ 2
⑩ 11
117/250

Surely only Donegan could turn a song about a British defeat into a major UK hit? Almost single handedly he had launched skiffle, which *NME* called 'the biggest musical craze Britain has ever known'. He was the most influential UK performer before The Beatles and inspired many of the 1960s beat boom stars to pick up guitars and form groups. Although now out of the spotlight, the first UK beat singer to crack the US chart remains one of Britain's most respected artists.

DUANE EDDY
PETER GUNN THEME
London American

▲ 6
⑩ 1
—/250

In the US, Ray Anthony hit with the Henry Mancini-composed TV theme, and Eddy's interpretation was not released until 1960. However, in the UK both this track and its flip side 'Yep' cracked the Top 20. Eddy's 1986 re-recording with Art Of Noise also reached the UK Top 10.

UNITED STATES
July 1959

STONEWALL JACKSON
WATERLOO
Columbia

▲ 4
⑩ 1•
—/250

The great grandson of confederate General Thomas 'Stonewall' Jackson followed fellow Columbia country artist Johnny Horton into the Top 5. North Carolina-born Jackson's follow-up to his first major country hit, 'Life To Go', was the biggest of the distinctive vocalist's three dozen country Top 40 entries. It was a rousing John D. Loudermilk song which told how certain people (including Napoleon and Tom Dooley) had met their Waterloos. The singer, who had been the first artist to join the Grand Ole Opry without a record deal, was voted Most Promising Male Artist of 1959.

FRANKIE AVALON
BOBBY SOX TO STOCKINGS
Chancellor

▲ 8
⑩ 4
—/250

Thanks in part to headlining appearances on both Alan Freed's and Dick Clark's stage shows, Avalon built up a formidable female following. This single, aimed straight at his fans who were 'trading baby toys for boys', ensured his place in their hearts.

CONNIE FRANCIS
FRANKIE
MGM

▲ 9
⑩ 4
—/250

Apparently, Connie asked Neil Sedaka to write a song about her boyfriend Bobby Darin. However, the composer penned this teen ballad about another Italian American star, Frankie Avalon. It joined the A side, 'Lipstick On Your Collar', which was already in the Top 10.

FABIAN
TIGER
Chancellor

▲ 3
⑩ 2
—/250

Stuffed tigers were to Fabulous Fabian what teddy bears were to Elvis, and it was therefore natural that he should record a song with this title. His biggest seller was written by R&B tunesmith Ollie Jones, who had previously penned hits for Nat 'King' Cole and Perry Como.

CARL DOBKINS JR
MY HEART IS AN OPEN BOOK
Decca

▲ 3
⑩ 1•
—/250

After releasing a single on his local Cincinnati label Fraternity, this teenage vocalist joined Decca, who sent him to Nashville to record with top producer Owen Bradley and the noted Anita Kerr Singers. For Dobkins' second Decca single, Bradley chose this Hal David and Lee Pockriss-penned puppy-love lament, which Jimmy Dean had earlier released, and after a slightly slow start it took off with the teen and pre-teen brigade. Soon afterwards Dobkins was drafted into the National Guard at Fort Knox and no more gold records came his way.

FRANKIE AVALON
A BOY WITHOUT A GIRL
Chancellor

▲ 10
⑩ 5
—/250

America's foremost teen balladeer saw this lilting love song join the other side, 'Bobby Sox To Stockings', in the Top 10. It came from the pen of Sid Jacobson, the composer of Earl Grant's gold disc 'The End' a year earlier.

ELVIS PRESLEY
BIG HUNK O' LOVE
RCA

▲ 1
⑩ 17
131/250

On his last hit of the decade the century's bestselling, best-known and most influential solo artist coupled one of his wildest rockers with one of his straightest ballads, 'My Wish Came True'. There is not room to list all of Presley's achievements and record-breaking feats, as he holds or held so many on both sides of the Atlantic. During Elvis' lifetime the King won almost every conceivable award and reached a plateau of worldwide fame that no other entertainer has ever achieved.

DRIFTERS
THERE GOES MY BABY
Atlantic

▲ 2
⑩ 1
—/250

Clyde McPhatter formed The Drifters in 1953 and they notched up nine R&B Top 10 entries by 1955. After a disagreement, their manager fired the whole group and replaced them with The Five Crowns. 'There Goes My Baby', which had little melody and few rhymes, was co-written by lead singer Ben E. King. Producers Leiber & Stoller added strings (a rarity in R&B) and the track sounded as if it was recorded in a tunnel. It took a year to convince Atlantic to release the first of the legendary act's numerous pop hits.

DUANE EDDY
FORTY MILES OF BAD
ROAD
Jamie

▲ 9
⑩ 2
—/250

One of the most frequent guests on Dick Clark's TV shows came up with this unusual title after overhearing two guys talking about a girl 'whose face looked like 40 miles of bad road'. Eddy, the first rock instrumentalist to reach super stardom, continued his run of transatlantic hits in the early 1960s, and was voted into the Rock and Roll Hall of Fame in 1994.

UNITED KINGDOM
July 1959

ANTHONY NEWLEY
PERSONALITY
Decca

▲ 6
⑩ 2
—/250

Anthony Newley is arguably the only Briton to have achieved international recognition as a singer, songwriter, producer, director, actor and cabaret performer. The entertainer with the unmistakable theatrical vocal style and distinctive quavering voice, scored the third of his ten UK Top 20 singles with a personality-packed rendition of this hit, which pipped the original US recording by Lloyd Price at the post.

LLOYD PRICE
PERSONALITY
HMV

▲ 9
⑩ 2•
—/250

See US entry (May).

RUBY MURRAY
GOODBYE JIMMY,
GOODBYE
Columbia

▲ 10
⑩ 8•
—/250

After a sensational run of hits in 1955, the unmistakable Irish songstress sold relatively few records, and returned only briefly to the Top 10 with her interpretation of a wistful ballad that Kathy Linden had taken into the US Top 20. Incidentally, no female performer came near to matching Murray's mid-1950s UK track record until Madonna over 30 years later.

CLIFF RICHARD
LIVING DOLL
Columbia

▲ 1
⑩ 4
17/250

A reworked version of a Lionel Bart song he performed in his debut film, *Serious Charge*, earned Cliff a gold record and introduced him to the US Top 40. A 1986 re-recording with comedy team The Young Ones also topped the UK chart.

CONNIE FRANCIS
LIPSTICK ON YOUR COLLAR
MGM

▲ 3
⑩ 4
167/250

See US entry (June).

ELVIS PRESLEY
BIG HUNK O' LOVE
RCA

▲ 4
⑩18
—/250

See US entry.

UNITED STATES
August 1959

SAMMY TURNER
LAVENDER-BLUE
Big Top

▲ 3
⑩ 1•
—/250

The New Jersey native's doo-wop roots were clearly showing on his Leiber & Stoller-produced revival of this 'dilly dilly' ditty. Turner (born Samuel Black) stretched out the neo-nursery rhyme and added vocal gymnastics that teens loved and most adults abhorred. For a follow-up, the flexible voiced ex-leader of The Twisters gave Irving Berlin's 'Always' a similar workover and it, too, reached the Top 20.

RICKY NELSON
SWEETER THAN YOU
Imperial

▲ 9
⑩10
—/250

Once again Nelson had a double-sided Top 10 entry, coupling a sweet teen ballad and an up-tempo pop/rocker. His regular hit provider Baker Knight composed the ballad, which The Gaylords also recorded.

DINAH WASHINGTON
WHAT A DIFFERENCE A DAY MAKES
Mercury

▲ 8
⑩ 1
—/250

Fifteen years after debuting on the R&B chart, the unique song stylist (born Ruth Lee Jones) from Alabama debuted on the pop list with her fortieth R&B hit. She clicked with a 25-year-old ballad that later gave Washington-soundalike Esther Phillips her only transatlantic Top 20 entry. This Grammy winner was the first of Washington's four pop Top 20s in 12 months. In 1993, the singer, who died from an overdose in 1963, was voted into the Rock and Roll Hall of Fame and also featured on a US postage stamp.

RAY CHARLES
WHAT'D I SAY (PART 1)
Atlantic

▲ 6
⑩ 1
—/250

Like fellow Top 10 entrants The Drifters and Dinah Washington, this blind singer/songwriter/pianist and bandleader (born Ray Charles Robinson) from Georgia had been a frequent visitor to the R&B charts before finding pop fame. He finally broke down the barriers with a seemingly untamed, gospel-based call-and-response stomper that helped launch the soul explosion of the next decade. The innovative and influential performer was one of the top artists of the 1960s, and continued adding to his collection of hits in the 1970s, 1980s and 1990s.

BROWNS
THE THREE BELLS
RCA

▲ 1
🔟 1
79/250

Siblings Jim Ed, Maxine and Bonnie Brown were already country headliners when their update of the French opus 'Les Trois Cloches' transported them into the transatlantic Top 10. The song had first been recorded in English as 'When The Angelus Was Ringing' in 1949, and charted as 'The Three Bells' in 1952 by Les Compagnons De La Chanson. Jim Ed sang lead on the song about his namesake, Jimmy Brown. The trio's next singles, revivals of 'Scarlet Ribbons' and 'The Lamp Lighter', also made the US Top 20.

RICKY NELSON
JUST A LITTLE TOO MUCH
Imperial

▲ 9
🔟 11
—/250

Although not the most powerful rock'n'roll vocalist, Nelson was one of the most popular. Johnny Burnette, later a hit maker in his own right, penned the consistently successful singer's eleventh and last Top 10 entry of the decade. Nelson, who moved into country rock in the mid-1960s, died in a plane crash in 1985.

PHIL PHILLIPS WITH THE TWILIGHTS
SEA OF LOVE
Mercury

▲ 2
🔟 1•
—/250

One of the decade's most haunting and hypnotic songs was written and performed by this Louisiana vocalist, born John Phillip Baptiste. Noted local band The Cupcakes backed him and he received strong vocal support from The Twilights. Mercury picked it up from Khoury, and after a slow start it narrowly missed the top. Phillips, who wrote 'Sea Of Love' for his girlfriend Verdie Mae, subsequently produced a version by The Five Ants (five of his children). In 1984 it sailed back into the Top 3 recorded by Led Zeppelin off-shoot The Honeydrippers.

SANTO & JOHNNY
SLEEP WALK
Canadian American

▲ 1
🔟 1•
111/250

The last instrumental No 1 of the decade came from New Yorkers Santo and Johnny Farina, who also composed their memorable million seller. This dreamy mid-tempo track, which featured Santo's haunting Hawaiian steel guitar, was the brothers' first and most successful single. Like many other records in the 1950s, it languished in the doldrums until Alan Freed put his weight behind it. The distinctive duo's other chart entries did not include their 1968 update of 'Sleep Walk'.

FATS DOMINO
I WANT TO WALK YOU HOME
Imperial

▲ 8
🔟 7
—/250

Domino's first transatlantic Top 20 entry for 30 months was another self-written song that highlighted his unique Creole pronunciation, which enabled him to rhyme words that other artists simply would not dare to attempt. Advertisements claimed sales of 300,000 in the first week.

LLOYD PRICE
I'M GONNA GET MARRIED
ABC Paramount

▲ 3
🔟 3•
—/250

This distinctive performer's fourth R&B No 1 was another self-written crossover classic with a catchy chorus. Interestingly, Titus Turner (who had recorded a sequel to Price's 'Stagger Lee') charted with an answer record 'We Told You Not To Marry'. Price, who added a handful more hits to his tally in the early 1960s, received a Pioneer Award from the R&B Foundation in 1995.

JOHNNY & THE HURRICANES
RED RIVER ROCK
Warwick

▲ 5
🔟 1•
—/250

At a time when many people were busy writing rock'n'roll's obituary, the sax-fronted instrumental quintet from Ohio rocked up the transatlantic charts with their frantic treatment of the traditional western tune 'Red River Valley'. The group, who first recorded on Twirl in 1958, were led by saxophonist Johnny Paris (real name Pocisk), a veteran of rockabilly performer Mack Vickery's band. Over the next couple of years this influential act logged several more transatlantic hits, and in 1962 The Beatles supported them at the Star Club, Hamburg.

UNITED KINGDOM
August 1959

PAUL ANKA
LONELY BOY
Columbia

▲ 3
⑩ 5
180/250

See US entry (June).

FRANKIE VAUGHAN
THE HEART OF A MAN
Philips

▲ 5
⑩ 8
—/250

Curiously, the Paddy Roberts-penned title song from Vaughan's fifth film was the only British composition among his 14 Top 20 entries in the 1950s. The hit came soon after he became the first British entertainer to headline at New York's Copacabana club. Frankie then went to Hollywood and starred alongside Marilyn Monroe in *Let's Make Love*. The British legend, who had spasmodic hits throughout the 1960s, received an OBE from the Queen in 1965.

CRAIG DOUGLAS
ONLY SIXTEEN
Top Rank

▲ 1
⑩ 4
8/250

Three versions of this singalong teen anthem made the UK charts, with clean-cut Douglas (real name Terence Perkins) taking the lion's share of sales. The teen idol from the Isle of Wight was only 18 when the single gave him the biggest of his nine UK Top 20 entries and helped him scoop the *NME* award for Best New Artist of 1959. The song, which was co-written by Sam Cooke, Lou Adler and Herb Alpert, finally made the US Top 10 in 1976 when revived by Dr Hook.

RUSS CONWAY
CHINA TEA
Columbia

▲ 5
⑩ 4
—/250

For the third time in six months one of pianist Conway's compositions headed the UK sheet music chart. There is no doubt that the one-time accompanist for acts such as Gracie Fields, Joan Regan and Lita Roza was the year's surprise superstar in the UK.

JOHNNY MATHIS
SOMEONE
Fontana

▲ 6
⑩ 2
—/250

Only Frank Sinatra and Elvis Presley have had more US chart albums than this critically acclaimed balladeer, who has amassed over five dozen entries to date. The stylish singer, who has packed houses around the world for 40 years, scored his second UK Top 10 single with a tender love song on which he was accompanied by the Ray Ellis Orchestra.

UNITED STATES
September 1959

EVERLY BROTHERS
('TIL) I KISSED YOU
Cadence

▲ 4
⑩ 6
—/250

The era's most successful duo ended the decade with their first self-penned smash. They were backed on the track by Buddy Holly's ex-band The Crickets. The duo continued to add to their transatlantic hit portfolio in the early 1960s, and there is no doubt that the brothers' very individual harmony vocal style had a powerful influence on many of the British and American groups that followed them.

SARAH VAUGHAN
BROKEN-HEARTED MELODY
Mercury

▲ 7
⑩ 2•
—/250

One of the most respected vocalists of the era had her biggest hit with a contemporary jazz-slanted song composed by Hal David and Sherman Edwards. The popular New Jersey-born performer, who boasted a very wide vocal range, was regarded by many as one of the great song interpreters. 'The Divine One' was awarded a Lifetime Achievement Grammy in 1989, just months before she died from cancer.

BOBBY DARIN
MACK THE KNIFE
Atco

The US' top song of 1959 was over 30 years old and had first been performed by composer Kurt Weill's wife Lotte Lenya (who is mentioned in it). Even though it was banned on some stations (for promoting violence), 'Mack The Knife' was a transatlantic No 1 and won the Grammy for Best Record of the Year. Darin, who successfully moved from *Bandstand* to Las Vegas, remained a popular entertainer until his death in 1973.

JAN & DEAN
BABY TALK
Dore

▲ 10
⑩ 2
—/250

At the outset, this single was released as by Jan & Arnie, to cash in on that duo's 1958 smash 'Jennie Lee'. However, when their version of the novelty number, first cut by composer Melvin Schwartz, started flying out of the shops the act's name was corrected to Jan (Berry) & Dean (Torrence). It was the first single the future surf stars had recorded under the wing of manager/producers Herb Alpert and Lou Adler.

PAUL ANKA
PUT YOUR HEAD ON MY SHOULDER
ABC Paramount

▲ 2
⑩ 4
194/250

As he headlined Dick Clark's *Caravan Of Stars* (alongside such acts as Duane Eddy, Lloyd Price and Annette), Anka clocked up his last transatlantic Top 10 entry for 15 years with another self-composed teen-ballad classic.

SANDY NELSON
TEEN BEAT
Original Sound

When he noticed that drummer Cozy Cole and bongo player Preston Epps ('Bongo Rock') were having Top 20 hits, session drummer Nelson decided to record his own rock instrumental. He personally financed 'Teen Beat', which also featured top guitarist Barney Kessel and future Beach Boy Bruce Johnston, and placed it with Epps' label Original Sound (owned by noted DJ Art Laboe). The single darted up the transatlantic charts and quickly established Nelson as rock's best-known drummer.

UNITED KINGDOM

September 1959

JERRY KELLER
HERE COMES SUMMER
London American

▲ 1
⑩ 1•
95/250

This self-penned summertime anthem gave the one-time demo singer from Arkansas his only chart entry on either side of the Atlantic. Curiously, the happy-go-lucky teen tune, which started as the B side to the ballad 'Time Has A Way', climbed to the top in the UK as autumn replaced summer. It is perhaps even more strange that a song about the joys of drive-in movies should have been so successful in a country that had none.

CONWAY TWITTY
MONA LISA
MGM

▲ 5
⑩ 2•
—/250

Hit maker Twitty was in the studio when 16-year-old Carl Mann recorded a rockabilly rendition of this 1950 million seller by Nat 'King' Cole. The Mississippi-born performer covered Mann's single and his version returned him to the UK Top 10. However, in the US Mann's interpretation outsold Twitty's treatment.

EVERLY BROTHERS
('TIL) I KISSED YOU
London American

▲ 2
⑩ 6
136/250

See US entry.

UNITED STATES

October 1959

FLEETWOODS
MR BLUE
Dolton

▲ 1
⑩ 2
100/250

Mellow Washington trio The Fleetwoods scored their second No 1 in six months with a song written by Dewayne Blackwell for The Platters. This unique act amassed nine Top 40 singles in the pre-Beatles era and may have fared better had Gary Troxel not been drafted. 'Mr Blue' was later included on the 13 million-selling album *No Fences* by Garth Brooks.

COASTERS
POISON IVY
Atco

Although their run of Top 10 singles did not spill over into the 1960s, The Coasters' records were revived by many later groups including The Beatles, Rolling Stones and Hollies. In fact, both sides of the quintet's last major hits, the catchy R&B No 1 'Poison Ivy' and it's coupling 'I'm A Hog For You', were musts for every British R&B band.

FRANKIE AVALON
JUST ASK YOUR HEART
Chancellor

▲ 7
⑩ 6
—/250

No one had more Top 10 singles in 1959 than this extremely popular teen celebrity. The singer, who frequently appeared on both *Bandstand* and the top-rated Saturday night *Dick Clark Show*, added to his hits with another rapturously received teenage love song.

ANDY WILLIAMS
LONELY STREET
Cadence

▲ 5
⑩ 4
—/250

One of the biggest-selling MOR artists of all time had his last hit of the 1950s with a lost-love lament penned and previously recorded by country singer Carl Belew. It was the eighth Top 20 entry by the relaxed performer who was voted Personality of the Year, thanks in part to his successful summer CBS-TV series. *Lonely Street* was also the title of the first of his numerous chart albums.

DELLA REESE
DON'T YOU KNOW
RCA

▲ 2
⑩ 1•
224/250

Detroit-born Delloreese Early's bestseller was adapted from Puccini's 'Musetta's Waltz' from *La Boheme* (which, due to copyright problems, was not released in the UK at the time). The vocalist, who as a teenager had sung in the groups of top gospel stars Mahalia Jackson and Clara Ward, was equally at home on the nightclub and rock'n'roll circuits. RCA paid a big advance for the soulful song stylist, whose first solo single was issued in 1953, and who subsequently starred in the TV series *The Jeffersons*.

JERRY WALLACE
PRIMROSE LANE
Challenge

▲ 8
⑩ 1•
—/250

This bouncy Wayne Shanklin-composed pop pearl earned the clean-cut singer from Missouri his only gold disc. Wallace, who often appeared on Dick Clark shows, had been recording with little success since 1952 (including a spell with the 49 cent cover label, Tops). He returned to the Top 20 with 'In The Misty Moonlight' in 1964, and a year later started a run of country hits which culminated in the 1972 No 1 'If You Leave Me Tonight I'll Cry'.

WINK MARTINDALE
DECK OF CARDS
Dot

▲ 7
⑩ 1•
—/250

T. Texas Tyler wrote the memorable monologue about a soldier playing cards in church, and in 1948 his version narrowly missed the top of the country chart. It was turned into a transatlantic pop hit by the host of KHV-TV's *Teenage Dance Party*. Tennessee-born Martindale, who started as a radio DJ, had recorded a few small-selling singles before lady luck dealt him a good hand. Astonishingly, in the UK this single reached the Top 40 in 1959, 1963 (peaking at No 5) and 1973.

UNITED KINGDOM
October 1959

BOBBY DARIN
MACK THE KNIFE
London American

▲ 1
⑩ 2
81/250

See US entry (September).

BROWNS
THE THREE BELLS
RCA

▲ 6
⑩ 1•
—/250

See US entry (August).

FRANK SINATRA
HIGH HOPES
Capitol

▲ 6
⑩ 6
—/250

Yet again the year's Academy Award winner was penned by Sammy Cahn and came from a Frank Sinatra film. This time it was an uplifting children's anthem on which the internationally celebrated performer was joined by 13-year-old Eddie Hodges. Sinatra, who many consider to be a song's best friend, continued to rack up hits in the 1960s. He retired for the first (of many) times in 1970, and was still breaking house records and selling millions of albums in the 1990s.

MARTY WILDE
SEA OF LOVE
Philips

▲ 3
⑩ 4
220/250

The host of the top-rated new pop TV show *Boy Meets Girls* continued his run of Top 10 singles with a cover of Phil Phillips' self-composed US million seller. Joe Meek (later a leading producer/writer) engineered the track which, as usual, Johnny Franz produced. Wilde added to his hit portfolio in the early 1960s and subsequently turned his hand most successfully to songwriting.

CLIFF RICHARD
TRAVELLIN' LIGHT
Columbia

▲ 1
⑩ 5
31/250

Top American songsmiths Tepper & Bennett composed the ballad that quickly returned Cliff to the No 1 slot, and its rockin' B side, 'Dynamite', gave him his eighth Top 20 entry in a year. Sir Cliff Richard (as he is now known) has had a UK career without parallel; he has amassed more Top 10 hits than any other act and sold nearly 100 million records overall.

SARAH VAUGHAN
BROKEN-HEARTED
MELODY
Mercury

▲ 7
⑩ 1•
—/250

See US entry (September).

JOHNNY & THE HURRICANES
RED RIVER ROCK
London American

▲ 3
⑩ 1
190/250

See US entry (August).

UNITED STATES
November 1959

PAUL EVANS & THE CURLS
SEVEN LITTLE GIRLS SITTING IN THE BACK SEAT
Guaranteed

▲ 9
⑩ 1
—/250

After recording without success for RCA, Decca and Atlantic, the New York singer/songwriter, who composed the Kalin Twin's million seller 'When', became the first act signed to Carlton Records' Guaranteed subsidiary. The label loved Evans' demo of this cute novelty so much that they released it as it was, and had enough faith to take

a (very rare) double-page advertisement in the trade papers. The story song about Paul's lucky friend Fred was the first of his three Top 20 entries.

GUY MITCHELL
HEARTACHES BY THE NUMBER
Columbia

▲ 1
⑩ 8•
101/250

After a couple of relatively quiet sales years, one of the most popular show business personalities of the 1950s had his last major hit with a cover of Ray Price's recent country charter. Like many of his peers, Mitchell's later career was dogged by personal problems, and his infrequent recordings sold far fewer copies.

BROOK BENTON
SO MANY WAYS
Mercury

▲ 6
🔟 2
—/250

Before he found fame, this distinctive vocalist had recorded without success for Columbia and RCA and sung on over 500 song demos. The one-time gospel singer scored his eighth US chart entry of the year with another standout R&B ballad. Benton was one of the top-selling artists of the early 1960s, racking up total sales in the region of 20 million.

ERNIE FIELDS
IN THE MOOD
Rendezvous

▲ 4
🔟 1•
—/250

'In The Mood' was first performed by the Edgar Hayes Band (who included its composer Joe Garland) and was later made famous by the orchestras of Glenn Miller and Joe Loss in the UK. Veteran Texan R&B/jazz bandleader/arranger Fields, whose studio band included such noted musicians as Plas Johnson, Earl Palmer and Rene Hall, had the biggest hit of his long career with this rocking rendition. Fields (who didn't actually play on this record) followed the transatlantic Top 20

entry with a similar treatment of Miller's 'Chattanooga Choo Choo'.

BOBBY RYDELL
WE GOT LOVE
Cameo

▲ 6
🔟 1
—/250

As the 1950s faded and Alan Freed and Dick Clark were drawn into the US Government's payola ('pay for play') probe, Philadelphia produced yet another photogenic teen idol. Like Fabian, Rydell (born Robert Ridarelli) was not an instant hit but, after a few best-forgotten flops, he strung together a run of bestsellers that lasted until The Beatles appeared. Chart regulars Mann & Lowe composed this singalong teen beat tune which the youthful showbiz veteran duly performed on stage and TV with Freed and Clark.

FATS DOMINO
BE MY GUEST
Imperial

▲ 8
🔟 8
—/250

Future hit singer/songwriter Tommy Boyce was just 14 when he co-wrote this bouncy bopper for Fats. It was the last hit of the decade for the legendary performer who had been rockin' and rollin' long before the term was coined. Domino, who amassed more than five dozen US chart entries, was rightfully among the first acts voted into the Rock and Roll Hall of Fame.

UNITED KINGDOM
November 1959

EMILE FORD & THE CHECKMATES
WHAT DO YOU WANT
TO MAKE THOSE EYES
AT ME FOR
Pye

▲ 1
🔟 1
19/250

West Indian vocalist Ford (real name Emile Sweatman) and his multi-racial pop/R&B band

intended to release a cover of Don Gibson's 'Don't Tell Me Your Troubles' as their debut single. However, it was the group's rush-recorded B side revival of this World War I music hall favourite that went on to sell over a million in the UK alone, and became the forerunner of many other Ford hits. The Michael Barclay-produced track employed an arrangement similar to that used a year earlier by The Johnny Otis Show.

PAUL ANKA
PUT YOUR HEAD ON MY
SHOULDER
Columbia

See US entry (September).

FLOYD ROBINSON
MAKIN' LOVE
RCA

After his composition 'Little Space Girl' rocketed up the chart by Jesse Lee Turner, RCA released this Nashville native's own version of another novelty, 'My Girl'. However, the public preferred the B side, on which Robinson wondered what people would think and say if they knew he 'was with you making love' (which then was presumed to mean simply a little kissing and hugging). Later releases, including the similarly titled 'The Art Of Making Love' and an early treatment of 'Let It Be Me' failed to follow it into the transatlantic Top 20.

NEIL SEDAKA
OH! CAROL
RCA

Up-and-coming singer/songwriter Carole King was not only the inspiration for one of the year's most memorable pop songs, but also recorded a humorous answer version, 'Oh Neil'. The first of his six transatlantic Top 20 singles re-entered the UK Top 20 in 1972 and a revival of its title-dropping B side, 'One Way Ticket', was a UK Top 5 hit by Eruption in 1979.

ADAM FAITH
WHAT DO YOU WANT
Parlophone

Londoner Faith (born Terry Nelhams) recorded for HMV and Top Rank before joining Parlophone and giving George Martin's label the first of its numerous No 1s. This Buddy Holly-influenced pop pearl was written (and recorded) by Johnny Worth, who had worked with Faith on the TV series *Drumbeat*. It was the first of a record seven successive Top 5 singles by the popular teen pin-up, although the single was an also-ran in the US where it fought cover versions by Bobby Vee, rocker Ersel Hickey and the UK's Craig Douglas.

UNITED STATES
December 1959

NEIL SEDAKA
OH! CAROL
RCA

See US Entry.

CONWAY TWITTY
DANNY BOY
MGM

His rock treatment of 'Londonderry Air' returned the distinctive 'growling' baritone to the US Top 10. However, in the UK, due to copyright problems,

Twitty had to re-vocal the track and the revised 'Rosalena' sold few. He followed it with another Danny ditty, 'Lonely Blue Boy' (originally titled 'Danny'). When the pop hits stopped, Twitty moved into country music and notched up more No 1 singles than any other artist.

FRANKIE AVALON
WHY
Chancellor

Like his first hit, 'Dede Dinah', Avalon's last Top 20 entry was penned by Bob Marcucci and Peter De

Angelis. The decade's final No 1 was a somewhat dated easy-on-the-ear ballad that some considered musically similar to 'In A Little Spanish Town'. When his record sales slipped, Avalon moved successfully on to the big screen (making a bevy of 'Beach' movies) and later to the supper club circuit. A part share in the musical *Grease* reputedly made him a millionaire.

PAUL ANKA
IT'S TIME TO CRY
ABC Paramount

One of the late 1950's most popular performers had his eighth US Top 20 entry with yet another self-composed song. The teenager continued clocking up hits in the early 1960s and returned for another chart run in the 1970s. This Songwriters' Hall of Fame member also penned huge hits for such acts as Buddy Holly, Tom Jones and Frank Sinatra ('My Way').

MISS TONI FISHER
THE BIG HURT
Signet

Three weeks after Jerry Wallace's 'Primrose Lane' left the Top 10, another notable Wayne Shanklin composition replaced it – thanks in no small part to the ear-catching arrangement employed on this petite Los Angeles nightclub entertainer's version. The ballad itself was by no means run-of-the-mill, and the addition of a striking guitar reverb sound helped it stand out from other records. 'The Big Hurt' was the big hit the one-time child prodigy had waited for; sadly, though, most of Miss Fisher's later releases were misses.

MARTY ROBBINS
EL PASO
Columbia

During his 30 year recording career, the legendary Tex-Mex pioneer notched up 62 Top 20 country entries, the biggest being a Grammy-winning four-minute tale about a murder that took place at Rosa's Cantina. It was the first UK hit for the act whose recent releases, 'Story Of My Life' and 'Stairway Of Love', had been covered successfully by several UK artists. A later sequel, 'El Paso City', headed the country chart by Robbins in 1976.

FREDDY CANNON
WAY DOWN YONDER IN NEW ORLEANS
Swan

Every track on the energetic entertainer's first album, *The Explosive Freddy Cannon*, included the name of a place in America. The performer, who is sometimes tagged 'the last rock'n' roll star', scored his biggest transatlantic hit with a distinctive 'boom boom' update of this 1922 standard, which was taken from that UK No 1 album.

CONNIE FRANCIS
AMONG MY SOUVENIRS
MGM

The 'Queen of Pop' notched up her fifth transatlantic Top 20 entry with this revival of a British song from 1927. Francis, who ended the decade as the world's bestselling female vocalist, continued to add to her portfolio of hits in the early 1960s. She set many records for female singers that remained unchallenged until Madonna arrived on the scene.

FABIAN
HOUND DOG MAN
Chancellor

In 1959 this much maligned performer scored six Top 40 singles and two Top 5 albums, and was arguably the US' most popular teen idol. Fabian ended the year with two songs from his debut movie *Hound Dog Man* in the Top 20. Pomus and Shuman penned the up-tempo A side and Ken Darby (who had also worked on Elvis' first film) composed the ballad flip.

STEVE LAWRENCE
PRETTY BLUE EYES
ABC Paramount

Q: What have 'Fabulous', 'The Banana Boat Song' and 'Party Doll' got in common? A: Well, apart from being Top 10 hits, they were all covered by this classy cabaret performer from New York (born Steve Leibowitz). The song stylist, who was frequently seen on Steve Allen's *Tonight Show*, finally started his own run of Top 10 entries with a teen-targeted ballad co-written by early rock'n'roller Teddy Randazzo, ex-member of The Three Chuckles.

UNITED KINGDOM
December 1959

AVONS
SEVEN LITTLE
GIRLS SITTING IN
THE BACK SEAT
Columbia

▲ 3
🔟 1•
219/250

After a couple of singles as the Avon Sisters failed to tempt record buyers, sisters-in-law Valerie and Elaine Murtagh added Jersey native Ray Adams and became The Avons. Their first release as a trio was a spirited cover of the winning novelty that composer Paul Evans had driven up the US chart. It was the act's only noticeable hit, although they wrote The Shadows' 1963 No 1, 'Dance On'. Interestingly, another British treatment by Al Saxon featured future chart regular Dusty Springfield on backing vocals.

SANDY NELSON
TEEN BEAT
Top Rank

▲ 9
🔟 1
—/250

See US entry (September).

RUSS CONWAY
SNOW COACH
Columbia

▲ 7
🔟 5
—/250

In 1959 no recording artist spend longer on the UK chart than the prolific pianist, who took an amazing six singles into the Top 10. Surprisingly, this foot-tapping seasonal single was Conway's last self-composed Top 10 entry.

RUSS CONWAY
MORE AND MORE PARTY
POPS
Columbia

▲ 5
🔟 6•
—/250

Producer Norman Newell started the decade with a string of Steve Conway chart entries and ended it with a run of hits by a performer that he had renamed after that earlier star. A year after 'More Party Pops' introduced this personable pianist to the Top 10, Conway clicked with another selection of party songs. It was one of the last hits by the entertainer, whose music appeared to be unaffected by the arrival of rock.

FRANKIE LAINE
RAWHIDE
Philips

▲ 6
🔟 18•
—/250

As the decade closed, one of its most consistently enjoyable performers rode up the UK Top 10 for the final time. Like many of his earlier successes, Laine's last hit was a western theme song – this time taken from a popular TV series. The man whose robust vocal style had helped crush crooners now found himself replaced by rock'n'roll stars less than half his age. Nevertheless, he was still topping bills when the majority of them were long forgotten.

WINIFRED ATWELL
PIANO PARTY
Decca

▲ 10
🔟 11•
—/250

The rise of rock and fellow pianist Russ Conway helped halt Atwell's amazing run of hits. Her last bestselling medley included the standards 'Baby Face', 'Apple Blossom Time' and 'I'll See You In My Dreams' – which had all recently been revived successfully. The bubbling, vivacious performer sold over 20 million records in the 1950s. Atwell was equally popular in Australia, to where she relocated in the 1970s.

ELMER BERNSTEIN & HIS ORCHESTRA
STACCATO'S THEME
Capitol

▲ 4
⑩ 1•
—/250

Few people can claim to have written as many successful film scores as this New York-born composer and conductor. In 1956, Bernstein's recording of his ground-breaking main title theme from the film *The Man With The Golden Arm* reached the US Top 20, although in the UK Billy May's Orchestra took the honours. His big British hit came with the title theme from TV's popular *Johnny Staccato Show* – which had negligible sales in the US.

TOMMY STEELE
LITTLE WHITE BULL
Decca

▲ 6
⑩ 6
—/250

The UK's first rock star always wanted to be an all-round entertainer, and by the end of the decade Steele was well on his way to this goal. The final hit of the 1950s by the one-time target of teen worship was a children's novelty written for his fifth film, *Tommy The Toreador*, by Lionel Bart. Steele's only US success came in the 1960s, when he appeared in several Hollywood musicals.

THE US
TOP 100 ARTISTS
1950–1959

1 ELVIS PRESLEY	35 CREW-CUTS	69 ROGER WILLIAMS
2 PERRY COMO	36 FONTANE SISTERS	70 VAUGHN MONROE
3 EDDIE FISHER	37 FOUR LADS	71 FRANK CHACKSFIELD
4 PATTI PAGE	38 CHUCK BERRY	72 JULIUS LA ROSA
5 PAT BOONE	39 CONNIE FRANCIS	73 FABIAN
6 LES PAUL	40 MCGUIRE SISTERS	74 ANTON KARAS
7 NAT 'KING' COLE	41 MARIO LANZA	75 AL HIBBLER
8 RICKY NELSON	42 DEAN MARTIN	76 DON CHERRY
9 FRANKIE LAINE	43 GUY LOMBARDO	77 PERCY FAITH
10 KAY STARR	44 TENNESSEE ERNIE FORD	78 LEROY ANDERSON
11 GUY MITCHELL	45 BILL HALEY & HIS COMETS	79 GALE STORM
12 FOUR ACES	46 GEORGIA GIBBS	80 DIAMONDS
13 ROSEMARY CLOONEY	47 JIMMIE RODGERS	81 JOHNNY MATHIS
14 AMES BROTHERS	48 KITTY KALLEN	82 CONWAY TWITTY
15 JOHNNIE RAY	49 PERCY FAITH	83 LITTLE RICHARD
16 TONY BENNETT	50 LLOYD PRICE	84 DINAH SHORE
17 PLATTERS	51 CHORDETTES	85 ANDREWS SISTERS
18 JO STAFFORD	52 GAYLORDS	86 FREDDY CANNON
19 EVERLY BROTHERS	53 PEREZ PRADO	87 BROOK BENTON
20 GORDON JENKINS	54 BILLY VAUGHN	88 RAY ANTHONY
21 TONY MARTIN	55 HUGO WINTERHALTER	89 GOGI GRANT
22 LES BAXTER	56 GARY CROSBY	90 BILL HAYES
23 DORIS DAY	57 ANDY WILLIAMS	91 NELSON RIDDLE
24 FATS DOMINO	58 MITCH MILLER	92 JACK SCOTT
25 TERESA BREWER	59 SAMMY KAYE	93 GENE AUTRY
26 FRANKIE AVALON	60 FLEETWOODS	94 TOMMY EDWARDS
27 BING CROSBY	61 JERRY LEE LEWIS	95 FOUR PREPS
28 WEAVERS	62 MILLS BROTHERS	96 DELL-VIKINGS
29 PAUL ANKA	63 DEBBIE REYNOLDS	97 DANNY & THE JUNIORS
30 FRANK SINATRA	64 HILLTOPPERS	98 EARTHA KITT
31 DON CORNELL	65 VERA LYNN	99 EDDY HOWARD
32 JONI JAMES	66 MARTY ROBBINS	100 AL MARTINO
33 COASTERS	67 BILLY ECKSTINE	
34 BOBBY DARIN	68 CHIPMUNKS	

THE UK
TOP 100 ARTISTS
Nov 1952–1959

1 FRANKIE LAINE
2 ELVIS PRESLEY
3 GUY MITCHELL
4 DAVID WHITFIELD
5 LONNIE DONEGAN
6 PAT BOONE
7 JOHNNIE RAY
8 WINIFRED ATWELL
9 PERRY COMO
10 NAT 'KING' COLE
11 BILL HALEY & HIS COMETS
12 DEAN MARTIN
13 DORIS DAY
14 EDDIE FISHER
15 RUBY MURRAY
16 DICKIE VALENTINE
17 FRANKIE VAUGHAN
18 EVERLY BROTHERS
19 FRANK SINATRA
20 PAUL ANKA
21 RUSS CONWAY
22 CLIFF RICHARD
23 ROSEMARY CLOONEY
24 AL MARTINO
25 CONNIE FRANCIS
26 TOMMY STEELE
27 JIMMY YOUNG
28 EDDIE CALVERT
29 RONNIE HILTON
30 BING CROSBY
31 STARGAZERS
32 KAY STARR
33 MAX BYGRAVES
34 HARRY BELAFONTE
35 PLATTERS

36 TENNESSEE ERNIE FORD
37 MARTY WILDE
38 SLIM WHITMAN
39 MALCOLM VAUGHAN
40 ALMA COGAN
41 LITTLE RICHARD
42 JOAN REGAN
43 MANTOVANI
44 CRICKETS
45 BUDDY HOLLY
46 FOUR ACES
47 PETULA CLARK
48 SHIRLEY BASSEY
49 VERA LYNN
50 BOBBY DARIN
51 TED HEATH
52 TERESA BREWER
53 JOHNSTON BROTHERS
54 RICKY NELSON
55 TAB HUNTER
56 JERRY LEE LEWIS
57 FRANK CHACKSFIELD
58 CONWAY TWITTY
59 FRANKIE LYMON & THE
   TEENAGERS
60 MICHAEL HOLLIDAY
61 PEREZ PRADO
62 JO STAFFORD
63 BILLY COTTON & HIS BAND
64 TONY MARTIN
65 JIMMY BOYD
66 ANTHONY NEWLEY
67 JOHNNY MATHIS
68 BILLY ECKSTINE
69 GOONS

70 NEIL SEDAKA
71 PEGGY LEE
72 EMILE FORD & THE
   CHECKMATES
73 DON CORNELL
74 MUDLARKS
75 KALIN TWINS
76 KITTY KALLEN
77 BEVERLEY SISTERS
78 CHARLIE GRACIE
79 DREAM WEAVERS
80 LORD ROCKINGHAM'S XI
81 CRAIG DOUGLAS
82 LOUIS ARMSTRONG
83 ANNE SHELTON
84 OBERNKIRCHEN
   CHILDREN'S CHOIR
85 TOMMY EDWARDS
86 ADAM FAITH
87 TONY BENNETT
88 MARVIN RAINWATER
89 VIC DAMONE
90 CHORDETTES
91 LLOYD PRICE
92 MARIO LANZA
93 ANDY WILLIAMS
94 TONY BRENT
95 LITA ROZA
96 JERRY KELLER
97 JANE MORGAN
98 KAYE SISTERS
99 RON GOODWIN
100 GRACE KELLY

THE US
TOP 250 SINGLES
1950–1959

1 VAYA CON DIOS
LES PAUL & MARY FORD
CAPITOL

2 GOODNIGHT IRENE
GORDON JENKINS & THE WEAVERS
DECCA

3 *THE THIRD MAN* THEME
ANTON KARAS
LONDON

4 CRY
JOHNNIE RAY
OKEH

5 HOUND DOG/DON'T BE CRUEL
ELVIS PRESLEY
RCA

6 BECAUSE OF YOU
TONY BENNETT
COLUMBIA

7 SONG FROM MOULIN ROUGE
PERCY FAITH & FELICIA SANDERS
COLUMBIA

8 CHERRY PINK AND APPLE BLOSSOM WHITE
PEREZ PRADO
RCA

9 LITTLE THINGS MEAN A LOT
KITTY KALLEN
DECCA

10 BLUE TANGO
LEROY ANDERSON
DECCA

11 THE TENNESSEE WALTZ
PATTI PAGE
MERCURY

12 HOW HIGH THE MOON
LES PAUL & MARY FORD
CAPITOL

13 WHEEL OF FORTUNE
KAY STARR
CAPITOL

14 ROCK AROUND THE CLOCK
BILL HALEY & HIS COMETS
DECCA

15 SINGING THE BLUES
GUY MITCHELL
COLUMBIA

16 WANTED
PERRY COMO
RCA

17 THE DOGGIE IN THE WINDOW
PATTI PAGE
MERCURY

18 TOO YOUNG
NAT 'KING' COLE
CAPITOL

19 MACK THE KNIFE
BOBBY DARIN
ATCO

20 MONA LISA
NAT 'KING' COLE
CAPITOL

21 AUF WIEDERSEH'N SWEETHEART
VERA LYNN
LONDON

22 COLD, COLD HEART
TONY BENNETT
COLUMBIA

23 OH! MY PA-PA
EDDIE FISHER
RCA

24 HEY THERE
ROSEMARY CLOONEY
COLUMBIA

25 SH-BOOM
CREW-CUTS
MERCURY

26 RAGS TO RICHES
TONY BENNETT
COLUMBIA

27 HEARTBREAK HOTEL
ELVIS PRESLEY
RCA

28 MR SANDMAN
CHORDETTES
CADENCE

29 TILL I WALTZ AGAIN WITH YOU
TERESA BREWER
CORAL

30 SIXTEEN TONS
TENNESSEE ERNIE FORD
CAPITOL

31 JAILHOUSE ROCK
ELVIS PRESLEY
RCA

32 YOU BELONG TO ME
JO STAFFORD
COLUMBIA

33 DON'T LET THE STARS GET IN YOUR EYES
PERRY COMO
RCA

34 THE YELLOW ROSE OF TEXAS
MITCH MILLER
COLUMBIA

35 IF
PERRY COMO
RCA

36 TEDDY BEAR
ELVIS PRESLEY
RCA

37 AUTUMN LEAVES
ROGER WILLIAMS
KAPP

38 LOVE LETTERS IN THE SAND
PAT BOONE
DOT

39 THE WAYWARD WIND
GOGI GRANT
ERA

40 BE MY LOVE
MARIO LANZA
RCA

41 I WENT TO YOUR WEDDING
PATTI PAGE
MERCURY

42 THE BALLAD OF DAVY CROCKETT
BILL HAYES
CADENCE

43 ALL SHOOK UP
ELVIS PRESLEY
RCA

44 COME ON-A MY HOUSE
ROSEMARY CLOONEY
COLUMBIA

45 SINCERELY
MCGUIRE SISTERS
CORAL

46 WHY DON'T YOU BELIEVE ME
JONI JAMES
MGM

47 LOVE ME TENDER
ELVIS PRESLEY
RCA

48 LISBON ANTIGUA
NELSON RIDDLE
CAPITOL

49 MEMORIES ARE MADE OF THIS
DEAN MARTIN
CAPITOL

50 I NEED YOU NOW
EDDIE FISHER
RCA

51 IT'S ALL IN THE GAME
TOMMY EDWARDS
MGM

52 THIS OLE HOUSE
ROSEMARY CLOONEY
COLUMBIA

53 I'M WALKING BEHIND YOU
EDDIE FISHER
RCA

54 MAKE LOVE TO ME!
JO STAFFORD
COLUMBIA

55 HARBOR LIGHTS
SAMMY KAYE
COLUMBIA

56 AT THE HOP
DANNY & THE JUNIORS
ABC PARAMOUNT

57 THE POOR PEOPLE OF PARIS
LES BAXTER
CAPITOL

58 MUSIC! MUSIC! MUSIC!
TERESA BREWER
LONDON

59 SIN
EDDY HOWARD
MERCURY

60 SECRET LOVE
DORIS DAY
COLUMBIA

61 TAMMY
DEBBIE REYNOLDS
DOT

62 LOVE IS A MANY-SPLENDOURED THING
FOUR ACES
DECCA

63 HERE IN MY HEART
AL MARTINO
BBS

64 NEL BLU DIPINTO DI BLU (VOLARE)
DOMENICO MODUGNO
DECCA

65 CHATTANOOGIE SHOE SHINE BOY
RED FOLEY
DECCA

66 THE THING
PHIL HARRIS
RCA

67 YOU YOU YOU
AMES BROTHERS
RCA

68 IT'S IN THE BOOK
JOHNNY STANDLEY
CAPITOL

69 THE PURPLE PEOPLE EATER
SHEB WOOLEY
MGM

70 TEQUILA
CHAMPS
CHALLENGE

71 ALL I HAVE TO DO IS DREAM
EVERLY BROTHERS
CADENCE

72 VENUS
FRANKIE AVALON
CHANCELLOR

73 DELICADO
PERCY FAITH
COLUMBIA

74 DON'T/I BEG OF YOU
ELVIS PRESLEY
RCA

75 YOUNG LOVE
TAB HUNTER
DOT

76 MY PRAYER
PLATTERS
MERCURY

77 LONELY BOY
PAUL ANKA
ABC PARAMOUNT

78 TO KNOW HIM, IS TO LOVE HIM
TEDDY BEARS
DORE

79 THE THREE BELLS
BROWNS
RCA

80 STAGGER LEE
LLOYD PRICE
ABC PARAMOUNT

81 THE LOVELIEST NIGHT OF THE YEAR
MARIO LANZA
RCA

82 THE BATTLE OF NEW ORLEANS
JOHNNY HORTON
COLUMBIA

83 SMOKE GETS IN YOUR EYES
PLATTERS
MERCURY

84 APRIL LOVE/WHEN THE SWALLOWS COME BACK TO CAPISTRANO
PAT BOONE
DOT

85 YOU SEND ME
SAM COOKE
KEEN

86 ST GEORGE AND THE DRAGONET
STAN FREBERG
CAPITOL

87 COME SOFTLY TO ME
FLEETWOODS
DOLPHIN

88 LET ME GO, LOVER
JOAN WEBER
COLUMBIA

89 ROCK AND ROLL WALTZ
KAY STARR
RCA

90 WITCH DOCTOR
DAVID SEVILLE
LIBERTY

91 IF I KNEW YOU WERE COMIN' I'D'VE BAKED A CAKE
EILEEN BARTON
NATIONAL

92 HONEYCOMB
JIMMIE RODGERS
ROULETTE

93 I WANT YOU, I NEED YOU, I LOVE YOU
ELVIS PRESLEY
RCA

94 HEARTS OF STONE
FONTANE SISTERS
DOT

95 IT'S ONLY MAKE BELIEVE
CONWAY TWITTY
MGM

96 TOM DOOLEY
KINGSTON TRIO
CAPITOL

97 TOO MUCH
ELVIS PRESLEY
RCA

98 I GET IDEAS
TONY MARTIN
RCA

99 DIANA
PAUL ANKA
ABC PARAMOUNT

100 MR BLUE
FLEETWOODS
DOLTON

101 HEARTACHES BY THE NUMBER
GUY MITCHELL
COLUMBIA

102 THAT'S AMORE
DEAN MARTIN
CAPITOL

103 EL PASO
MARTY ROBBINS
COLUMBIA

104 I BELIEVE
FRANKIE LAINE
COLUMBIA

105 *THE THIRD MAN* THEME
GUY LOMBARDO
DECCA

106 THE CHIPMUNK SONG
CHIPMUNKS
LIBERTY

107 ROUND AND ROUND
PERRY COMO
RCA

108 EBB TIDE
FRANK CHACKSFIELD
LONDON

109 WAKE UP LITTLE SUSIE
EVERLY BROTHERS
CADENCE

110 POOR LITTLE FOOL
RICKY NELSON
IMPERIAL

111 SLEEP WALK
SANTO & JOHNNY
CANADIAN AMERICAN

112 THE GREEN DOOR
JIM LOWE
DOT

113 NO OTHER LOVE
PERRY COMO
RCA

114 HALF AS MUCH
ROSEMARY CLOONEY
COLUMBIA

115 GLOW WORM
MILLS BROTHERS
DECCA

116 LITTLE STAR
ELEGANTS
APT

117 ON TOP OF OLD SMOKY
WEAVERS
DECCA

118 APRIL IN PORTUGAL
LES BAXTER
CAPITOL

119 RAG MOP
AMES BROTHERS
CORAL

120 TWILIGHT TIME
PLATTERS
MERCURY

121 UNCHAINED MELODY
LES BAXTER
CAPITOL

122 KANSAS CITY
WILBERT HARRISON
FURY

123 YOUNG-AT-HEART
FRANK SINATRA
CAPITOL

124 MY HEART CRIES FOR YOU
GUY MITCHELL
COLUMBIA

125 JEZEBEL
FRANKIE LAINE
COLUMBIA

126 ANY TIME
EDDIE FISHER
RCA

127 MOMENTS TO REMEMBER
FOUR LADS
COLUMBIA

128 PARTY DOLL
BUDDY KNOX
ROULETTE

129 TELL ME WHY
FOUR ACES
DECCA

130 KISS OF FIRE
GEORGIA GIBBS
MERCURY

131 BIG HUNK O' LOVE
ELVIS PRESLEY
RCA

132 WHY
FRANKIE AVALON
CHANCELLOR

133 OH!
PEE WEE HUNT
CAPITOL

134 IT ISN'T FAIR
SAMMY KAYE & DON CORNELL
RCA

135 TELL ME YOU'RE MINE
GAYLORDS
MERCURY

136 JUST WALKING IN THE RAIN
JOHNNIE RAY
COLUMBIA

137 HARD HEADED WOMAN
ELVIS PRESLEY
RCA

138 THAT'LL BE THE DAY
CRICKETS
BRUNSWICK

139 THE LITTLE WHITE CLOUD THAT CRIED
JOHNNIE RAY
OKEH

140 I GET SO LONELY
FOUR KNIGHTS
CAPITOL

141 MELODY OF LOVE
BILLY VAUGHN
DOT

142 EH CUMPARI
JULIUS LA ROSA
CADENCE

143 MOONGLOW AND THEME FROM *PICNIC*
MORRIS STOLOFF
DECCA

144 WISH YOU WERE HERE
EDDIE FISHER
RCA

145 AIN'T THAT A SHAME
PAT BOONE
DOT

146 MOCKIN' BIRD HILL
LES PAUL & MARY FORD
CAPITOL

147 BYE BYE LOVE
EVERLY BROTHERS
CADENCE

148 A BLOSSOM FELL/IF I MAY
NAT 'KING' COLE
CAPITOL

149 THE LITTLE SHOEMAKER
GAYLORDS
MERCURY

150 THE HAPPY ORGAN
DAVE 'BABY' CORTEZ
CLOCK

151 SENTIMENTAL ME
AMES BROTHERS
CORAL

152 THE GREAT PRETENDER
PLATTERS
MERCURY

153 HONKY TONK (PARTS 1 & 2)
BILL DOGGETT
KING

154 STRANGER IN PARADISE
TONY BENNETT
COLUMBIA

155 LEARNIN' THE BLUES
FRANK SINATRA
CAPITOL

156 HOT DIGGITY (DOG ZIGGITY BOOM)
PERRY COMO
RCA

157 THERE'S NO TOMORROW
TONY MARTIN
RCA

158 RUDOLPH THE RED-NOSED REINDEER
GENE AUTRY
COLUMBIA

159 PRETEND
NAT 'KING' COLE
CAPITOL

160 SAM'S SONG
BING CROSBY & GARY CROSBY
DECCA

161 SO RARE
JIMMY DORSEY
FRATERNITY

162 THE CRAZY OTTO (MEDLEY)
JOHNNY MADDOX
DOT

163 WHATEVER WILL BE WILL BE (QUE SERA SERA)
DORIS DAY
COLUMBIA

164 BLUEBERRY HILL
FATS DOMINO
IMPERIAL

165 PLAY A SIMPLE MELODY
BING CROSBY & GARY CROSBY
DECCA

166 THREE COINS IN THE FOUNTAIN
FOUR ACES
DECCA

167 JAMBALAYA
JO STAFFORD
COLUMBIA

168 DANCE WITH ME HENRY (WALLFLOWER)
GEORGIA GIBBS
MERCURY

169 HERNANDO'S HIDEAWAY
ARCHIE BLEYER
CADENCE

170 I SAW MOMMY KISSING SANTA CLAUS
JIMMY BOYD
COLUMBIA

171 MOCKIN' BIRD HILL
PATTI PAGE
MERCURY

172 LITTLE DARLIN'
DIAMONDS
MERCURY

173 TZENA, TZENA, TZENA
GORDON JENKINS & THE WEAVERS
DECCA

174 SEARCHIN'/YOUNG BLOOD
COASTERS
ATCO

175 RUBY
RICHARD HAYMAN
MERCURY

176 I WANNA BE LOVED
ANDREWS SISTERS
DECCA

177 CANADIAN SUNSET
HUGO WINTERHALTER & EDDIE HEYWOOD
RCA

178 HARBOR LIGHTS
GUY LOMBARDO
DECCA

179 I ALMOST LOST MY MIND
PAT BOONE
DOT

180 ALL MY LOVE
PATTI PAGE
MERCURY

181 BLACKSMITH BLUES
ELLA MAE MORSE
CAPITOL

182 CROSS OVER THE BRIDGE
PATTI PAGE
MERCURY

183 MY FOOLISH HEART
GORDON JENKINS
DECCA

184 CHANGING PARTNERS
PATTI PAGE
MERCURY

185 TEACH ME TONIGHT
DE CASTRO SISTERS
ABBOTT

186 BIRD DOG
EVERLY BROTHERS
CADENCE

187 TWEEDLE DEE
GEORGIA GIBBS
MERCURY

188 PATRICIA
PEREZ PRADO
RCA

189 BOTCH-A-ME
ROSEMARY CLOONEY
COLUMBIA

190 SLOW POKE
PEE WEE KING
RCA

191 RICOCHET
TERESA BREWER
CORAL

192 DONNA
RITCHIE VALENS
DEL-FI

193 SIN
FOUR ACES
VICTORIA

194 PUT YOUR HEAD ON MY SHOULDER
PAUL ANKA
ABC PARAMOUNT

195 BEWITCHED
BILL SNYDER
TOWER

196 I HEAR YOU KNOCKING
GALE STORM
DOT

197 PS I LOVE YOU
HILLTOPPERS
DOT

198 SHRIMP BOATS
JO STAFFORD
COLUMBIA

199 THE WORLD IS WAITING FOR THE SUNRISE
LES PAUL & MARY FORD
CAPITOL

200 ROCK-IN' ROBIN/OVER AND OVER
BOBBY DAY
CLASS

201 I'LL NEVER BE FREE
KAY STARR & TENNESSEE ERNIE FORD
CAPITOL

202 YOUNG LOVE
SONNY JAMES
CAPITOL

203 SWEET VIOLETS
DINAH SHORE
RCA

204 HE'S GOT THE WHOLE WORLD (IN HIS HANDS)
LAURIE LONDON
CAPITOL

205 DON'T FORBID ME
PAT BOONE
DOT

206 A GUY IS A GUY
DORIS DAY
COLUMBIA

207 DREAM LOVER
BOBBY DARIN
ATCO

208 PERSONALITY
LLOYD PRICE
ABC PARAMOUNT

209 THE HAPPY WANDERER
FRANK WEIR
LONDON

210 BONAPARTE'S RETREAT
KAY STARR
CAPITOL

211 CHANCES ARE/THE TWELFTH OF NEVER
JOHNNY MATHIS
COLUMBIA

212 A WHITE SPORT COAT (AND A PINK CARNATION)
MARTY ROBBINS
COLUMBIA

213 BLUE SUEDE SHOES
CARL PERKINS
SUN

214 GREAT BALLS OF FIRE
JERRY LEE LEWIS
SUN

215 HE
AL HIBBLER
DECCA

216 A TEENAGERS ROMANCE/I'M WALKIN'
RICKY NELSON
VERVE

217 SKOKIAAN
RALPH MARTERIE
MERCURY

218 THE NAUGHTY LADY OF SHADY LANE
AMES BROTHERS
RCA

219 RAUNCHY
BILL JUSTIS
PHILLIPS

220 THINKING OF YOU
DON CHERRY
DECCA

221 16 CANDLES
CRESTS
COED

222 IF YOU LOVE ME (REALLY LOVE ME)
KAY STARR
CAPITOL

223 WEAR MY RING AROUND YOUR NECK
ELVIS PRESLEY
RCA

224 DON'T YOU KNOW
DELLA REESE
RCA

225 CATCH A FALLING STAR/MAGIC MOMENTS
PERRY COMO
RCA

226 PAPA LOVES MAMBO
PERRY COMO
RCA

227 YAKETY YAK
COASTERS
ATCO

228 JEALOUSY (JALOUSIE)
FRANKIE LAINE
COLUMBIA

229 ABA DABA HONEYMOON
CARLETON CARPENTER & DEBBIE REYNOLDS
MGM

230 PEGGY SUE
BUDDY HOLLY
CORAL

231 CHARLIE BROWN
COASTERS
ATCO

232 MY HAPPINESS
CONNIE FRANCIS
MGM

233 STOOD UP/WAITIN' IN SCHOOL
RICKY NELSON
IMPERIAL

234 STANDING ON THE CORNER
FOUR LADS
COLUMBIA

235 GET A JOB
SILHOUETTES
EMBER

236 NO, NOT MUCH!
FOUR LADS
COLUMBIA

237 SOUND OFF
VAUGHN MONROE
RCA

238 BE-BOP BABY/HAVE I TOLD YOU LATELY THAT I LOVE YOU?
RICKY NELSON
IMPERIAL

239 TRUE LOVE
BING CROSBY
CAPITOL

240 DRAGNET
RAY ANTHONY
CAPITOL

241 SILHOUETTES
RAYS
CAMEO

242 SWEET LITTLE SIXTEEN
CHUCK BERRY
CHESS

243 HOOP-DE-HOO
PERRY COMO & THE FONTANE SISTERS
RCA

244 TONIGHT YOU BELONG TO ME
PATIENCE & PRUDENCE
LIBERTY

245 BALLAD OF DAVY CROCKETT
FESS PARKER
COLUMBIA

246 I'M IN LOVE AGAIN
FATS DOMINO
IMPERIAL

247 IF I GIVE MY HEART TO YOU
DORIS DAY
COLUMBIA

248 SORRY (I RAN ALL THE WAY HOME)
IMPALAS
CUB

249 TEEN-AGE CRUSH
TOMMY SANDS
CAPITOL

250 PROBLEMS
EVERLY BROTHERS
CADENCE

THE UK
TOP 250 SINGLES
Nov 1952–1959

1 I BELIEVE
FRANKIE LAINE
PHILIPS

2 ROCK AROUND THE CLOCK
BILL HALEY & HIS COMETS
BRUNSWICK

3 SECRET LOVE
DORIS DAY
PHILIPS

4 CARA MIA
DAVID WHITFIELD
DECCA

5 MARY'S BOY CHILD
HARRY BELAFONTE
RCA

6 ROSE MARIE
SLIM WHITMAN

7 PRETTY-EYED BABY
JO STAFFORD & FRANKIE LAINE
COLUMBIA

7 OH MEIN PAPA
EDDIE CALVERT
COLUMBIA

8 DIANA
PAUL ANKA
COLUMBIA

9 GIVE ME YOUR WORD
TENNESSEE ERNIE FORD
CAPITOL

10 HERE IN MY HEART
AL MARTINO
CAPITOL

11 ANSWER ME
FRANKIE LAINE
PHILIPS

12 ALL I HAVE TO DO IS DREAM/CLAUDETTE
EVERLY BROTHERS
LONDON AMERICAN

13 ALL SHOOK UP
ELVIS PRESLEY
HMV

14 MAGIC MOMENTS
PERRY COMO
RCA

15 JUST WALKIN' IN THE RAIN
JOHNNIE RAY
PHILIPS

16 WHO'S SORRY NOW
CONNIE FRANCIS
MGM

17 LIVING DOLL
CLIFF RICHARD
COLUMBIA

18 YOUNG LOVE
TAB HUNTER
LONDON AMERICAN

19 WHAT DO YOU WANT TO MAKE THOSE EYES AT ME FOR
EMILE FORD & THE CHECKMATES
PYE

20 WHATEVER WILL BE WILL BE
DORIS DAY
PHILIPS

21 SIDE SADDLE
RUSS CONWAY
COLUMBIA

22 I'LL BE HOME
PAT BOONE
LONDON AMERICAN

23 HOLD MY HAND
DON CORNELL
VOGUE

24 CHERRY PINK AND APPLE BLOSSOM WHITE
EDDIE CALVERT
COLUMBIA

25 CAROLINA MOON/STUPID CUPID
CONNIE FRANCIS
MGM

26 I SEE THE MOON
STARGAZERS
DECCA

27 LOOK AT THAT GIRL
GUY MITCHELL
PHILIPS

28 SOFTLY SOFTLY
RUBY MURRAY
COLUMBIA

29 SINGING THE BLUES
GUY MITCHELL
PHILIPS

30 A WOMAN IN LOVE
FRANKIE LAINE
PHILIPS

31 TRAVELLIN' LIGHT
CLIFF RICHARD
COLUMBIA

32 MOULIN ROUGE
MANTOVANI
DECCA

33 DON'T LET THE STARS GET IN YOUR EYES
PERRY COMO
HMV

34 NO OTHER LOVE
RONNIE HILTON
HMV

35 A FOOL SUCH AS I/I NEED YOUR LOVE TONIGHT
ELVIS PRESLEY
RCA

36 WHEN
KALIN TWINS
BRUNSWICK

37 LITTLE THINGS MEAN A LOT
KITTY KALLEN
BRUNSWICK

38 IT DOESN'T MATTER ANYMORE
BUDDY HOLLY
CORAL

39 SHE WEARS RED FEATHERS
GUY MITCHELL
COLUMBIA

40 DREAM LOVER
BOBBY DARIN
LONDON AMERICAN

41 THREE COINS IN THE FOUNTAIN
FRANK SINATRA
CAPITOL

42 IT'S ONLY MAKE BELIEVE
CONWAY TWITTY
MGM

43 AS I LOVE YOU
SHIRLEY BASSEY
PHILIPS

44 IT'S ALMOST TOMORROW
DREAM WEAVERS
BRUNSWICK

45 UNCHAINED MELODY
JIMMY YOUNG
DECCA

46 HOOTS MON
LORD ROCKINGHAM'S XI
DECCA

47 MEMORIES ARE MADE OF THIS
DEAN MARTIN
CAPITOL

48 ONLY SIXTEEN
CRAIG DOUGLAS
TOP RANK

49 FINGER OF SUSPICION
DICKIE VALENTINE
DECCA

50 YOU BELONG TO ME
JO STAFFORD
COLUMBIA

51 WHY DO FOOLS FALL IN LOVE
FRANKIE LYMON & THE TEENAGERS
COLUMBIA

52 LAY DOWN YOUR ARMS
ANNE SHELTON
PHILIPS

53 CUMBERLAND GAP
LONNIE DONEGAN
PYE NIXA

54 CHERRY PINK AND APPLE BLOSSOM WHITE
PEREZ PRADO
HMV

55 SUCH A NIGHT
JOHNNIE RAY
PHILIPS

56 THE MAN FROM LARAMIE
JIMMY YOUNG
DECCA

57 POOR PEOPLE OF PARIS
WINIFRED ATWELL
DECCA

58 ROCK AND ROLL WALTZ
KAY STARR
HMV

59 I'M WALKING BEHIND YOU
EDDIE FISHER
HMV

60 GARDEN OF EDEN
FRANKIE VAUGHAN
PHILIPS

61 HAPPY WANDERER
OBERNKIRCHEN CHILDREN'S
CHOIR
PARLOPHONE

62 MAMBO ITALIANO
ROSEMARY CLOONEY
PHILIPS

63 IT'S ALL IN THE GAME
TOMMY EDWARDS
MGM

64 ROULETTE
RUSS CONWAY
COLUMBIA

65 YES TONIGHT JOSEPHINE
JOHNNIE RAY
PHILIPS

**66 GAMBLIN' MAN/PUTTING
ON THE STYLE**
LONNIE DONEGAN
PYE NIXA

67 WHAT DO YOU WANT
ADAM FAITH
PARLOPHONE

68 *LIMELIGHT*
FRANK CHACKSFIELD
DECCA

69 LET'S HAVE A PARTY
WINIFRED ATWELL
PHILIPS

70 OUTSIDE OF HEAVEN
EDDIE FISHER
HMV

71 STRANGER IN PARADISE
TONY BENNETT
PHILIPS

**72 SMOKE GETS IN YOUR
EYES**
PLATTERS
MERCURY

73 DREAMBOAT
ALMA COGAN
HMV

74 WHOLE LOTTA WOMAN
MARVIN RAINWATER
MGM

75 JAILHOUSE ROCK
ELVIS PRESLEY
RCA

76 SIXTEEN TONS
TENNESSEE ERNIE FORD
CAPITOL

77 THE STORY OF MY LIFE
MICHAEL HOLLIDAY
COLUMBIA

78 THIS OLE HOUSE
ROSEMARY CLOONEY
PHILIPS

79 THAT'LL BE THE DAY
CRICKETS
VOGUE CORAL

80 MY SON MY SON
VERA LYNN
DECCA

81 MACK THE KNIFE
BOBBY DARIN
LONDON AMERICAN

**82 ON THE STREET WHERE
YOU LIVE**
VIC DAMONE
PHILIPS

83 ANSWER ME
DAVID WHITFIELD
DECCA

84 COMES A-LONG A-LOVE
KAY STARR
CAPITOL

85 HERNANDO'S HIDEAWAY
JOHNSTON BROTHERS
DECCA

86 ONE NIGHT/I GOT STUNG
ELVIS PRESLEY
RCA

87 BECAUSE YOU'RE MINE
MARIO LANZA
HMV

88 BUTTERFLY
ANDY WILLIAMS
LONDON AMERICAN

89 COOL WATER
FRANKIE LAINE
PHILIPS

**90 LET'S HAVE ANOTHER
PARTY**
WINIFRED ATWELL
DECCA

91 HOUND DOG
ELVIS PRESLEY
HMV

92 GREAT BALLS OF FIRE
JERRY LEE LEWIS
LONDON AMERICAN

**93 (HOW MUCH IS) THAT
DOGGIE IN THE WINDOW**
LITA ROZA
DECCA

94 CHRISTMAS ALPHABET
DICKIE VALENTINE
DECCA

95 HERE COMES SUMMER
JERRY KELLER
LONDON AMERICAN

96 BROKEN WINGS
STARGAZERS
DECCA

97 THE DAY THE RAINS CAME
JANE MORGAN
LONDON AMERICAN

**98 LOVE LETTERS IN THE
SAND**
PAT BOONE
LONDON AMERICAN

99 HEY JOE
FRANKIE LAINE
PHILIPS

100 PRETEND
NAT 'KING' COLE
CAPITOL

**101 TERRY'S THEME FROM
*LIMELIGHT***
RON GOODWIN
PARLOPHONE

102 SWEDISH RHAPSODY
MANTOVANI
DECCA

103 ROCK-A-BILLY
GUY MITCHELL
PHILIPS

104 HEARTBREAK HOTEL
ELVIS PRESLEY
HMV

**105 SEE YOU LATER
ALLIGATOR**
BILL HALEY & HIS COMETS
BRUNSWICK

106 TRUE LOVE
BING CROSBY & GRACE KELLY
CAPITOL

107 EV'RYWHERE
DAVID WHITFIELD
DECCA

108 SINGING THE BLUES
TOMMY STEELE
DECCA

109 ONLY YOU
HILLTOPPERS
LONDON AMERICAN

**110 YOU NEED HANDS/TULIPS
FROM AMSTERDAM**
MAX BYGRAVES
DECCA

111 WHEN I FALL IN LOVE
NAT 'KING' COLE
CAPITOL

112 ISLAND IN THE SUN
HARRY BELAFONTE
RCA

113 UNCHAINED MELODY
AL HIBBLER
BRUNSWICK

**114 HOLD ME THRILL ME
KISS ME**
MURIEL SMITH
PHILIPS

115 PETITE FLEUR
CHRIS BARBER'S JAZZ BAND
PYE NIXA

116 CLOUD LUCKY SEVEN
GUY MITCHELL
PHILIPS

117 BATTLE OF NEW ORLEANS
LONNIE DONEGAN
PYE

**118 ROCKIN' THROUGH THE
RYE**
BILL HALEY & HIS COMETS
BRUNSWICK

119 SMILE
NAT 'KING' COLE
CAPITOL

120 DON'T FORBID ME
PAT BOONE
LONDON AMERICAN

121 ZAMBESI
LOU BUSCH
CAPITOL

122 GREEN DOOR
FRANKIE VAUGHAN
PHILIPS

**123 ST THERESE OF THE
ROSES**
MALCOLM VAUGHAN
HMV

124 RETURN TO ME
DEAN MARTIN
CAPITOL

125 NO ONE BUT YOU
BILLY ECKSTINE
MGM

**126 MA HE'S MAKING EYES
AT ME**
JOHNNY OTIS SHOW
CAPITOL

**127 LOVE IS A MANY-
SPLENDOURED THING**
FOUR ACES
BRUNSWICK

**128 LAST TRAIN TO SAN
FERNANDO**
JOHNNY DUNCAN & THE BLUE
GRASS BOYS
COLUMBIA

129 MY SEPTEMBER LOVE
DAVID WHITFIELD
DECCA

130 MY FRIEND
FRANKIE LAINE
PHILIPS

131 TAMMY
DEBBIE REYNOLDS
VOGUE CORAL

132 BANANA BOAT SONG
HARRY BELAFONTE
HMV

133 LOST JOHN/STEWBALL
LONNIE DONEGAN
PYE NIXA

134 BIRD DOG
EVERLY BROTHERS
LONDON AMERICAN

135 IDLE GOSSIP
PERRY COMO
HMV

136 ('TIL) I KISSED YOU
EVERLY BROTHERS
LONDON AMERICAN

137 A TEENAGER IN LOVE
MARTY WILDE
PHILIPS

138 EVERMORE
RUBY MURRAY
COLUMBIA

139 BLOWING WILD
FRANKIE LAINE
PHILIPS

140 WE WILL MAKE LOVE
RUSS HAMILTON
ORIOLE

141 DON'T LAUGH AT ME
NORMAN WISDOM
COLUMBIA

142 YELLOW ROSE OF TEXAS
MITCH MILLER
PHILIPS

143 LEARNIN' THE BLUES
FRANK SINATRA
CAPITOL

144 EARTH ANGEL
CREW-CUTS
MERCURY

145 HEARTBEAT
RUBY MURRAY
COLUMBIA

146 A WONDERFUL TIME UP THERE
PAT BOONE
LONDON AMERICAN

147 THE GREAT PRETENDER/ONLY YOU
PLATTERS
MERCURY

148 PARTY
ELVIS PRESLEY
RCA

149 IT'S LATE
RICKY NELSON
LONDON AMERICAN

150 A TEAR FELL
TERESA BREWER
VOGUE/CORAL

151 DOWNHEARTED
EDDIE FISHER
HMV

152 ALL THE WAY
FRANK SINATRA
CAPITOL

153 WALK HAND IN HAND
TONY MARTIN
HMV

154 TEDDY BEAR
ELVIS PRESLEY
HMV

155 WHERE THE WIND BLOWS
FRANKIE LAINE
PHILIPS

156 OH! CAROL
NEIL SEDAKA
RCA

157 TOM HARK
ELIAS & HIS ZIGZAG JIVE FLUTES
COLUMBIA

158 VOLARE
DEAN MARTIN
CAPITOL

159 LITTLE DARLIN'
DIAMONDS
MERCURY

160 TEA FOR TWO CHA CHA
TOMMY DORSEY ORCHESTRA
BRUNSWICK

161 FRIENDLY PERSUASION
PAT BOONE
LONDON AMERICAN

162 BIG MAN
FOUR PREPS
CAPITOL

163 THAT'S AMORE
DEAN MARTIN
CAPITOL

164 FEET UP
GUY MITCHELL
COLUMBIA

165 WAKE UP LITTLE SUSIE
EVERLY BROTHERS
LONDON AMERICAN

166 BLUE STAR
CYRIL STAPLETON
DECCA

167 LIPSTICK ON YOUR COLLAR
CONNIE FRANCIS
MGM

168 PRETTY LITTLE BLACK EYED SUSIE
GUY MITCHELL
COLUMBIA

169 ISLE OF INNISFREE
BING CROSBY
BRUNSWICK

170 COME PRIMA
MARINO MARINI
DURIUM

171 NOW
AL MARTINO
CAPITOL

172 DON'T YOU ROCK ME DADDY-O
LONNIE DONEGAN
PYE NIXA

173 WANTED
AL MARTINO
CAPITOL

174 I'VE WAITED SO LONG
ANTHONY NEWLEY
DECCA

175 POPPA PICCOLINO
DIANA DECKER
COLUMBIA

176 BE MY GIRL
JIM DALE
PARLOPHONE

177 CHANGING PARTNERS
KAY STARR
CAPITOL

178 MEET ME ON THE CORNER
MAX BYGRAVES
HMV

179 TO KNOW HIM, IS TO LOVE HIM
TEDDY BEARS
LONDON AMERICAN

180 LONELY BOY
PAUL ANKA
COLUMBIA

181 LONG TALL SALLY
LITTLE RICHARD
LONDON AMERICAN

182 SANTO NATALE
DAVID WHITFIELD
DECCA

183 LET'S WALK THATA-WAY
DORIS DAY & JOHNNIE RAY
PHILIPS

184 I LOVE YOU BABY
PAUL ANKA
COLUMBIA

185 KISS ME HONEY HONEY KISS ME
SHIRLEY BASSEY
PHILIPS

186 CHIKA BOOM
GUY MITCHELL
PHILIPS

187 MY SPECIAL ANGEL
MALCOLM VAUGHAN
HMV

188 I STILL BELIEVE
RONNIE HILTON
HMV

189 MOVE IT
CLIFF RICHARD
COLUMBIA

190 RED RIVER ROCK
JOHNNY & THE HURRICANES
LONDON AMERICAN

191 TOM DOOLEY
LONNIE DONEGAN
PYE NIXA

192 AT THE HOP
DANNY & THE JUNIORS
HMV

193 SWEET OLD-FASHIONED GIRL
TERESA BREWER
VOGUE/CORAL

194 FRIENDS AND NEIGHBOURS
BILLY COTTON & HIS BAND
DECCA

195 THE SAINTS ROCK 'N ROLL
BILL HALEY & HIS COMETS
BRUNSWICK

196 OH, BOY!
CRICKETS
CORAL

197 DON'T
ELVIS PRESLEY
RCA

198 THE TENDER TRAP
FRANK SINATRA
CAPITOL

199 BABY FACE
LITTLE RICHARD
LONDON AMERICAN

200 WANTED
PERRY COMO
HMV

201 THE BALLAD OF DAVY CROCKETT
BILL HAYES
LONDON AMERICAN

202 RAGS TO RICHES
DAVID WHITFIELD
DECCA

203 KNEE DEEP IN THE BLUES
GUY MITCHELL
PHILIPS

204 A PUB WITH NO BEER
SLIM DUSTY
COLUMBIA

205 AROUND THE WORLD
RONNIE HILTON
HMV

206 DONNA
MARTY WILDE
PHILIPS

207 WITH ALL MY HEART
PETULA CLARK
PYE NIXA

208 LOLLIPOP
MUDLARKS
COLUMBIA

209 KING CREOLE
ELVIS PRESLEY
RCA

210 THE KID'S LAST FIGHT
FRANKIE LAINE
PHILIPS

211 THIS OLD HOUSE
BILLIE ANTHONY
COLUMBIA

212 HARD HEADED WOMAN
ELVIS PRESLEY
RCA

213 LET'S HAVE A DING DONG
WINIFRED ATWELL
DECCA

214 HALF AS MUCH
ROSEMARY CLOONEY
COLUMBIA

215 A CERTAIN SMILE
JOHNNY MATHIS
FONTANA

216 TELL ME A STORY
FRANKIE LAINE & JIMMY BOYD
PHILIPS

217 TWILIGHT TIME
PLATTERS
MERCURY

218 MOUNTAIN GREENERY
MEL TORME
VOGUE/CORAL

**219 SEVEN LITTLE GIRLS
SITTING IN THE BACK SEAT**
AVONS
COLUMBIA

220 SEA OF LOVE
MARTY WILDE
PHILIPS

221 I WONDER
DICKIE VALENTINE
DECCA

222 RIP IT UP
BILL HALEY & HIS COMETS
BRUNSWICK

223 ALL STAR HIT PARADE
VARIOUS ARTISTS
DECCA

**224 IF I GIVE MY HEART
TO YOU**
JOAN REGAN
DECCA

225 ENDLESS SLEEP
MARTY WILDE
PHILIPS

226 HOT DIGGITY
PERRY COMO
HMV

227 SHAKE, RATTLE AND ROLL
BILL HALEY & HIS COMETS
BRUNSWICK

**228 SWINGIN' SHEPHERD
BLUES**
TED HEATH
DECCA

229 IN A GOLDEN COACH
BILLY COTTON & HIS BAND
DECCA

**230 DOES YOUR CHEWING
GUM LOSE ITS FLAVOUR**
LONNIE DONEGAN
PYE NIXA

231 NAIROBI
TOMMY STEELE
DECCA

232 TENNESSEE WIG WALK
BONNIE LOU
PARLOPHONE

233 THE BOOK
DAVID WHITFIELD
DECCA

234 EVERY DAY OF MY LIFE
MALCOLM VAUGHAN
HMV

235 MY HAPPINESS
CONNIE FRANCIS
MGM

236 STAIRWAY OF LOVE
MICHAEL HOLLIDAY
COLUMBIA

237 A BLOSSOM FELL
NAT 'KING' COLE
CAPITOL

238 POOR LITTLE FOOL
RICKY NELSON
LONDON AMERICAN

239 MORE
JIMMY YOUNG
DECCA

240 MY PRAYER
PLATTERS
MERCURY

**241 IF I GIVE MY HEART
TO YOU**
DORIS DAY
PHILIPS

242 TWENTY TINY FINGERS
STARGAZERS
DECCA

243 LOVE AND MARRIAGE
FRANK SINATRA
CAPITOL

**244 BLOODNOK'S ROCK'N'
ROLL CALL/YING TONG SONG**
GOONS
DECCA

245 THE BREEZE AND I
CATERINA VALENTE
POLYDOR

246 CINDY, OH CINDY
EDDIE FISHER
HMV

247 LET ME GO, LOVER
DEAN MARTIN
CAPITOL

248 MOBILE
RAY BURNS
COLUMBIA

**249 SOMEWHERE ALONG
THE WAY**
NAT 'KING' COLE
CAPITOL

**250 MEMORIES ARE MADE
OF THIS**
DAVE KING
DECCA

Artist Index

(including month of entry)

Elmer Bernstein
Staccato's Theme 12/59

Chuck Berry
Johnny B. Goode 5/58
Maybellene 8/55
Rock & Roll Music 12/57
School Day 4/57
Sweet Little Sixteen 3/58

Beverley Sisters
*I Saw Mommy Kissing Santa
Claus* 12/53
The Little Drummer Boy 2/59

Big Ben Banjo Band
Let's Get Together No 1
12/54

Big Bopper
Chantilly Lace 10/58

Billy & Lillie
La Dee Dah 1/58

Mel Blanc
I Taut I Taw A Puddy Tat 2/51

Archie Bleyer
Hernando's Hideaway 6/54

Bobbettes
Mr Lee 9/57

Pat Boone
Ain't That A Shame 7/55
*April Love/When The Swallows
Come Back To Capistrano*
11/57
*At My Front Door (Crazy Little
Mama)* 11/55
Don't Forbid Me 1/57
*Friendly Persuasion/Chains Of
Love* 10/56
I Almost Lost My Mind 6/56
I'll Be Home 2/56
Love Letters In The Sand 5/57
*Remember You're Mine/There's
A Gold Mine In The Sky* 9/57
Sugar Moon/Cherie I Love You
5/58
*When The Swallows Come Back
To Capistrano* 11/57
Why Baby Why 3/57
*A Wonderful Time Up
There/It's Too Soon To Know*
3/58

Eve Boswell
Pickin' A Chicken 2/56

Jimmy Boyd
*I Saw Mommy Kissing Santa
Claus* 12/52
Tell Me A Story 5/53

Johnny Brandon
Tomorrow 3/55

Tony Brent
Make It Soon 1/53
Walkin' To Missouri 12/52

Bernard Bresslaw
Mad Passionate Love 9/58

Teresa Brewer
Let Me Go, Lover! 1/55
Music! Music! Music! 2/50
Ricochet 10/53
Sweet Old-Fashioned Girl 8/56
A Tear Fell 4/56
Till I Waltz Again With You
12/52

Les Brown
Undecided 10/51

Browns
The Three Bells 8/59

Buchanan & Goodman
The Flying Saucer (Parts 1 & 2)
8/56

Ray Burns
Mobile 3/55

Lou Busch
Zambesi 2/56

Red Buttons
The Ho Ho Song 5/53

Max Bygraves
Cowpuncher's Cantata 12/52
*Gilly Gilly Ossenfeffer
Katzenellen Bogen By The
Sea* 9/54
Heart Of My Heart 5/54
Meet Me On The Corner 12/55
*You Need Hands/Tulips From
Amsterdam* 5/58

**Edward Byrnes & Connie
Stevens**
*Kookie, Kookie (Lend Me Your
Comb)* 5/59

Eddie Calvert
*Cherry Pink And Apple Blossom
White* 4/55
John And Julie 9/55
Mandy 4/58

Oh, Mein Papa 12/53

Freddy Cannon
Tallahassee Lassie 6/59
*Way Down Yonder In New
Orleans* 12/59

Hoagy Carmichael
My Resistance Is Low 7/51

**Carleton Carpenter & Debbie
Reynolds**
Aba Daba Honeymoon 3/51

Cathy Carr
Ivory Tower 5/56

Joe 'Fingers' Carr
Sam's Song 8/50

David Carroll
Melody Of Love 2/55

George Cates
*Moonglow/Theme From
Picnic* 5/56

Frank Chacksfield
Ebb Tide 2/54
Limelight 5/53
Little Red Monkey 4/53

Champs
Tequila 3/58

Karen Chandler
Hold Me, Thrill Me, Kiss Me
1/53

Ray Charles
What'd I Say (Part 1) 8/59

Cheers
Black Denim Trousers 10/55

Don Cherry
Band Of Gold 1/56
Thinking Of You 10/50

Chipmunks
Alvin's Harmonica 3/59
The Chipmunk Song 12/58

Chordettes
Born To Be With You 7/56
Lollipop 3/58
Mr Sandman 11/54

Chords
Sh-Boom 7/54

Savannah Churchill
(It's No) Sin 11/51

Jimmy Clanton
Just A Dream 8/58

Bing Crosby & Gary Crosby
Play A Simple Melody 7/50
Sam's Song 7/50
*When You And I Were Young
 Maggie* 5/51

Bing Crosby & Grace Kelly
True Love 11/56

Bing Crosby & Jane Wyman
Zing A Little Zong 12/52

Gary Crosby
Play A Simple Melody 7/50
Sam's Song 7/50
*When You And I Were Young
 Maggie* 5/51

Jim Dale
Be My Girl 11/57

Vic Damone
On The Street Where You Live
 6/56
Tzena, Tzena, Tzena 8/50

Johnny Dankworth
Experiments With Mice 6/56

Danny & The Juniors
At The Hop 12/57

Bobby Darin
Dream Lover 5/59
Mack The Knife 9/59
Queen Of The Hop 11/58
Splish Splash 7/58

Sammy Davis Jr
Love Me Or Leave Me 9/55
Something's Gotta Give 7/55

Bobby Day
Rock-In' Robin/Over And Over
 9/58

Dennis Day
Christmas In Killarney 1/51

Doris Day
Bewitched 6/50
Black Hills Of Dakota 8/54
A Guy Is A Guy 3/52
If I Give My Heart To You
 10/54
My Love And Devotion 11/52
Ready Willing And Able 4/55
Secret Love 1/54
Shanghai 8/51
*Whatever Will Be Will Be (Que
 Sera Sera)* 7/56

Doris Day & Frankie Laine
Sugarbush 8/52

Doris Day & Johnnie Ray
Let's Walk That-a-Way 7/53

De Castro Sisters
Teach Me Tonight 11/54

Diana Decker
Poppa Piccolino 10/53

Dejohn Sisters
*(My Baby Don't Love Me) No
 More* 1/55

Dell-Vikings
Come Go With Me 4/57
Whispering Bells 7/57

Jackie Dennis
La Dee Dah 3/58

Martin Denny
Quiet Village 5/59

Johnny Desmond
The Yellow Rose Of Texas 8/55

Diamonds
Little Darlin' 3/57
The Stroll 1/58

Dinning Sisters
Once In A While 7/50

Dion & The Belmonts
A Teenager In Love 5/59

Carl Dobkins Jr
My Heart Is An Open Book
 7/59

Bill Doggett
Honky Tonk (Parts 1 & 2)
 9/56

Fats Domino
Be My Guest 11/59
Blue Monday 2/57
Blueberry Hill 10/56
I Want To Walk You Home
 8/59
I'm In Love Again 5/56
I'm Walkin' 3/57
Valley Of Tears/It's You I Love
 7/57
Whole Lotta Loving 12/58

Lonnie Donegan
Battle Of New Orleans 6/59
*Bring A Little Water
 Sylvie/Dead Or Alive* 9/56
Cumberland Gap 4/57

*Does Your Chewing Gum Lose
 Its Flavour* 2/59
Don't You Rock Me Daddy-O
 2/57
*Gamblin' Man/Putting On The
 Style* 6/57
Grand Coolie Dam 5/58
Lost John/Stewball 5/56
My Dixie Darling 11/57
Rock Island Line 1/56
Tom Dooley 11/58

Jimmy Dorsey
So Rare 5/57

Tommy Dorsey Orchestra
Tea For Two Cha Cha 10/58

Craig Douglas
Only Sixteen 8/59

Charlie Drake
Splish Splash 8/58

Rusty Draper
Gambler's Guitar 8/53
The Shifting, Whispering Sands
 10/55

Dream Weavers
It's Almost Tomorrow 12/55

Drifters
There Goes My Baby 7/59

**Johnny Duncan & The Blue
Grass Boys**
Last Train To San Fernando
 8/57

Slim Dusty
A Pub With No Beer 2/59

Billy Eckstine
Gigi 3/59
I Apologize 4/51
I Wanna Be Loved 7/50
My Foolish Heart 5/50
No One But You 11/54

Duane Eddy
Forty Miles Of Bad Road 7/59
Peter Gunn Theme 6/59
Rebel-'Rouser 7/58

Tommy Edwards
It's All In The Game 9/58

Elegants
Little Star 8/58

Elias & His Zigzag Jive Flutes
Tom Hark 5/58

Duke Ellington
Skin Deep 3/54

Paul Evans & The Curls
*Seven Little Girls Sitting In
The Back Seat* 11/59

Everly Brothers
All I Have To Do Is Dream
4/58
Bird Dog 8/58
Bye Bye Love 6/57
Problems 12/58
('Til) I Kissed You 9/59
Wake Up Little Susie 10/57

Fabian
Hound Dog Man 12/59
Tiger 7/59
Turn Me Loose 4/59

Adam Faith
What Do You Want 11/59

Percy Faith
Delicado 5/52

Percy Faith & Felicia Sanders
Song From Moulin Rouge 4/53

**Jose Ferrer & Rosemary
Clooney**
Woman (Uh-Huh)/Man 2/54

Ernie Fields
In The Mood 11/59

Gracie Fields
Around The World 6/57

Eddie Fisher
Any Time 12/51
Cindy, Oh Cindy 11/56
Count Your Blessings 12/54
Downhearted 5/53
Dungaree Doll 1/56
Everything I Have Is Yours
2/53
Forgive Me 3/52
A Girl, A Girl 4/54
I Need You Now 9/54
I'm Walking Behind You 5/53
I'm Yours 5/52
Lady Of Spain 11/52
Many Times 10/53
Maybe 6/52
Oh! My Pa-Pa 12/53
Outside Of Heaven 11/52
Tell Me Why 1/52
Thinking Of You 11/50

Turn Back The Hands Of Time
10/51
Wedding Bells 3/55
Wish You Were Here 8/52
With These Hands 8/53

Miss Toni Fisher
The Big Hurt 12/59

Ralph Flanagan
Rag Mop 3/50

Fleetwoods
Come Softly To Me 3/59
Mr Blue 10/59

Red Foley
Chattanoogie Shoe Shine Boy
1/50

Fontane Sisters
Hearts Of Stone 12/54
Hoop-De-Hoo 5/50
Seventeen 9/55
You're Just In Love 1/51

Emile Ford & The Checkmates
*What Do You Want To Make
Those Eyes At Me For* 11/59

Tennessee Ernie Ford
Ballad Of Davy Crockett 4/55
Give Me Your Word 1/55
I'll Never Be Free 9/50
Shotgun Boogie 6/51
Sixteen Tons 11/55

Four Aces
*The Gang That Sang 'Heart Of
My Heart'* 1/54
*Love Is A Many-Splendoured
Thing* 9/55
Mr Sandman 12/54
Perfidia 3/52
Sin 10/51
Stranger In Paradise 1/54
Tell Me Why 1/52
Three Coins In The Fountain
5/54

Four Knights
I Get So Lonely 2/54

Four Lads
Moments To Remember 9/55
No, Not Much! 2/56
Skokiaan 9/54
Standing On The Corner 5/56

Four Preps
Big Man 6/58
26 Miles 3/58

Four Tunes
*I Understand Just How You
Feel* 7/54

Connie Francis
Among My Souvenirs 12/59
Carolina Moon/Stupid Cupid
8/58
Frankie 7/59
Lipstick On Your Collar 6/59
My Happiness 1/59
Who's Sorry Now 3/58

Stan Freberg
St George And The Dragonet
10/53

Bobby Freeman
Do You Want To Dance 6/58

Frank Froeba
Mistakes 2/52

Gaylords
From The Vine Came The Grape
2/54
The Little Shoemaker 7/54
Tell Me You're Mine 1/53

Georgia Gibbs
*Dance With Me Henry
(Wallflower)* 4/55
Kiss Of Fire 4/52
Tweedle Dee 2/55

Don Gibson
*Oh Lonesome Me/I Can't Stop
Lovin' You* 5/58

**Terry Gilkyson & The Easy
Riders**
Marianne 2/57

Darrell Glenn
Crying In The Chapel 8/53

Ron Goodwin
Terry's Theme From Limelight
6/53

Goons
*Bloodnok's Rock'n'Roll
Call/Ying Tong Song* 9/56
*I'm Walking Backwards For
Christmas/Bluebottle Blues*
7/56

Barry Gordon
Nuttin' For Christmas 12/55

Charlie Gracie
Butterfly 3/57
Fabulous 8/57

*Wanderin' Eyes/I Love You So
  Much It Hurts* 9/57

Billy Grammer
Gotta Travel On 1/59

Earl Grant
The End 10/58

Gogi Grant
The Wayward Wind 5/56

Andy Griffith
What Is Was, Was Football
  1/54

Bonnie Guitar
Dark Moon 6/57

Bill Haley & His Comets
Don't Knock The Rock 2/57
Rip It Up 11/56
Rock Around The Clock 5/55
Rock-A-Beatin' Boogie 1/56
Rockin' Through The Rye 8/56
The Saints Rock 'n Roll 6/56
See You Later, Alligator 1/56
Shake, Rattle And Roll 10/54

George Hamilton IV
A Rose And A Baby Ruth
  12/56

Roy Hamilton
Unchained Melody 5/55

Russ Hamilton
Rainbow 6/57
We Will Make Love 6/57

Lionel Hampton
Rag Mop 2/50

Phil Harris
The Thing 11/50

Thurston Harris
Little Bitty Pretty One 11/57

Wilbert Harrison
Kansas City 5/59

Bill Hayes
The Ballad Of Davy Crockett
  3/55

Richard Hayes
The Old Master Painter 1/50

Richard Hayes & Kitty Kallen
Our Lady Of Fatima 9/50

Richard Hayman
Ruby 4/53

Dick Haymes
The Old Master Painter 1/50

Ted Heath
Blacksmith Blues 6/52
Dragnet 11/53
Hot Toddy 7/53
Skin Deep 2/54
Swingin' Shepherd Blues 4/58

Bobby Helms
Jingle Bell Rock 1/58
My Special Angel 11/57

Eddie Heywood
Canadian Sunset 8/56

Al Hibbler
He 10/55
Unchained Melody 4/55

Hilltoppers
Only You 2/56
PS I Love You 7/53
Till Then 2/54
Trying 9/52

Ronnie Hilton
Around The World 6/57
A Blossom Fell 4/55
I Still Believe 12/54
No Other Love 4/56
Who Are We 7/56

Edmund Hockridge
Young And Foolish 3/56

Michael Holliday
Stairway Of Love 6/58
The Story Of My Life 1/58

Buddy Holly
It Doesn't Matter Anymore
  3/59
Peggy Sue 12/57
Rave On 7/58

Leroy Holmes
The High And The Mighty 8/54

Bob Hope
Home Cookin'/Blind Date
  10/50

Johnny Horton
The Battle Of New Orleans
  5/59

Don Howard
Oh Happy Day 12/52

Eddy Howard
Sin 10/51

Pee Wee Hunt
Oh! 8/53

Tab Hunter
Ninety-Nine Ways 4/57
Young Love 1/57

Ferlin Husky
Gone 4/57

Betty Hutton
A Bushel And A Peck 11/50

Jane Hutton
Say You're Mine Again 8/53

Dick Hyman
*Moritat (A Theme From The
  Threepenny Opera)* 3/56

Impalas
*Sorry (I Ran All The Way
  Home)* 4/59

Ink Spots
Melody Of Love 5/55

Stonewall Jackson
Waterloo 7/59

Joni James
Have You Heard 1/53
How Important Can It Be 3/55
My Love, My Love 9/53
Why Don't You Believe Me
  11/52
Your Cheatin' Heart 3/53

Sonny James
Young Love 1/57

Jan & Arnie
Jennie Lee 6/58

Jan & Dean
Baby Talk 9/59

Gordon Jenkins
Bewitched 5/50
Lover 7/52
My Foolish Heart 4/50

**Gordon Jenkins & The
Weavers**
Goodnight Irene 7/50
So Long 1/51
Tzena, Tzena, Tzena 7/50

Johnnie & Joe
*Over The Mountain; Across The
  Sea* 7/57

Johnny & The Hurricanes
Red River Rock 8/59

Teddy Johnson
Beloved Be Faithful 11/50
Tennessee Waltz 3/51

Moulin Rouge 5/53
Swedish Rhapsody 10/53
White Christmas 12/52

Marino Marini
Come Prima 10/58

Ralph Marterie
Skokiaan 9/54

Dean Martin
Kiss 9/53
Let Me Go, Lover 3/55
Memories Are Made Of This 12/55
Naughty Lady Of Shady Lane 2/55
Return To Me 5/58
Sway 10/54
That's Amore 11/53
Under The Bridges Of Paris 4/55
Volare 9/58

Mary Martin
Go To Sleep, Go To Sleep, Go To Sleep 4/50

Ray Martin
Swedish Rhapsody 12/53

Tony Martin
Domino 11/51
Here 4/54
I Get Ideas 7/51
I Said My Pajamas And Put On My Pray'rs 2/50
Kiss Of Fire 6/52
La Vie En Rose 8/50
Stranger In Paradise 1/54
There's No Tomorrow 1/50
Walk Hand In Hand 7/56

Wink Martindale
Deck Of Cards 10/59

Al Martino
Here In My Heart 5/52
Now 1/53
Rachel 7/53
The Story Of Tina 10/54
Take My Heart 11/52
Wanted 6/54

Johnny Mathis
A Certain Smile 10/58
Chances Are/The Twelfth Of Never 9/57
It's Not For Me To Say 7/57
Someone 8/59

Billy May
Main Title Theme From The Man With The Golden Arm 5/56

Chas McDevitt Skiffle Group
Freight Train 5/57

McGuire Sisters
Goodnight, Sweetheart, Goodnight 8/54
Sincerely 1/55
Something's Gotta Give 6/55
Sugartime 1/58

Giselle McKenzie
Seven Lonely Days 8/53

Clyde McPhatter
A Lover's Question 12/58

Chuck Miller
The House Of Blue Lights 8/55

Gary Miller
Robin Hood 2/56

Mitch Miller
Theme Song From Song For A Summer Night *9/56*
Tzena, Tzena, Tzena 8/50
The Yellow Rose Of Texas 8/55

Mills Brothers
Daddy's Little Girl 4/50
Glow Worm 10/52
Nevertheless 12/50

Sal Mineo
Start Movin' (In My Direction) 6/57

Guy Mitchell
Chika Boom 11/53
Cloud Lucky Seven 1/54
Cuff Of My Shirt 2/54
Dime And A Dollar 4/54
Feet Up 10/52
Heartaches By The Number 11/59
Knee Deep In The Blues 2/57
Look At That Girl 8/53
My Heart Cries For You 12/50
My Truly, Truly Fair 6/51
Pittsburgh, Pennsylvania 4/52
Pretty Little Black Eyed Susie 4/53
Rock-A-Billy 5/57
The Roving Kind 1/51
She Wears Red Feathers 2/53
Singing The Blues 11/56

Sparrow In The Tree Top 3/51
There's Always Room At Our House 3/52

Domenico Modugno
Nel Blu Dipinto Di Blu (Volare) 8/58

Monotones
Book Of Love 4/58

Vaughn Monroe
Old Soldiers Never Die 5/51
On Top Of Old Smoky 6/51
Sound Off 5/51

Art Mooney
Honey-Babe 5/55

Al Morgan
Jealous Heart 2/50

Jane Morgan
The Day The Rains Came 12/58

Jaye P. Morgan
That's All I Want From You 1/55

Russ Morgan
Sentimental Me 5/50

Ella Mae Morse
Blacksmith Blues 3/52

Mudlarks
Book Of Love 6/58
Lollipop 5/58

Ruby Murray
Evermore 7/55
Goodbye Jimmy, Goodbye 7/59
Happy Days And Lonely Nights 2/55
Heartbeat 12/54
I'll Come When You Call 11/55
If Anyone Finds This I Love You 3/55
Let Me Go, Lover 3/55
Softly Softly 1/55

Ricky Nelson
Be-Bop Baby/Have I Told You Lately That I Love You 10/57
Believe What You Say/My Bucket's Got A Hole In It 4/58
I Got A Feeling 11/58
It's Late 3/59
Just A Little Too Much 8/59
Lonesome Town 11/58

Rays
Silhouettes 10/57

Della Reese
Don't You Know 10/59

Joan Regan
If I Give My Heart To You
  10/54
May You Always 6/59
Prize Of Gold 4/55
Ricochet 12/53
Someone Else's Roses 5/54

Henri Rene
The Happy Wanderer 6/54
I'm In Love Again 8/51

Debbie Reynolds
Aba Daba Honeymoon 3/51
Tammy 7/57

Jody Reynolds
Endless Sleep 6/58

Cliff Richard
High Class Baby 12/58
Living Doll 7/59
Mean Streak 5/59
Move It 10/58
Travellin' Light 10/59

Nelson Riddle
Lisbon Antigua 1/56

Tex Ritter
Wayward Wind 7/56

Marty Robbins
El Paso 12/59
*A White Sport Coat (And A Pink
  Carnation)* 5/57

Don Robertson
The Happy Whistler 6/56

Floyd Robinson
Makin' Love 11/59

Lord Rockingham's XI
Hoots Mon 10/58

Jimmie Rodgers
Are You Really Mine 9/58
Honeycomb 9/57
Kisses Sweeter Than Wine
  12/57
Secretly 6/58

Don Rondo
White Silver Sands 8/57

Royal Teens
Short Shorts 2/58

Lita Roza
Allentown Jail 12/51
*(How Much Is) That Doggie In
  The Window* 3/53

Marion Ryan
Love Me Forever 2/58

Bobby Rydell
We Got Love 11/59

Felicia Sanders
Song From Moulin Rouge 4/53

Tommy Sands
Teen-Age Crush 3/57

Santo & Johnny
Sleep Walk 8/59

Jack Scott
Goodbye Baby 1/59
My True Love/Leroy 7/58

Neil Sedaka
I Go Ape 5/59
Oh! Carol 12/59

David Seville
Witch Doctor 4/58

Georgie Shaw
Till We Two Are One 2/54

Anne Shelton
Lay Down Your Arms 9/56

Mervin Shiner
Peter Cottontail 4/50

Dinah Shore
Dear Hearts And Gentle People
  1/50
Sweet Violets 7/51

Dinah Shore & Buddy Clark
Baby It's Cold Outside 1/50

Silhouettes
Get A Job 1/58

Frank Sinatra
All The Way 12/57
Hey! Jealous Lover 12/56
High Hopes 10/59
Learnin' The Blues 6/55
Love And Marriage 12/55
The Tender Trap 1/56
Three Coins In The Fountain
  6/54
Young-At-Heart 2/54

Muriel Smith
Hold Me Thrill Me Kiss Me
  5/53

**Somethin' Smith & The
Redheads**
It's A Sin To Tell A Lie 7/55

Bill Snyder
Bewitched 4/50

Sportsmen
Me And My Shadow 6/50

Jo Stafford
Jambalaya 9/52
Keep It A Secret 12/52
Make Love To Me! 2/54
No Other Love 9/50
Shrimp Boats 12/51
You Belong To Me 8/52

Johnny Standley
It's In The Book 10/52

Cyril Stapleton
Blue Star 9/55

Stargazers
Broken Wings 3/53
Close The Door 9/55
I See The Moon 2/54
Twenty Tiny Fingers 11/55

Kay Starr
Bonaparte's Retreat 7/50
Changing Partners 3/54
Comes A-Long A-Love 12/52
Half A Photograph 7/53
*If You Love Me (Really Love
  Me)* 5/54
Man Upstairs 5/54
Rock And Roll Waltz 1/56
Side By Side 2/53
Wheel Of Fortune 2/52

**Kay Starr & Tennessee Ernie
Ford**
I'll Never Be Free 9/50

Tommy Steele
Butterfingers 7/57
Come On Let's Go 12/58
Little White Bull 12/59
Nairobi 3/58
Singing The Blues 1/57
Water Water/Handful Of Songs
  9/57

April Stevens & Henri Rene
I'm In Love Again 8/51

Connie Stevens
*Kookie, Kookie (Lend Me Your
  Comb)* 5/59

Billy Williams
I'm Gonna Sit Right Down And Write Myself A Letter 7/57

Larry Williams
Short Fat Fannie 7/57

Roger Williams
Autumn Leaves 9/55
Near You 9/58

Johnnie Lee Wills
Rag Mop 3/50

Jackie Wilson
Lonely Teardrops 1/59
Reet Petite 12/57

Hugo Winterhalter
Blue Tango 5/52
Count Every Star 8/50
The Little Shoemaker 7/54

Hugo Winterhalter & Eddie Heywood
Canadian Sunset 8/56

Norman Wisdom
Don't Laugh At Me 2/54

Del Wood
Down Yonder 10/51

Sheb Wooley
The Purple People Eater 6/58

Ruby Wright
Bimbo 4/54

Jane Wyman
Zing A Little Zong 12/52

Eve Young
Silver Dollar/If I Knew You Were Comin' I'd've Baked A Cake 9/50

Jimmy Young
Because Of You 10/51
Chain Gang 3/56
Eternally 8/53
The Man From Laramie 9/55
More 11/56
Too Young 9/51
Unchained Melody 5/55

Victor Young
The High And The Mighty 8/54
Mona Lisa 9/50

John Zacherle
Dinner With Drac (Part 1) 3/58

Title Index

(including month of entry)

Aba Daba Honeymoon
Carleton Carpenter & Debbie
  Reynolds 3/51

Adoration Waltz
David Whitfield 3/57

Ain't That A Shame
Pat Boone 7/55

All American Boy
Bill Parsons 2/59

All I Have To Do Is Dream
Everly Brothers 4/58

All My Love
Patti Page 9/50

(All Of A Sudden) My Heart Sings
Paul Anka 2/59

All Shook Up
Elvis Presley 4/57

All Star Hit Parade
Various Artists 7/56

All The Time And Everywhere
Dickie Valentine 3/53

All The Way
Frank Sinatra 12/57

Allegheny Moon
Patti Page 7/56

Allentown Jail
Lita Roza 12/51

Alone
Petula Clark 12/57

Along Came Jones
Coasters 6/59

Alvin's Harmonica
Chipmunks 3/59

Among My Souvenirs
Connie Francis 12/59

And So To Sleep Again
Patti Page 9/51

Anna
Silvana Mangano 5/53

Answer Me
Frankie Laine 10/53

Answer Me
David Whitfield 10/53

Answer Me, My Love
Nat 'King' Cole 3/54

Any Time
Eddie Fisher 12/51

Anywhere I Wander
Julius La Rosa 2/53

April In Portugal
Les Baxter 4/53

April Love
Pat Boone 11/57

Are You Really Mine
Jimmie Rodgers 9/58

Army Game
TV Cast 6/58

Around The World
Bing Crosby 6/57

Around The World
Gracie Fields 6/57

Around The World
Ronnie Hilton 6/57

As I Love You
Shirley Bassey 1/59

At The Hop
Danny & The Juniors 12/57

At My Front Door (Crazy Little Mama)
Pat Boone 11/55

Auf Wiederseh'n Sweetheart
Vera Lynn 6/52

Autumn Leaves
Roger Williams 9/55

Baby Baby
Frankie Lymon & The
  Teenagers 4/57

Baby Face
Little Richard 1/59

Baby It's Cold Outside
Dinah Shore & Buddy Clark
  1/50

Baby Talk
Jan & Dean 9/59

Ballad Of Davy Crockett
Tennessee Ernie Ford 4/55

The Ballad Of Davy Crockett
Bill Hayes 3/55

Ballad Of Davy Crockett
Fess Parker 3/55

Banana Boat (Day-O)
Harry Belafonte 1/57

Banana Boat Song
Shirley Bassey 3/57

The Banana Boat Song
Tarriers 12/56

Band Of Gold
Don Cherry 1/56

Battle Of New Orleans
Lonnie Donegan 6/59

The Battle Of New Orleans
Johnny Horton 5/59

Be My Girl
Jim Dale 11/57

Be My Guest
Fats Domino 11/59

Be My Life's Companion
Johnston Brothers 5/52

Be My Love
Mario Lanza 12/50

Be-Bop Baby
Ricky Nelson 10/57

Be-Bop-A-Lula
Gene Vincent & His Blue Caps
  7/56

Because Of You
Les Baxter 9/51

Because Of You
Tony Bennett 7/51

Because Of You
Jimmy Young 10/51

Because You're Mine
Nat 'King' Cole 12/52

Because You're Mine
Mario Lanza 11/52

Beep Beep
Playmates 11/58

Believe What You Say
Ricky Nelson 4/58

Bell Bottom Blues
Alma Cogan 3/54

Beloved Be Faithful
Teddy Johnson 11/50

Bermuda
Bell Sisters 1/52

Bewitched
Doris Day 6/50

Bewitched
Gordon Jenkins 5/50

Bewitched
Bill Snyder 4/50

Beyond The Stars
David Whitfield 3/55

The Bible Tells Me So
Don Cornell 10/55

Big Hunk O' Love
Elvis Presley 7/59

The Big Hurt
Miss Toni Fisher 12/59

Big Man
Four Preps 6/58

Bimbo
Ruby Wright 4/54

Bird Dog
Everly Brothers 8/58

Black Denim Trousers
Cheers 10/55

Black Hills Of Dakota
Doris Day 8/54

Blacksmith Blues
Ted Heath 6/52

Blacksmith Blues
Ella Mae Morse 3/52

Blind Date
Margaret Whiting & Bob Hope
  10/50

Bloodnok's Rock'n'Roll Call
Goons 9/56

A Blossom Fell
Nat 'King' Cole 5/55

A Blossom Fell
Ronnie Hilton 4/55

A Blossom Fell
Dickie Valentine 3/55

Blowing Wild
Frankie Laine 1/54

Blue Monday
Fats Domino 2/57

Blue Moon
Elvis Presley 11/56

Blue Star
Cyril Stapleton 9/55

Blue Suede Shoes
Carl Perkins 3/56

Blue Suede Shoes
Elvis Presley 6/56

Blue Tango
Leroy Anderson 2/52

Blue Tango
Hugo Winterhalter 5/52

Blueberry Hill
Fats Domino 10/56

Bluebottle Blues
Goons 7/56

Bobby Sox To Stockings
Frankie Avalon 7/59

Bonaparte's Retreat
Kay Starr 7/50

The Book
David Whitfield 2/54

Book Of Love
Monotones 4/58

Book Of Love
Mudlarks 6/58

Born To Be With You
Chordettes 7/56

Born Too Late
Poni-Tails 8/58

Botch-A-Me
Rosemary Clooney 7/52

A Boy Without A Girl
Frankie Avalon 7/59

Breathless
Jerry Lee Lewis 4/58

The Breeze And I
Caterina Valente 8/55

Bridge Of Sighs
David Whitfield 10/53

Bring A Little Water Sylvie
Lonnie Donegan 9/56

Britannia Rag
Winifred Atwell 1/53

Broken Wings
Art & Dotty Todd 2/53

Broken Wings
Stargazers 3/53

Broken-Hearted Melody
Sarah Vaughan 9/59

A Bushel And A Peck
Perry Como & Betty Hutton
  11/50

Butterfingers
Tommy Steele 7/57

Butterfly
Charlie Gracie 3/57

Butterfly
Andy Williams 3/57

Bye Bye Love
Everly Brothers 6/57

C'est Si Bon
Eartha Kitt 8/53

C'mon Everybody
Eddie Cochran 4/59

Can Anyone Explain
Ames Brothers 8/50

Can't I
Nat 'King' Cole 8/53

Canadian Sunset
Andy Williams 9/56

Canadian Sunset
Hugo Winterhalter & Eddie
  Heywood 8/56

Cara Mia
David Whitfield 6/54

Carolina Moon
Connie Francis 8/58

Catch A Falling Star
Perry Como 2/58

A Certain Smile
Johnny Mathis 10/58

Chain Gang
Jimmy Young 3/56

Domino
Tony Martin 11/51

Don't Be Cruel
Elvis Presley 8/56

Don't Forbid Me
Pat Boone 1/57

Don't Knock The Rock
Bill Haley & His Comets 2/57

Don't Laugh At Me
Norman Wisdom 2/54

Don't Let The Stars Get In Your Eyes
Perry Como 12/52

Don't You Know
Della Reese 10/59

Don't You Rock Me Daddy-O
Lonnie Donegan 2/57

Don't You Rock Me Daddy-O
Vipers Skiffle Group 2/57

Don't
Elvis Presley 2/58

Donna
Ritchie Valens 1/59

Donna
Marty Wilde 4/59

Down Yonder
Del Wood 10/51

Downhearted
Eddie Fisher 5/53

Dragnet
Ray Anthony 9/53

Dragnet
Ted Heath 11/53

Dream Lover
Bobby Darin 5/59

Dreamboat
Alma Cogan 6/55

Dreams Can Tell A Lie
Nat 'King' Cole 2/56

Dungaree Doll
Eddie Fisher 1/56

Earth Angel
Crew-Cuts 2/55

Earth Angel (Will You Be Mine)
Penguins 2/55

Ebb Tide
Frank Chacksfield 2/54

Eh Cumpari
Julius La Rosa 9/53

El Paso
Marty Robbins 12/59

The End
Earl Grant 10/58

Endless Sleep
Jody Reynolds 6/58

Endless Sleep
Marty Wilde 7/58

Enjoy Yourself
Guy Lombardo 3/50

Eternally
Jimmy Young 8/53

Evermore
Ruby Murray 7/55

Every Day Of My Life
Malcolm Vaughan 7/55

Everything I Have Is Yours
Eddie Fisher 2/53

Ev'rywhere
David Whitfield 7/55

Experiments With Mice
Johnny Dankworth 6/56

Fabulous
Charlie Gracie 8/57

Faith Can Move Mountains
Johnnie Ray 12/52

Feet Up
Guy Mitchell 10/52

Fever
Peggy Lee 8/58

Finger Of Suspicion
Dickie Valentine 12/54

Flirtation Waltz
Winifred Atwell 10/53

The Flying Saucer (Parts 1 & 2)
Buchanan & Goodman 8/56

The Flying Saucer
Billy Cotton & His Band 5/51

The Fool
Sanford Clark 9/56

A Fool Such As I
Elvis Presley 4/59

Forget Me Not
Vera Lynn 11/52

Forgive Me
Eddie Fisher 3/52

Forty Miles Of Bad Road
Duane Eddy 7/59

Frankie
Connie Francis 7/59

Freight Train
Chas McDevitt Skiffle Group 5/57

Friendly Persuasion
Pat Boone 10/56

Friends And Neighbours
Billy Cotton & His Band 5/54

From The Vine Came The Grape
Gaylords 2/54

Frosty The Snowman
Gene Autry 1/51

Gambler's Guitar
Rusty Draper 8/53

Gamblin' Man
Lonnie Donegan 6/57

The Gang That Sang 'Heart Of My Heart'
Four Aces 1/54

Garden Of Eden
Frankie Vaughan 1/57

Get A Job
Silhouettes 1/58

Giddy-Up-A-Ding-Dong
Freddie Bell & The Bellboys 10/56

Gigi
Billy Eckstine 3/59

Gilly Gilly Ossenfeffer Katzenellen Bogen By The Sea
Max Bygraves 9/54

Ginger Bread
Frankie Avalon 9/58

The Girl Can't Help It
Little Richard 4/57

A Girl, A Girl
Eddie Fisher 4/54

Give Me Your Word
Tennessee Ernie Ford 1/55

Glow Worm
Mills Brothers 10/52

Go To Sleep, Go To Sleep, Go To Sleep
Mary Martin 4/50

Gone
Ferlin Husky 4/57

Good Golly Miss Molly
Little Richard 3/58

Good Luck, Good Health, God Bless You
Steve Conway 5/51

Goodbye Baby
Jack Scott 1/59

Goodbye Jimmy, Goodbye
Ruby Murray 7/59

Goodnight Irene
Gordon Jenkins & The Weavers 7/50

Goodnight, Sweetheart, Goodnight
McGuire Sisters 8/54

Gotta Have Something In The Bank Frank
Frankie Vaughan & The Kaye Sisters 11/57

Gotta Travel On
Billy Grammer 1/59

Granada
Frankie Laine 3/54

Grand Coolie Dam
Lonnie Donegan 5/58

Great Balls Of Fire
Jerry Lee Lewis 12/57

The Great Pretender
Jimmy Parkinson 3/56

The Great Pretender
Platters 1/56

The Green Door
Jim Lowe 10/56

Green Door
Frankie Vaughan 11/56

Guitar Boogie Shuffle
Virtues 4/59

Guitar Boogie Shuffle
Bert Weedon 6/59

Gum Drop
Crew-Cuts 9/55

A Guy Is A Guy
Doris Day 3/52

Half A Photograph
Kay Starr 7/53

Half As Much
Rosemary Clooney 7/52

Handful Of Songs
Tommy Steele 9/57

Happy Days And Lonely Nights
Ruby Murray 2/55

The Happy Organ
Dave 'Baby' Cortez 4/59

The Happy Wanderer
Henri Rene 6/54

The Happy Wanderer
Frank Weir 5/54

Happy, Happy Birthday Baby
Tune Weavers 9/57

Happy Wanderer
Obernkirchen Children's Choir 1/54

The Happy Whistler
Don Robertson 6/56

Harbour Lights
Bing Crosby 12/50

Harbour Lights
Sammy Kaye 9/50

Harbour Lights
Guy Lombardo 11/50

Hard Headed Woman
Elvis Presley 7/58

Hard To Get
Giselle Mackenzie 7/55

Have I Told You Lately That I Love You
Ricky Nelson 10/57

Have I Told You Lately That I Love You
Bing Crosby & The Andrews Sisters 8/50

Have You Heard
Joni James 1/53

Hawkeye
Frankie Laine 12/55

He
Al Hibbler 10/55

He's Got The Whole World (In His Hands)
Laurie London 4/58

The Heart Of A Man
Frankie Vaughan 8/59

Heart Of My Heart
Max Bygraves 5/54

Heartaches By The Number
Guy Mitchell 11/59

Heartbeat
Ruby Murray 12/54

Heartbreak Hotel
Elvis Presley 3/56

Hearts Of Stone
Fontane Sisters 12/54

Here
Tony Martin 4/54

Here Am I – Broken Hearted
Johnnie Ray 3/52

Here Comes Summer
Jerry Keller 9/59

Here In My Heart
Al Martino 5/52

Hernando's Hideaway
Archie Bleyer 6/54

Hernando's Hideaway
Johnston Brothers 10/55

Hey Joe
Frankie Laine 10/53

Hey There
Rosemary Clooney 7/54

Hey There
Johnnie Ray 10/55

Hey! Jealous Lover
Frank Sinatra 12/56

The High And The Mighty
Les Baxter 8/54

The High And The Mighty
Leroy Holmes 8/54

The High And The Mighty
Victor Young 8/54

High Class Baby
Cliff Richard 12/58

High Hopes
Frank Sinatra 10/59

High Noon
Frankie Laine 8/52

The Ho Ho Song
Red Buttons 5/53

Hold Me, Thrill Me, Kiss Me
Karen Chandler 1/53

Hold Me Thrill Me Kiss Me
Muriel Smith 5/53

Hold My Hand
Don Cornell 9/54

Home Cookin'
Margaret Whiting & Bob Hope
10/50

Homing Waltz
Vera Lynn 8/52

Honey-Babe
Art Mooney 5/55

Honeycomb
Jimmie Rodgers 9/57

Honky Tonk (Parts 1 & 2)
Bill Doggett 9/56

Hoop-De-Hoo
Perry Como & The Fontane
Sisters 5/50

Hoots Mon
Lord Rockingham's XI 10/58

Hot Diggity (Dog Ziggity Boom)
Perry Como 3/56

Hot Toddy
Ted Heath 7/53

Hound Dog Man
Fabian 12/59

The House Of Blue Lights
Chuck Miller 8/55

How Can You Believe Me When I Say...
Fred Astaire & Jane Powell
4/51

How High The Moon
Les Paul & Mary Ford 4/51

How Important Can It Be?
Joni James 3/55

(How Much Is) That Doggie In The Window
Lita Roza 3/53

Hummingbird
Les Paul & Mary Ford 8/55

I Almost Lost My Mind
Pat Boone 6/56

I Am
Tony Bennett 9/57

I Apologise
Billy Eckstine 4/51

I Beg Of You
Elvis Presley 2/58

I Believe
Frankie Laine 2/53

I Can't Stop Lovin' You
Don Gibson 5/58

I Can't Tell A Waltz From A Tango
Alma Cogan 1/55

I Cried A Tear
Lavern Baker 2/59

I Get Ideas
Tony Martin 7/51

I Get So Lonely
Four Knights 2/54

I Go Ape
Neil Sedaka 5/59

I Got A Feeling
Ricky Nelson 11/58

I Got Stung
Elvis Presley 11/58

I Hear You Knocking
Gale Storm 11/55

I Like Your Kind Of Love
Andy Williams 7/57

I Love You Baby
Paul Anka 11/57

I Love You So Much It Hurts
Charlie Gracie 9/57

I Need You Now
Eddie Fisher 9/54

I Need Your Love Tonight
Elvis Presley 4/59

I Said My Pajamas And Put On My Pray'rs
Tony Martin 2/50

I Saw Mommy Kissing Santa Claus
Beverley Sisters 12/53

I Saw Mommy Kissing Santa Claus
Jimmy Boyd 12/52

I Saw Mommy Kissing Santa Claus
Spike Jones 12/52

I See The Moon
Stargazers 2/54

I Still Believe
Ronnie Hilton 12/54

I Taut I Taw A Puddy Tat
Mel Blanc 2/51

I Understand Just How You Feel
Four Tunes 7/54

I Wanna Be Loved
Andrews Sisters 6/50

I Wanna Be Loved
Billy Eckstine 7/50

I Wanna Say Hello
Sir Hubert Pimm 1/52

I Want To Walk You Home
Fats Domino 8/59

I Want You, I Need You, I Love You
Elvis Presley 6/56

I Went To Your Wedding
Patti Page 9/52

I Wonder
Dickie Valentine 7/55

I'll Be Home
Pat Boone 2/56

I'll Come When You Call
Ruby Murray 11/55

I'll Never Be Free
Kay Starr & Tennessee Ernie
Ford 9/50

I'll Take You Home Again Kathleen
Slim Whitman 5/57

I'll Walk Alone
Don Cornell 4/52

I'm A Fool To Care
Les Paul & Mary Ford 8/54

I'm Gonna Get Married
Lloyd Price 8/59

I'm Gonna Sit Right Down And Write Myself A Letter
Billy Williams 7/57

I'm In Love Again
Fats Domino 5/56

I'm In Love Again
April Stevens & Henri Rene
8/51

I'm Walkin'
Fats Domino 3/57

Kisses Sweeter Than Wine
Jimmie Rodgers 12/57

Kisses Sweeter Than Wine
Frankie Vaughan 1/58

Knee Deep In The Blues
Guy Mitchell 2/57

Ko Ko Mo (I Love You So)
Crew-Cuts 2/55

Ko Ko Mo (I Love You So)
Perry Como 2/55

Kookie, Kookie (Lend Me Your Comb)
Edward Byrnes & Connie Stevens 5/59

La Dee Dah
Billy & Lillie 1/58

La Dee Dah
Jackie Dennis 3/58

La Vie En Rose
Tony Martin 8/50

Lady Of Spain
Eddie Fisher 11/52

Last Train To San Fernando
Johnny Duncan & The Blue Grass Boys 8/57

Lavender-Blue
Sammy Turner 8/59

Lay Down Your Arms
Anne Shelton 9/56

Learnin' The Blues
Frank Sinatra 6/55

Leroy
Jack Scott 7/58

Let Me Go, Lover!
Teresa Brewer 1/55

Let Me Go, Lover
Dean Martin 3/55

Let Me Go, Lover
Ruby Murray 3/55

Let Me Go, Lover
Joan Weber 12/54

Let's Get Together No. 1
Big Ben Banjo Band 12/54

Let's Have A Ball
Winifred Atwell 12/57

Let's Have A Ding Dong
Winifred Atwell 11/55

Let's Have A Party
Winifred Atwell 12/53

Let's Have Another Party
Winifred Atwell 11/54

Let's Walk Thata-Way
Doris Day & Johnnie Ray 7/53

Limelight
Frank Chacksfield 5/53

Lipstick On Your Collar
Connie Francis 6/59

Lisbon Antigua
Nelson Riddle 1/56

Little Bitty Pretty One
Thurston Harris 11/57

Little Darlin'
Diamonds 3/57

The Little Drummer Boy
Beverley Sisters 2/59

Little Red Monkey
Frank Chacksfield 4/53

The Little Shoemaker
Petula Clark 7/54

The Little Shoemaker
Gaylords 7/54

The Little Shoemaker
Hugo Winterhalter 7/54

Little Star
Elegants 8/58

Little Things Mean A Lot
Kitty Kallen 5/54

Little White Bull
Tommy Steele 12/59

The Little White Cloud That Cried
Johnnie Ray 12/51

Living Doll
Cliff Richard 7/59

Lollipop
Chordettes 3/58

Lollipop
Mudlarks 5/58

Lonely Boy
Paul Anka 6/59

Lonely Street
Andy Williams 10/59

Lonely Teardrops
Jackie Wilson 1/59

Lonesome Town
Ricky Nelson 11/58

Long Tall Sally
Little Richard 5/56

Look At That Girl
Guy Mitchell 8/53

Look Homeward Angel
Johnnie Ray 4/57

Looking Back
Nat 'King' Cole 5/58

Lost John
Lonnie Donegan 5/56

Love And Marriage
Frank Sinatra 12/55

Love Is A Many-Splendoured Thing
Four Aces 9/55

Love Letters In The Sand
Pat Boone 5/57

Love Makes The World Go Round
Perry Como 11/58

Love Me
Elvis Presley 12/56

Love Me Forever
Marion Ryan 2/58

Love Me Or Leave Me
Sammy Davis Jr. 9/55

Love Me Tender
Elvis Presley 10/56

The Loveliest Night Of The Year
Mario Lanza 5/51

The Loveliest Night Of The Year
Fred Waring 11/51

Lover
Peggy Lee 7/52

A Lover's Question
Clyde McPhatter 12/58

Lucille
Little Richard 8/57

Ma He's Making Eyes At Me
Johnny Otis Show 11/57

Mack The Knife
Bobby Darin 9/59

Mad Passionate Love
Bernard Bresslaw 9/58

My Friend
Frankie Laine 8/54

My Happiness
Connie Francis 1/59

My Heart Cries For You
Guy Mitchell 12/50

My Heart Is An Open Book
Carl Dobkins Jr 7/59

My Love And Devotion
Doris Day 11/52

My Love, My Love
Joni James 9/53

My Personal Possession
Nat 'King' Cole 7/57

My Prayer
Platters 7/56

My Resistance Is Low
Hoagy Carmichael 7/51

My September Love
David Whitfield 4/56

My Son My Son
Vera Lynn 10/54

My Special Angel
Bobby Helms 11/57

My Special Angel
Malcolm Vaughan 12/57

My True Love
Jack Scott 7/58

My Truly, Truly Fair
Guy Mitchell 6/51

Nairobi
Tommy Steele 3/58

The Naughty Lady Of Shady Lane
Ames Brothers 12/54

Naughty Lady Of Shady Lane
Dean Martin 2/55

Near You
Roger Williams 9/58

Nel Blu Dipinto Di Blu (Volare)
Domenico Modugno 8/58

Never Be Anyone Else But You
Ricky Nelson 3/59

Never Do A Tango With An Eskimo
Alma Cogan 12/55

Nevertheless
Mills Brothers 12/50

Nevertheless
Paul Weston 11/50

Ninety-Nine Ways
Tab Hunter 4/57

No One But You
Billy Eckstine 11/54

No Other Love
Perry Como 6/53

No Other Love
Ronnie Hilton 4/56

No Other Love
Jo Stafford 9/50

No, Not Much!
Four Lads 2/56

Nola
Les Paul 8/50

Now
Al Martino 1/53

Nuttin' For Christmas
Barry Gordon 12/55

Oh Happy Day
Don Howard 12/52

Oh Happy Day
Johnston Brothers 4/53

Oh Julie
Crescendos 2/58

Oh Lonesome Me
Don Gibson 5/58

Oh!
Pee Wee Hunt 8/53

Oh, Boy!
Crickets 1/58

Oh! Carol
Neil Sedaka 12/59

Oh, Mein Papa
Eddie Calvert 12/53

Oh! My Pa-Pa
Eddie Fisher 12/53

Old Cape Cod
Patti Page 7/57

The Old Master Painter
Richard Hayes 1/50

The Old Master Painter
Dick Haymes 1/50

Old Soldiers Never Die
Vaughn Monroe 5/51

On The Street Where You Live
Vic Damone 6/56

On Top Of Old Smoky
Vaughn Monroe 6/51

On Top Of Old Smoky
Weavers 4/51

Once In A While
Dinning Sisters 7/50

One Night
Elvis Presley 11/58

Only Sixteen
Craig Douglas 8/59

Only You
Hilltoppers 2/56

Only You
Platters 10/55

Only You
Frank Pourcel's French Fiddles 5/59

Open Up Your Heart (And Let The Sunshine In)
Cowboy Church Sunday School 3/55

Our Lady Of Fatima
Richard Hayes & Kitty Kallen 9/50

Outside Of Heaven
Eddie Fisher 11/52

Over And Over
Bobby Day 9/58

Over The Mountain; Across The Sea
Johnnie & Joe 7/57

PS I Love You
Hilltoppers 7/53

Papa Loves Mambo
Perry Como 10/54

Paralysed
Elvis Presley 9/57

Party
Elvis Presley 10/57

Party Doll
Buddy Knox 3/57

Patricia
Perry Como 11/50

Patricia
Perez Prado 7/58

Round And Round
Perry Como 3/57

The Roving Kind
Guy Mitchell 1/51

Ruby
Les Baxter 6/53

Ruby
Richard Hayman 4/53

Rudolph The Red-Nosed Reindeer
Gene Autry 12/50

Sail Along Silvery Moon
Billy Vaughn 1/58

The Saints Rock 'n Roll
Bill Haley & His Comets 6/56

Sam's Song
Joe 'Fingers' Carr 8/50

Sam's Song
Bing Crosby & Gary Crosby 7/50

Santa Baby
Eartha Kitt 12/53

Santa Bring My Baby Back To Me
Elvis Presley 12/57

Santo Natale
David Whitfield 11/54

Say You're Mine Again
Perry Como 5/53

Say You're Mine Again
Jane Hutton 8/53

School Day
Chuck Berry 4/57

Sea Of Love
Phil Phillips With The Twilights 8/59

Sea Of Love
Marty Wilde 10/59

Searchin'
Coasters 6/57

Secret Love
Doris Day 1/54

Secretly
Jimmie Rodgers 6/58

See You Later, Alligator
Bill Haley & His Comets 1/56

Send For Me
Nat 'King' Cole 7/57

Sentimental Me
Ames Brothers 4/50

Sentimental Me
Russ Morgan 5/50

Serenade
Slim Whitman 8/56

Seven Little Girls Sitting In The Back Seat
Avons 12/59

Seven Little Girls Sitting In The Back Seat
Paul Evans & The Curls 11/59

Seven Lonely Days
Giselle McKenzie 8/53

Seventeen
Boyd Bennett & His Rockets 8/55

Seventeen
Fontane Sisters 9/55

Sh-Boom
Chords 7/54

Sh-Boom
Crew-Cuts 7/54

Shake, Rattle And Roll
Bill Haley & His Comets 10/54

Shanghai
Doris Day 8/51

She Wears Red Feathers
Guy Mitchell 2/53

The Shifting Whispering Sands (Parts 1 & 2)
Billy Vaughn 10/55

The Shifting, Whispering Sands
Rusty Draper 10/55

Short Fat Fannie
Larry Williams 7/57

Short Shorts
Royal Teens 2/58

Shotgun Boogie
Tennessee Ernie Ford 6/51

Shrimp Boats
Jo Stafford 12/51

Side By Side
Kay Starr 2/53

Side Saddle
Russ Conway 3/59

Silent Night
Bing Crosby 12/52

Silhouettes
Rays 10/57

Silver Dollar
Eve Young 9/50

Sin
Four Aces 10/51

Sin
Eddy Howard 10/51

Sincerely
McGuire Sisters 1/55

Singing The Blues
Guy Mitchell 11/56

Singing The Blues
Tommy Steele 1/57

16 Candles
Crests 1/59

Sixteen Tons
Tennessee Ernie Ford 11/55

Sixteen Tons
Frankie Laine 1/56

Skin Deep
Duke Ellington 3/54

Skin Deep
Ted Heath 2/54

Skokiaan
Four Lads 9/54

Skokiaan
Ralph Marterie 9/54

Sleep Walk
Santo & Johnny 8/59

Slow Poke
Pee Wee King 12/51

Smile
Nat 'King' Cole 9/54

Smoke Gets In Your Eyes
Platters 12/58

Snow Coach
Russ Conway 12/59

So Long
Gordon Jenkins & The Weavers 1/51

So Many Ways
Brook Benton 11/59

So Rare
Jimmy Dorsey 5/57

Tell Me Why
Four Aces 1/52

Tell Me You're Mine
Gaylords 1/53

The Tender Trap
Frank Sinatra 1/56

Tenderly
Nat 'King' Cole 4/54

Tennessee Waltz
Teddy Johnson 3/51

Tennessee Waltz
Guy Lombardo 1/51

The Tennessee Waltz
Patti Page 11/50

Tennessee Waltz
Les Paul & Mary Ford 2/51

Tennessee Wig Walk
Bonnie Lou 2/54

Tequila
Champs 3/58

Terry's Theme From *Limelight*
Ron Goodwin 6/53

That'll Be The Day
Crickets 8/57

That's All I Want From You
Jaye P. Morgan 1/55

That's Amore
Dean Martin 11/53

Theme From *Picnic*
Morris Stoloff 6/56

Theme From *The Threepenny Opera*
Louis Armstrong 5/56

Theme Song From *Song For A Summer Night*
Mitch Miller 9/56

There Goes My Baby
Drifters 7/59

There Must Be A Reason
Frankie Laine 10/54

There's A Gold Mine In The Sky
Pat Boone 9/57

There's Always Room At Our House
Guy Mitchell 3/52

There's No Tomorrow
Tony Martin 1/50

The Thing
Billy Cotton & His Band 1/51

The Thing
Phil Harris 11/50

Thinking Of You
Don Cherry 10/50

Thinking Of You
Eddie Fisher 11/50

The Third Man Theme
Anton Karas 4/50

The Third Man Theme
Guy Lombardo 4/50

This Old House
Billie Anthony 10/54

This Ole House
Rosemary Clooney 8/54

The Three Bells
Browns 8/59

Three Coins In The Fountain
Four Aces 5/54

Three Coins In The Fountain
Frank Sinatra 6/54

Tiger
Fabian 7/59

Tiger Rag
Les Paul 1/52

('Til) I Kissed You
Everly Brothers 9/59

Till I Waltz Again With You
Teresa Brewer 12/52

Till Then
Hilltoppers 2/54

Till We Two Are One
Georgie Shaw 2/54

Tina Marie
Perry Como 9/55

To Know Him, Is To Love Him
Teddy Bears 11/58

Tom Dooley
Lonnie Donegan 11/58

Tom Dooley
Kingston Trio 10/58

Tom Hark
Elias & His Zigzag Jive Flutes 5/58

Tomboy
Perry Como 4/59

Tomorrow
Johnny Brandon 3/55

Tonight You Belong To Me
Patience & Prudence 9/56

Too Much
Elvis Presley 2/57

Too Young
Nat 'King' Cole 4/51

Too Young
Jimmy Young 9/51

Too Young To Go Steady
Nat 'King' Cole 6/56

Topsy II
Cozy Cole 10/58

Tragedy
Thomas Wayne 3/59

Transfusion
Nervous Norvus 6/56

Travellin' Light
Cliff Richard 10/59

True Love
Bing Crosby 11/56

Trying
Hilltoppers 9/52

Tulips And Heather
Fred Waring 11/51

Tulips From Amsterdam
Max Bygraves 5/58

Turn Back The Hands Of Time
Eddie Fisher 10/51

Turn Me Loose
Fabian 4/59

Tweedle Dee
Georgia Gibbs 2/55

The Twelfth Of Never
Johnny Mathis 9/57

26 Miles
Four Preps 3/58

Twenty Tiny Fingers
Stargazers 11/55

Twilight Time
Platters 4/58

Tzena, Tzena, Tzena
Vic Damone 8/50

Tzena, Tzena, Tzena
Gordon Jenkins & The Weavers 7/50

Wild Horses
Perry Como 3/53

Willie And The Hand Jive
Johnny Otis Show 8/58

Wish You Were Here
Eddie Fisher 8/52

Witch Doctor
Don Lang 6/58

Witch Doctor
David Seville 4/58

With All My Heart
Petula Clark 8/57

With These Hands
Eddie Fisher 8/53

Woman (Uh-Huh)
Jose Ferrer & Rosemary
 Clooney 2/54

A Woman In Love
Frankie Laine 9/56

Wonderful Copenhagen
Danny Kaye 2/53

A Wonderful Time Up There
Pat Boone 3/58

**The World Is Waiting For The
Sunrise**
Les Paul & Mary Ford 9/51

**Would I Love You (Love You,
Love You)**
Patti Page 2/51

Yakety Yak
Coasters 6/58

The Yellow Rose Of Texas
Johnny Desmond 8/55

The Yellow Rose Of Texas
Mitch Miller 8/55

Yes Tonight Josephine
Johnnie Ray 5/57

Ying Tong Song
Goons 9/56

You Alone
Perry Como 11/53

You Are My Destiny
Paul Anka 2/58

You Belong To Me
Patti Page 9/52

You Belong To Me
Jo Stafford 8/52

You Don't Owe Me A Thing
Johnnie Ray 2/57

You Need Hands
Max Bygraves 5/58

You Send Me
Sam Cooke 10/57

You You You
Ames Brothers 7/53

You're Just In Love
Perry Como & The Fontane
 Sisters 1/51

(You've Got) The Magic Touch
Platters 4/56

Young And Foolish
Edmund Hockridge 3/56

Young Blood
Coasters 6/57

Young Love
Tab Hunter 1/57

Young Love
Sonny James 1/57

Young-At-Heart
Frank Sinatra 2/54

Your Cheatin' Heart
Joni James 3/53

Yours
Vera Lynn 11/52

Zambesi
Lou Busch 2/56

Zing A Little Zong
Bing Crosby & Jane Wyman
 12/52